GERHART HAUPTMANN

GERHART HAUPTMANN

THE WEAVERS
HANNELE
THE BEAVER COAT

*Translated from the German by Horst Frenz
and Miles Waggoner*

INTRODUCTION BY HORST FRENZ

———————

Holt, Rinehart and Winston
NEW YORK

Fourth Printing, April, 1962

Translation copyright, 1951, by Horst Frenz

Introduction copyright, 1951, by Horst Frenz

Typography Design by Stefan Salter

Printed in the United States of America

22937-0111

INTRODUCTION

I

In 1932, Thomas Mann said on the occasion of the seventieth birthday of Gerhart Hauptmann: "He did not speak in his own guise, but let life itself talk with the tongues of changing, active human beings. He was neither a man of letters nor a rhetorician, neither an analyst nor a formal dialectician; his dialectic was that of life itself; it was human drama." This was a fitting comment on the rich and varied activities of a writer who occupies a unique position in contemporary German literature. In his long span of life (1862–1946) Hauptmann's works and personality merged, to become a kind of symbol to three generations of Germans, a symbol of humaneness, understanding, and power of vision.

Hauptmann is best known as a dramatist, and the 1912 award of the Nobel Prize in Literature, "principally for his rich, versatile, and prominent activity in the realm of the drama," gave international recognition to the contributions he has made to the development of modern drama. Hauptmann reawakened the dramatic form to new life. Rooted deeply in the modern world of turmoil, doubt, and searching, he realized that the simplest motions of everyday life themselves produce the friction which makes up the drama of life. He found the essence of dynamic impact in the motivation for action rather than in action itself. For his material he chose men and women in their struggle to grow, to transcend the limitations imposed upon them by environment and heredity. Thus he created a drama that deals with modern man in a modern world, leaving behind much that is old, worn, and external in the tradition of the drama and theater.

Until Hauptmann knew that he would be a writer, he was —in school and in other activities—disillusioned and restless. Traveling from place to place, he was constantly searching for the realization of his inner purpose and mission. A turning point came with his marriage to Marie Thienemann in 1885. His earlier urge for sculpturing turned into the desire to become a "sculptor of words." Almost symbolically, his works of sculpture were destroyed in Rome by an artist friend in a fit of madness, as if these imperfect creations had no right to exist side by side with Hauptmann's great dramatic plastics of life. After a brief digression into the field of acting, Hauptmann ventured upon his path as a writer, never to depart from it again, save occasionally for the role of stage director. He settled down in the quiet atmosphere of Erkner, near Berlin, where he found the material for many of his famous character studies, such as Mrs. Wolff in *The Beaver Coat*. It was then that Hauptmann came in contact with a literary group in Berlin, called "Durch," which advocated the theories of naturalism.

Hauptmann proved a good disciple of this important movement. He reproduced the more unpleasant aspects of life, gave a picture of crime, primitive instincts, and morbid passion, portrayed the conditions in the lower strata of society, and showed heredity and environment as the prime movers of man's actions. His elaborate and overdetailed stage directions reflected the demands of the naturalistic school. For instance, that a chair is made of soft wood, that a man has a wart on his nose, or that the beer served in a tavern comes from Bavaria is of little importance either for the course of the action or for the immediate optical stage effect. The naturalists simply insisted on the most careful observance of details. Furthermore, in their effort to view life as realistically as possible, they avoided the traditional plot with its unfolding, climax, and conclusion, and presented slices of life in episodes often running concurrently and not always tightly knit together.

Hauptmann wrote most of his dramatic works between 1889 and the First World War, and some of his best from 1891 to 1903. He described the lives of people he knew well and laid the action in places with which he was thoroughly familiar—predominantly the Silesian mountains and the Berlin area. The result was a series of impressive dramas which carried his fame all over Europe. Their stage productions contributed greatly to the growth of the art of the modern theater. Hauptmann expected from the stage designer accuracy in the reproduction of real-life scenes; he taught the actors to avoid unnatural and stilted declamations and monologues to which they had been accustomed. He insisted on the expression of simple yet deep emotions and on natural and convincing movements and speech —even dialect, if that seemed natural to the character portrayed —and used the stage directions for minute details on physical characteristics, background description, and topography. Above all, he treated subjects and themes which had been taboo on the stage up to then.

In *Before Dawn* (1889), Hauptmann shows, in a powerful and frank manner, how environment and heredity can tragically enslave man beyond the power of his will. The play reflects not only the playwright's strong interest in the natural sciences and sociological studies but also his aversion to those socialists of his day who lived on theory exclusively, thinking that by mere adherence to it mankind can be elevated and the course of nature defeated. The first production of *Before Dawn,* sponsored by the Freie Buehne—an independent stage society which helped with the performance of plays that the state-supported and more conventional theaters refused to put on—received a stormy reception and became the starting point of a heated controversy between the advocates and opponents of naturalism. As a result, Hauptmann became known in Germany almost overnight.

Before Dawn was followed by *The Festival of Peace* (1890), "a family catastrophe," and *Lonely Lives* (1891), the portrait of an intellectual man caught in an environment of convention and routine and too weak to realize his idealism in a world full of disillusionment. Characteristic of Hauptmann's dramatic technique, there is very little exterior action in both plays, only the inner conflict between the characters and their friction with the outer world. In *The Weavers* (1892), his best-known work, Hauptmann recorded the tragic fate of the weavers who had become deprived of their life's subsistence through the rise of the factories. For many years, the play was the center of bitter debate in Germany as well as in other countries. There were those who called Hauptmann an advocate of nihilism and drawing-room anarchism, others who tried to use him for purposes of social and political propaganda. Some early critics objected to the "undramatic" presentation of the milieu and the static arrangement of episodes lacking a "real" plot; others hailed him as the most consistent and thoroughgoing representative of the naturalistic movement.

There were other plays in which Hauptmann applied the naturalistic technique to the treatment of social and psychological problems. In *Drayman Henschel* (1898), *Rose Bernd* (1903), and *Gabriel Schilling's Flight* (1907), he dealt with individuals who, for various reasons unable to cope with life, go down in defeat and failure. In his comedies, *Colleague Crampton* (1892) and *The Beaver Coat* (1893), he treated with light humor, surprising for the author of *The Weavers*, man's inadequacies and hopes for happiness. In a historical drama, *Florian Geyer* (1896), he presented with naturalistic techniques the social and political conflicts of the past—in this case, the German Peasants' War in the sixteenth century.

Here was a writer who felt called upon to express, through the medium of the drama, his sympathies with men and women in physical or spiritual troubles, with victims of love and rivalry, with personal failure or human limitations. His compassion was directed primarily toward the lower and suppressed classes of society; in his desire to present their dismal lot, Hauptmann, the son of a Silesian innkeeper, went into the backyards, factories, and taverns, and the dingy and cramped quarters of working-men and farm hands. "A barber or a scrubwoman," he asserted, "might as fittingly be the protagonist of a tragedy as Lady Macbeth or King Lear." He shared with his masters in France and Scandinavia, particularly Zola and Ibsen, a predilection for "unheroic" characters, characters who, he felt, needed his pity and sympathy. Yet Hauptmann was not a rebel. Although by no means a pensive and detached writer, he preferred to observe rather than to participate in the social and political decisions of his day. Deeply moved and concerned over the misery in this world, he did not hesitate to treat highly controversial subjects, but his approach was never that of the propagandist; first and foremost, he was the creative artist.

Hauptmann's artistry becomes more apparent when he fuses realistic and symbolic elements in such works as *Hannele* (1893), a dream play with poetic lines and heavenly visions. Here Hauptmann goes beyond naturalism; the poet takes over. *The Sunken Bell* (1896) departs even further from naturalism and enters the symbolic realm. Paralleling a serious crisis in his own life—his decision to break the marriage ties with Marie Thienemann and to marry Margarete Marschalk, who became for him a profound source of inspiration—Hauptmann wrote the story of the bell-founder Heinrich who is torn between his earthly wife Magda and the elf Rautendelein and (like the artist for whom Heinrich is the symbol) is doomed to restlessness and dissatisfaction. There is no final solution for the artist but growth—a message that reminds one strongly of Goethe's *Faust*. Increasingly Hauptmann is attracted to legendary material with its symbolic possibilities and the emphasis on mood and atmosphere—*Henry of Aue* (1901), *Charlemagne's Hostage* (1908), *Griselda* (1909).

This period of Hauptmann's life ends with the *Commemoration Masque* (1913) which he wrote on a commission from the city of Breslau in celebration of the anniversary of the German Wars of Liberation (against Napoleon I). In the form of a puppet play, this *Masque* closes with a procession of all representatives of Germany's good qualities—from the peasants and workers to the great musicians, poets, philosophers, and artists and to the few statesmen whom Hauptmann deemed worthy to appear. It was a grandiose procession in honor of peace and prosperity; ironically, one year later, Germany entered the First World War.

II

Hauptmann's contribution to world literature consists of his great dramas of the nineties. In German literature, however, he ranks high not only as a dramatist but also as a writer of narratives, and even of poetry. As early as 1887 he published an excellent novelette, *Flagman Thiel*. Outward expansion in form went alongside an increasing breadth of vision. In reaching artistic maturity, he searched for symbols more universal and more representative of western civilization than anything he had tried before. Jesus Christ was the first of these great figures to occupy Hauptmann, and the religious novel, *The Fool in Christ, Emmanuel Quint* (1910), lays bare the chaos of the modern world, the resulting degradation of man, and the decline of absolute values.

Another universal theme deals with Eulenspiegel, a hero of German folklore. In Hauptmann's symbolic epic, *Till Eulenspiegel* (1928), the figure is a World War hero who becomes, like Goethe's Faust, a symbol of the German soul. Till's prankish foolery is given an undertone of longing, and at the end of his tortuous journey toward redemption a kind of Faustian synthesis takes place between the north and antiquity, a polarity symbolic of all unsolvable conflicts within man. This conflict—which frequently takes on the form of a conflict between Christianity and paganism—showed itself concretely in Hauptmann's constant yearning for the south. His frequent visits to Italy, and particularly his journey to Greece in 1907, had had a deep influence on him. Associating with the South a free and unrestrained life and the concept of self-fulfillment, Hauptmann gave expression to these ideas in *The Heretic of Soana*

(1918), a novelette generally conceded to be Hauptmann's masterwork in fiction, and *The Isle of the Great Mother* (1924). The sensuality of subject matter and background in these novels is heightened rather than softened by the chaste and classical prose in which they are written.

The strong autobiographical current of nearly all of Hauptmann's works came more and more to the surface. It was undisguised in a novel like *Atlantis* (1912), which describes a shipwreck and a trip to America, and became profuse in the lengthy reflections on his youth and development, *Im Wirbel der Berufung* (1936), and *Das Abenteuer meiner Jugend* (1937). These two works are more characteristic of the late period of his productivity than dramas like *Hamlet in Wittenberg* (1936) or the Atreus tetralogy, which he wrote during the Second World War. Following the Wagnerian trend of revealing the complete history of human beings and their fates, Hauptmann, having begun with the final part of the tetralogy, *Iphigenie in Delphi* (1941), went back to unfold its beginning in *Iphigenie in Aulis* (1942) and finally added to the two full-length dramas the two one-act plays, *Agamemnons Tod* and *Elektra* (published posthumously). One important autobiographical work, *Der Grosse Traum,* was begun during the First World War, tentatively finished in 1932, but not published until the Second World War. Modeled on Dante's *Divine Comedy,* it is an epic poem concerning the artist whose searching and suffering merge into the searching and suffering of all mankind. Hauptmann regarded this work as the most profound and personal revelation of his soul. According to his wishes, he had a copy buried with him.

The time of the Weimar Republic saw the poet—then in his sixties—at the height of his fame. The irony of fate which had him write a peace masque shortly before the outbreak of the First World War repeated itself when, in 1932, he delivered an address at several American universities—on his second trip to this country—in commemoration of the hundredth anniversary of Goethe's death. Praising the kind of progress that Goethe had advocated, a progress brought about by "perpetual quiet reformation," he denounced in the name of Goethe all fanaticism, all subjugation of the mind, misanthropy and persecution, and urged that in an existence which makes tremendous demands upon mankind, we attempt "to live resolutely in the Whole, the Good, the True"—using Carlyle's version of this Goethe maxim. The next year, Hitler came to power. Hauptmann's position as the grand old man of German letters was unshakable—the most lavish edition of his works, in seventeen volumes, appeared for his eightieth birthday in 1942. However, life in Hitler Germany—he was too old and too much a part of his native soil to be transplanted—was stifling and painful to a man whose nature was as deeply opposed to such a regime. This is revealed in a manuscript written but kept hidden during the Nazi years. The work, called *Die Finsternisse*, laments the tragic fate of the Jews and hints at Germany's coming downfall; the biblical quotation, "Woe to him who buildeth a town with blood!" is used as the basis for the prophecy.

Hauptmann's dramatic work, various and abundant (he has written more than forty dramas), is not without consistency. The tetralogy of the last decade is not too far removed from the early plays that he wrote in the 1890's. Hauptmann has simply advanced from the immediate—although no less universal—problems of individuals and their environment to broader issues of mankind, irrespective of time and place. However, the deep compassion and feeling for humanity have remained the same.

This is indeed the distinguishing mark of Hauptmann's dramatic work: social sympathy, social pity, social compassion. His social feeling is not intellectual; it is intuitive. Thanks to this elemental feeling for his fellow men, Hauptmann has remained the foremost social poet of Germany. And thanks to this deep feeling for humanity he is counted among those modern dramatists who, like Ibsen, Strindberg, and Shaw, have outlasted the changes of time and fashion.

III

The three plays selected for this volume, *The Weavers, Hannele,* and *The Beaver Coat,* belong to the early and dramatically most important period of Hauptmann's creative life. They show his great versatility, for only a versatile mind like Hauptmann's could produce a tragedy, a dream play, and a comedy in the same year.

In *The Weavers* Hauptmann has written a drama of misery and pity—a play born out of actual experiences and the memories of stories of his grandfather's life as a weaver in Silesia. In dedicating it to his father he wrote: "Your tale of my grandfather, who in his youth was a poor weaver like those portrayed here sitting behind the loom, has become the germ of my drama which, whether it be vigorous as life or rotten to the core, is still the best that 'so poor a man as Hamlet is' can offer."

The Weavers lacks a developed plot; Hauptmann has written a series of tense scenes, each one of which could be played almost independently. He has created more than forty characters, each one individualized sufficiently to convey a realistic picture of the suffering of the Silesian home workers in the cotton and linen mills during the 1840's. Outsiders—a traveler, a doctor, a forester, and others—are brought into the play to round out this case study as completely as possible. In scene after scene Hauptmann reveals the inner struggle of these down-trodden weavers whose aspirations are aptly expressed in the peddler's words at the end of the third act: "Well, every man has his dream." First patient and humble, they become toward the end of the play a furious and howling mob. Their suffering moves them, their utter despair drives them to action, to revolt. Here is the outcry for the righting of a terrible wrong, but no suggestion of a reform, no solution; the drama ends on a note of hopelessness, with the ironical touch of having the one old weaver who up to the very end has condemned the revolt and trusted in God's judgment killed by a stray bullet. André Antoine, the founder of the Théâtre Libre in Paris and the first to produce a Hauptmann play on the French stage, once expressed the great power that this play has had over audiences everywhere: "More than once that evening while the drama proceeded to its tragic ending, a feeling of fear and horror went through the house—a feeling that was visibly reflected on the face of the audience."

Atmosphere is all-important, and it is interesting to see how Hauptmann succeeds in intensifying it throughout the play. The first act provides the setting, explains the reasons for the later revolt, presents the rumblings of discontent but, in general, shows the weavers docile and cowed. The first signs of unrest (in Act II) are limited to one weaver's room in Kaschbach, then the rebellion spreads to Peterswaldau (the tavern in Act III and Dreissiger's home in Act IV), and finally to the weavers in Langenbielau (Act V). "Bloody Justice," first introduced by the soldier Jaeger who has returned to his home village, and then taken up by the weavers, becomes the theme song—almost like a *Leitmotif* in an opera or a choral song in a Greek play. This is another effective device by which Hauptmann heightens the tension throughout the drama. Thus, two factors—the broadening of the field of operation and the heightening of the atmosphere—become essential for the dramatic action: they give the play unity.

The Weavers is more than an historical drama. In this vivid picture of human agony, of degradation and wretchedness brought about by social conditions—factories, tariff walls, and other factors—Hauptmann has written a play that transcends the sufferings of the Silesian weavers of more than a hundred years ago. With the present world in turmoil, with millions of starving people begging to be fed, it strikes a universal note. Its meaning belongs to all ages and all lands.

In *Hannele,* certain elements—the juxtaposition of scenes and the portrayal of the inhabitants of the poorhouse—remind one of the naturalistic technique. Adherence to this technique also accounts—at least to some extent—for the peculiar fact that the teacher Gottwald carries Hannele into the poorhouse instead of leaving her in his own home (which would have been more humane). But Hauptmann wanted to present the environment in which Hannele has to live, with its filth, its immorality and vulgarity, in order to give a convincing picture of Hannele's miserable life, her loneliness and her innocence.

Hannele, the abused child of a cruel stepfather, has followed a voice calling from the hole in the frozen pond. Still alive, she is pulled out, and in the ensuing agony, reality, dream, and fantasy weave together a pattern of childish desires and aspirations. Some of Hannele's fantasies may be explained realistically, for they have their psychological motivation—in the milieu in which she has been brought up, in the age of puberty, in the things she has learned in school and church. She knows her Bible, fairy tales, and legends well. There are, however, symbolic elements in the play that cannot be understood in terms of what is passing through the mind and soul of a dying child. Hannele, longing for heaven and eager to join her mother who has died before her, lives in a dream world. In a dream anything is possible: persons suddenly vanish or become transformed; time and space no longer exist. Toward the end of the play, the two characters who have been kind to her on earth—the deaconess and the teacher—appear (to her) as mother and Lord Jesus.

Again, as in *The Weavers,* Hauptmann is the poet of misery, but this time he is not satisfied to view earthly sorrows alone. Now he moves between poorhouse and paradise, between misery on earth and joy in heaven. Prose no longer suffices to convey adequately the vision of heaven, and the Angels as well as the Stranger express themselves in verse.

Both plays have been produced on the American stage. On the other hand, *The Beaver Coat,* widely played and popular on the European Continent, is hardly known in this country. In contrast to *Hannele* and *The Weavers,* with their difficult stage settings and unusual characters—the fairy tale figures and the half-dwarfed, flat-chested weavers—*The Beaver Coat* tells the humorous story of a washerwoman in the country near Berlin.

Mrs. Wolff, endowed by nature with a great deal of energy and shrewdness, soon realizes that in this world one cannot advance very far through honest labor alone. Stealing becomes her weapon in the struggle for existence, although she continues to work, in the words of one of the characters, "as hard as four men." Mrs. Wolff is not an ordinary thief who steals out of depravity; she is never vicious—she doesn't steal from the poor, just from the rich who can afford to be robbed. While her victims sleep comfortably in their beds, she works vigorously to deprive them of some of their surplus goods. She takes advantage of every opportunity—sells a deer killed illegally, steals a large load of wood or an expensive beaver coat. Each move is designed to help her and her family one step farther on the road to success and happiness. If everything goes right—and there is no reason why it should not—she will eventually move to Berlin with her husband and daughters, who, she thinks, are destined for the stage, and then she will have fulfilled her heart's desire. After all, "if you're once rich," she explains to her considerably less intelligent husband, "and can sit in a carriage, then nobody asks ya where ya got your money."

Hauptmann's sympathies with the underdog turn the old thief into a likable character. She is industrious, helpful, and generally popular. Her clever thieving is supported, unwittingly, by the local authorities and their unlimited confidence in her. It is particularly the narrowminded and presumptuous judge, Von Wehrhahn, who carries the brunt of Hauptmann's satire. Wehrhahn, priding himself on his wide experience and his ability to discern people, indicts harmless characters but believes in Mrs. Wolff as "an honest soul." He is no match for her, although it might be said in his defense that even less stupid characters are taken in by her acting abilities. Just as the scene alternates between Mrs. Wolff's kitchen and Wehrhahn's court room, most of the interest in this play is divided between the washerwoman and the judge.

The egotistical officer of the law has developed a mania for smelling political sabotage around him, and it is his prejudice that prevents him from showing good sense in his investigations and in dispensing fair justice. This blind spot, too, provides much of the humor. Hauptmann likes to make fun of the law and its ministers. There is not a little contempt and malice in his characterization of the dumb policeman, Mitteldorf, and Glasenapp, the secretary who, in the judge's absence, tries to imitate Wehrhahn's superior airs. Such a treatment of officials is not unusual in Hauptmann; it is almost an obsession with him that policemen and judges are of necessity imbeciles or charlatans.

The Beaver Coat does not end on a note of conventional morality. Mrs. Wolff's thievery is not discovered, "poetic justice" is not done. Against a social background, Hauptmann has written a pithy satire and created the splendid character of Mrs. Wolff.

It is characteristic of all three plays in this collection that Hauptmann does not give a definite conclusion to his conflict. More than once, he has pointed out that true drama has no ending and that a decision is often imposed upon a playwright who finds no clear-cut ending in life, who always sees new variations, new possibilities for breaking off the action. All that is closely connected with Hauptmann's belief that man's inner struggle is more important and more dramatic than the outcome of the struggle, his searching after truth more significant than the truth itself. It is because of this fundamentally new approach to the problem of dramatic structure that the modern English-speaking drama can hardly be imagined without the pioneer work of Gerhart Hauptmann.

Indiana University,   HORST FRENZ.
May, 1951.

BIBLIOGRAPHICAL NOTE

There is no full-length study in English of Gerhart Hauptmann's life and works. However, short accounts may be found in articles and book chapters: L. Lewisohn, "The Life of Gerhart Hauptmann" in *The German Classics* (1914); Camillo Von Klenze, *From Goethe to Hauptmann* (1926); Felix Bertaux, *A Panorama of German Literature, 1871–1921* (1935); Philo Buck, *Directions in Contemporary Literature* (1942); Walter A. Reichart, "The Totality of Hauptmann's Work," *Germanic Review,* XXI (1946), 143–149; and the excellent comprehensive analysis of Hauptmann's complete work by Hugo F. Garten, "Gerhart Hauptmann, a Revaluation," *German Life and Letters,* III (October, 1949), 32–41.

Certain aspects of Hauptmann's work have been investigated in a number of published American dissertations; among them F. A. Klemm, *The Death Problem in the Life and Works of Gerhart Hauptmann* (1939), John Jacob Weisert, *The Dream in Gerhart Hauptmann* (1949), Mary Quimby, *The Nature Background in the Drama of Gerhart Hauptmann* (1918), and Siegfried H. Muller, *Gerhart Hauptmann and Goethe* (1949). His relationship to the Nazi regime is treated in two articles by Walter A. Reichart, "Gerhart Hauptmann since 1933" in *Books Abroad,* XX (1946), 125–129, and Max Lederer, "Gerhart Hauptmann," *German Quarterly,* XX (1947), 46–48.

Almost every book on the modern drama discusses the German dramatist, e.g.: Ludwig Lewisohn, *Modern Drama* (1916), T. H. Dickinson, *An Outline of Contemporary Drama* (1927), F. W. Chandler, *Aspects of Modern Drama* (1924) and *Modern Continental Playwrights* (1931), John Gassner, *Masters of the Drama* (1940), and Barrett H. Clark and George Freedley, *A History of Modern Drama* (1947). The best treatment of Hauptmann's dramatic qualities is to be found in F. B. Wahr, "Theory and Composition of the Hauptmann Drama," *Germanic Review*, XVII (1942), 163–173. Most of Hauptmann's plays in translation have been collected by Ludwig Lewisohn in his nine volume edition of the *Dramatic Works* (1912–1929). For bibliographical purposes, the reader is referred to Walter A. Reichart, "Fifty Years of Hauptmann Study in America (1894–1944)," in *Monatshefte fuer Deutschen Unterricht*, XXXVII (1945), 1–31.

A NOTE ON THE TRANSLATION

Anyone attempting to translate the plays of Gerhart Hauptmann into the American idiom is faced with the problem of Hauptmann's extensive use of dialect. Instead of finding a substitute for the Berlin or Silesian dialect, we have decided to use speech mannerisms that are common to the United States as a whole. This is, in a way, unfortunate, for Hauptmann used German dialects frequently and effectively. We felt, however, that a more readable version could be thus obtained than by attempting to equate Berlin dialect with, for example, New York, and the Silesian speech with New England, or the hills of Kentucky.

We are grateful to Professor H. H. Remak of Indiana University and Professor Thomas F. Marshall of Western Maryland College for reading the translations and making useful suggestions.

HORST FRENZ
MILES WAGGONER

CONTENTS

INTRODUCTION   v

BIBLIOGRAPHICAL NOTE   xxi

A NOTE ON THE TRANSLATION   xxiii

THE WEAVERS   I

HANNELE   99

THE BEAVER COAT   145

GERHART HAUPTMANN

THE WEAVERS

A Play of the Eighteen-Forties

DRAMATIS PERSONAE

DREISSIGER, a cotton manufacturer

MRS. DREISSIGER, his wife

PFEIFER, a manager

NEUMANN, a cashier — at Dreissiger's

AN APPRENTICE

JOHANN, a coachman

A YOUNG GIRL

WEINHOLD, a tutor for Dreissiger's sons

PASTOR KITTELHAUS

MRS. KITTELHAUS, his wife

HEIDE, the Chief of Police

KUTSCHE, a policeman

WELZEL, an innkeeper

MRS. WELZEL, his wife

ANNA WELZEL

WIEGAND, a carpenter

A TRAVELING SALESMAN

A FARMER

A FORESTER

SCHMIDT, a physician

HORNIG, a rag picker

OLD WITTIG, a smith

WEAVERS: *Baecker — Moritz Jaeger — Old Baumert — Mother Baumert — Bertha Baumert — Emma Baumert — Fritz, Emma's son, four years old — August Baumert — Ansorge — Mrs. Heinrich — Old Hilse — Gottlieb Hilse — Luise, Gottlieb's wife — Mielchen, his daughter, six years old — Reimann — Heiber — A weaver woman — A boy, eight years old — A large crowd of young and old weavers and weaver women.*

The action of the play takes place in the 1840's in Kaschbach, Peterswaldau, and Langenbielau, cities at the foot of the mountains known as the Eulengebirge.

ACT ONE

SCENE: *A spacious whitewashed room in Dreissiger's house at Peterswaldau, where the weavers must deliver their finished webs. At the left are uncurtained windows; in the back wall, a glass door. At the right is a similar door through which weavers, men, women, and children continuously come and go. Along the right wall, which, like the others, is almost entirely hidden by wooden stands for cotton, there is a bench on which the weavers, as they come in, spread out their finished webs to be examined. They step forward in the order of their arrival and offer their finished products.* PFEIFER, *the manager, stands behind a large table on which the weavers lay their webs for inspection. He makes the inspection with the use of dividers and a magnifying glass. When he is finished, he lays the cotton on the scales, where an apprentice tests its weight. The same apprentice shoves the goods taken from the scales onto the stock shelves.* PFEIFER *calls out the amount to be paid to each weaver to* NEUMANN, *the cashier, who sits at a small table.*

It is a sultry day toward the end of May. The clock points to twelve. Most of the waiting weavers stand like men before the bar of justice where, tortured and anxious, they must await a life-and-death decision. They all give the impression of being crushed, like beggars. Passing from humiliation to humiliation and convinced that they are only tolerated, they are used to making themselves as inconspicuous as possible. Also, they have

2

a stark, irresolute look—gnawing, brooding faces. Most of the
men resemble each other, half-dwarf, half-schoolmaster. They
are flat-chested, coughing creatures with ashen gray faces:
creatures of the looms, whose knees are bent with much sitting. At first glance, their women folk are less typical. They
are broken, harried, worn out, while the men still have a certain look of pathetic gravity. The women's clothes are ragged,
while those of the men are patched. Some of the young girls
are not without charm—they have pale waxen complexions,
delicate figures, large protruding melancholy eyes.

CASHIER NEUMANN. (Counting out money.) That leaves 16
silver groschen and 2 pfennigs.

FIRST WEAVER WOMAN. (In her thirties, very emaciated, puts
the money away with trembling fingers.) Thank ya, kindly, sir.

NEUMANN. (As the woman does not move on.) Well, is
something wrong again?

FIRST WEAVER WOMAN. (Excitedly, in begging tone.) I'd like
a few pfennigs in advance. I need it awful bad.

NEUMANN. And I need a few hundred thalers. If it was just
a matter of needing—! (Already busy counting out money to
another weaver, curtly.) Mr. Dreissiger himself has to decide
about advances.

FIRST WEAVER WOMAN. Then, maybe I could talk to Mr.
Dreissiger hisself?

PFEIFER. (He was formerly a weaver. The type is unmistak-
able; only he is well-groomed, well-fed, well-clothed, clean-
shaven; also, a heavy user of snuff. He calls across brusquely.)
MR. DREISSIGER would have plenty to do, God knows, if he had
to bother himself with every trifle. That's what we're here for.

(*He measures and inspects a web with the magnifying glass.*) Damn it all! There's a draft! (*He wraps a heavy scarf around his neck.*) Shut the door when ya come in.

THE APPRENTICE. (*In a loud voice to* PFEIFER.) It's just like talkin' to a block of wood.

PFEIFER. That's settled then! Weigh it! (*The weaver lays his web on the scales.*) If ya only understood your work better. It's got lumps in it again—I can tell without looking. A good weaver doesn't put off the winding who knows how long.

BAECKER. (*Enters. A young, exceptionally strong weaver whose behavior is free and easy, almost impertinent.* PFEIFER, NEUMANN, *and* THE APPRENTICE *glance at each other understandingly when he enters.*) Damn it, I'm sweatin' like a dog again.

FIRST WEAVER. (*Softly.*) Feels like rain.

OLD BAUMERT. (*Pushes through the glass door at the right. Behind the door, waiting weavers are seen jammed together, shoulder to shoulder.* OLD BAUMERT *has hobbled forward and has laid his bundle on a bench near* BAECKER'S. *He sits down next to it and wipes the sweat from his face.*) Ya sure earn a rest here.

BAECKER. Rest is better than money.

OLD BAUMERT. Ya need money too. Good day to ya, Baecker!

BAECKER. And good day to you, Father Baumert! Who knows how long we'll have to be waitin' around here again.

FIRST WEAVER. It don't matter whether a weaver has to wait an hour or a day. He just don't count.

PFEIFER. Be quiet, back there. I can't hear myself think.

BAECKER. (*Softly.*) Today's one of his bad days again.

PFEIFER. (*To the weavers standing in front of him.*) How many times have I told you already. Ya ought to clean up the

4

webs better. What sort of a mess is this? There are chunks of dirt in it, as long as my finger—and straw, and all kinds of rubbish.

WEAVER REIMANN. I guess I need a new pair of pincers.

THE APPRENTICE. (*Has weighed the web.*) And it's short weight, too.

PFEIFER. The kind of weavers ya have nowadays! You hate to hand out the yarn. Oh, Lord, in my time! My master would've made me pay for it. I tell you, weaving was a different thing in those days. Then, a man had to understand his business. Today it's not necessary anymore. Reimann, 10 groschen.

WEAVER REIMANN. Yes, but one pound is allowed for waste.

PFEIFER. I haven't time. That's settled. (*To the next weaver.*) What have you got?

WEAVER HEIBER. (*Puts his web up on the counter. While* PFEIFER *is inspecting it,* HEIBER *steps up to him and speaks softly and eagerly.*) Please, forgive me, Mr. Pfeifer, I would like to ask ya, sir, if perhaps ya would be so kind as to do me a favor and not deduct my advance this time.

PFEIFER. (*Measuring with the dividers and inspecting, jeers.*) Well, now! That's just fine. It looks as if about half the woof has been left on the spool again.

HEIBER. (*Continuing, as before.*) I'd be glad to make it up next week for sure. Last week I had to put in two days' work on the estate. And my wife's home, sick in bed. . . .

PFEIFER. (*Putting the web on the scales.*) Here's another piece of real sloppy work. (*Already taking a new web for inspection.*) What a selvage—now it's broad, then it's narrow. In one place the woof's all gathered together, who knows how much, then the reed has been pulled apart. And scarcely

5

seventy threads to the inch. Whatever happened to the rest? Is that honest work? I never saw such a thing!

HEIBER, *suppressing tears, stands humiliated and helpless.*

BAECKER. (*Low, to* BAUMERT.) I guess this riffraff would like us to pay for the yarn, too.

FIRST WEAVER WOMAN. (*Who has withdrawn only a few steps from the cashier's table, stares about from time to time, seeking help, without moving from the spot. Then she takes heart and once more turns imploringly to the cashier.*) I can hardly . . . I don't know . . . if ya don't give me an advance this time . . . O, Lord, Lord. . . .

PFEIFER. (*Calls across.*) All this calling on the Lord! Just leave the Lord in peace. You haven't been bothering much about the Lord up to now. It'd be better if you'd look after your husband instead, so he isn't seen sitting in the tavern window all day long. We can't give advances. We have to account for every cent. It's not our own money. Later they'd be asking us for it. People who are industrious and understand their business and do their work in fear of God don't ever need advances. So, that's settled.

NEUMANN. And if a Bielau weaver got four times as much pay, he'd squander four times as much and be in debt in the bargain.

FIRST WEAVER WOMAN. (*In a loud voice, as if appealing to everyone's sense of justice.*) I'm certainly not lazy, but I just can't go on this way much longer. I've had two miscarriages, and my husband, he can't do no more than half the work neither; he went up to the shepherd at Zerlau, but he couldn't do nothin' for his trouble either . . . there's just so much a body can do. . . . We sure do work as much as we can. I ain't had much sleep for weeks, and everything'll be all right again if I can only get a bit of this weakness out of my bones. But ya got to have a little consideration. (*Beseeching him and fawning.*) Ya'll have to be good enough to let me have a few groschen, this time.

PFEIFER. (*Unperturbed.*) Fiedler, 11 groschen.

FIRST WEAVER WOMAN. Just a few groschen, so we can get some bread. The farmer won't give us no more credit. We got a house full of children. . . .

NEUMANN. (*Softly and with mock seriousness to* THE APPRENTICE.) Once a year the linen weaver has a brat, fa, la, la, la, la.

THE APPRENTICE. (*Chiming in.*) The first six weeks it's blind as a bat, fa, la, la, la, la.

REIMANN. (*Not touching the money that the cashier has counted out for him.*) We've always been gettin' 13½ groschen for a web.

PFEIFER. (*Calls across.*) If it doesn't suit you, Reimann, all you have to do is say the word. There are plenty of weavers. Especially weavers like you. For full weight, you'll get full pay.

REIMANN. That something should be wrong with the weight. . . .

PFEIFER. If there's nothing wrong with the cotton you bring, there'll be nothing wrong with your pay.

REIMANN. It really can't be that this web, here, should have too many flaws in it.

PFEIFER. (*Inspecting.*) He who weaves well, lives well.

HEIBER. (*He has stayed close to* PFEIFER *waiting for a favorable opportunity. He smiled with the others at* PFEIFER's *remark; now he steps forward and speaks to him as he did before.*) I would like to ask ya, sir, if perhaps ya would be so

7

kind and not deduct the 5 groschen advance this time. My wife's been sick in bed since before Ash Wednesday. She can't do a lick of work. And I have to pay a girl to tend the bobbin. And so—

PFEIFER. (*Takes a pinch of snuff.*) Heiber, you're not the only one I have to attend to. The others want their turn, too.

REIMANN. The way the warp was given to me—that's the way I wound it and that's the way I took it off again. I can't bring back better yarn than I take home.

PFEIFER. If ya don't like it, ya simply don't need to get any more warp here. There are plenty who'd run their feet off for it.

NEUMANN. (*To* REIMANN.) Aren't you going to take the money?

REIMANN. I just can't take such pay.

NEUMANN. (*Without troubling himself further about* REI-MANN.) Heiber, 10 groschen—take off the 5 groschen advance —leaves 5 groschen.

HEIBER. (*Steps up, looks at the money, stands there, shakes his head as if there were something he could not believe, and then quietly and carefully pockets the money.*) O my God—! (*Sighing.*) Ah, well!

OLD BAUMERT. (*Looking straight at* HEIBER.) Yes, yes, Franz! You've got cause for sighing there.

HEIBER. (*Speaking wearily.*) Ya see, I've got a sick girl layin' home. She needs a bottle of medicine.

OLD BAUMERT. What's wrong with her?

HEIBER. Ya see, she's been a sickly little thing from the time she was born. I really don't know . . . well, I can tell you: she brought it into the world with her. Such trouble's in the blood, and it keeps breakin' out over and over again.

8

OLD BAUMERT. There's something the matter everywhere. When you're poor, there's nothing but bad luck. There's no end to it and no salvation.

HEIBER. What have ya got in that bundle?

OLD BAUMERT. We haven't got a thing in the house. So I had our little dog killed. There ain't much to him, he was half-starved. He was a nice little dog. I couldn't kill him myself. I didn't have the heart.

PFEIFER. (*Has inspected* BAECKER's *web, calls out.*) Baecker, 13½ groschen.

BAECKER. That's a measly hand-out for a beggar, not pay.

PFEIFER. Those who are done, have to get out. It's so crowded, we can't move around in here.

BAECKER. (*To those standing about, without lowering his voice.*) That's a measly hand-out, that's all it is. And for that a man's to work the treadle from early morning till late at night. And after a man's been workin' behind a loom for eighteen days, evenin' after evenin'—worn out, dizzy with the dust and terrible heat, then he's lucky if he gets 13½ groschen for his drudgery.

PFEIFER. We'll have no back-talk here.

BAECKER. You can't make me hold my tongue.

PFEIFER. (*Jumps up, shouting.*) We'll see about that. (*Walks toward the glass door and calls into the office.*) Mr. Dreissiger! Mr. Dreissiger, if you'll be so kind!

DREISSIGER. (*Enters. He is about forty, fat, asthmatic. With a severe look.*) What's—the matter, Pfeifer?

PFEIFER. (*Angrily.*) Baecker won't hold his tongue.

DREISSIGER. (*Draws himself up, throws his head back, and stares at* BAECKER *with quivering nostrils.*) Oh, yes—Baecker— (*to* PFEIFER.) Is that him—? (*The clerk nods.*)

9

BAECKER. (*Impudently.*) Yes, indeed, Mr. Dreissiger! (*Pointing to himself.*) That's him. (*Pointing to* DREISSIGER.) And that's him.

DREISSIGER. (*Indignantly.*) How can he dare?

PFEIFER. He's too well off, that's what he is. He'll skate on thin ice once too often.

BAECKER. (*Roughly.*) You shut up, you fool! Once, in the new moon, your mother must have been ridin' a broomstick with Satan to beget such a devil as you for a son.

DREISSIGER. (*In sudden anger, bellows.*) Shut up! Shut up this minute, or else—(*He trembles, takes a few steps forward.*)

BAECKER. (*With determination, standing up to him.*) I'm not deaf. I still hear good.

DREISSIGER. (*Controls himself, asks with apparent businesslike calm.*) Isn't he one of those—?

PFEIFER. He's a Bielau weaver. They can always be found where trouble is brewing.

DREISSIGER. (*Trembling.*) Then I'm warning you: if it happens once more, and if such a gang of half-drunken young louts passes my house once again, as they did last night, singing that vile song. . . .

BAECKER. I guess you mean "Bloody Justice"?

DREISSIGER. You know exactly what I mean. Let me tell you, if I hear that song once more, I'll get hold of one of you, and—on my honor, joking aside, I promise you I'll turn him over to the state's attorney. And if I find out who wrote this wretched song. . . .

BAECKER. That's a beautiful song—it is!

DREISSIGER. Another word and I'll send for the police—immediately. I won't lose any time! We know how to deal with young fellows like you. I've taken care of your kind before.

BAECKER. Well, now, that I can believe. A real manufacturer like you can gobble up two or three hundred weavers before a person has time to turn around . . . and not so much as a bone left over. Such a man's got four stomachs like a cow and teeth like a wolf. No, indeed—that's nothing at all to him!

DREISSIGER. (*To the clerks.*) See to it that that fellow doesn't get another stick of work from us.

BAECKER. Oh, it's all the same to me whether I starve behind the loom or in a ditch by the side of the road.

DREISSIGER. Get out, this minute! Get out of here!

BAECKER. (*Firmly.*) I'll take my pay first.

DREISSIGER. How much has the man got coming, Neumann?

NEUMANN. Twelve groschen and five pfennigs.

DREISSIGER. (*Takes the money from the cashier in great haste and throws it down on the counter so that a few coins roll onto the floor.*) There you are—and now hurry—get out of my sight!

BAECKER. I'll take my pay first.

DREISSIGER. There's your pay; and if you don't hurry and get out. . . . It's exactly twelve . . . my dyers are taking off for lunch. . . .

BAECKER. My pay belongs in my hand. My pay belongs here. (*He points to the palm of his left hand.*)

DREISSIGER. (*To* THE APPRENTICE.) Pick it up, Tilgner.

THE APPRENTICE *picks up the money and lays it in* BAECKER's hand.

BAECKER. Everything's got to be done right. (*He puts the money slowly in an old purse.*)

DREISSIGER. Well? (As BAECKER *still does not leave, impatiently.*) Shall I help you?

There is excited movement among the crowd of weavers. A long, deep sigh is heard, then a fall. Everyone's attention is turned to this new event.

DREISSIGER. What's happened there?

VARIOUS WEAVERS *and* WEAVER WOMEN. Someone's fainted. It's a sickly little boy. What's wrong? Is it consumption, maybe?

DREISSIGER. Why . . . what's that? Fainted? (*He goes up closer.*)

AN OLD WEAVER. He's layin' there. (*They make room. A little boy, about eight years old, is seen lying on the floor as if dead.*)

DREISSIGER. Does somebody know this boy?

OLD WEAVER. He's not from our village.

OLD BAUMERT. He looks like one of Heinrich's boys. (*He looks at him more closely.*) Yes, indeed! That is Heinrich's little Gustav.

DREISSIGER. Where do they live, these people?

OLD BAUMERT. Why, near us in Kaschbach, Mr. Dreissiger. He goes around playin' music, and in the daytime he works at the loom. They have nine children and the tenth's on the way.

VARIOUS WEAVERS *and* WEAVER WOMEN. They sure got a lot of trouble. Their roof leaks. The woman ain't got two shirts for the nine children.

OLD BAUMERT. (*Taking hold of the boy.*) Why, my child, what's wrong with ya? Wake up, there now!

DREISSIGER. Take hold of him—here, help me—we'll pick him up. It's incomprehensible that anybody should let a weak

12

child like that come such a long way. Bring some water, Pfeifer!

WEAVER WOMAN. (*Helps him sit up.*) Don't ya up and die on us, boy!

DREISSIGER. Or brandy, Pfeifer, brandy is better.

BAECKER. (*Forgotten by everybody, has been watching. Now, with one hand on the doorknob, he calls across in a loud voice, mockingly.*) Give him something to eat, too, and he'll come to all right.

Exit.

DREISSIGER. That fellow will come to no good. Take him under the arm, Neumann. Slowly—slowly . . . that's it . . . there, now . . . we'll take him into my room. Why, what is it?

NEUMANN. He's said something, Mr. Dreissiger! He's moving his lips.

DREISSIGER. What is it, little boy?

THE BOY. (*Whispers.*) I'm—hungry!

DREISSIGER. (*Turns pale.*) I can't understand him.

WEAVER WOMAN. I think he said. . . .

DREISSIGER. Well, we'll see. Let's not lose any time—he can lie on my sofa. We'll hear, then, what the doctor says.

DREISSIGER, NEUMANN, *and the* WEAVER WOMAN *carry the boy into the office. There is a commotion among the weavers, as among school children when the teacher leaves the classroom. They stretch, they whisper, they shift from one foot to the other. Soon there is loud and general conversation among them.*

OLD BAUMERT. I really do believe Baecker is right.

SEVERAL WEAVERS *and* WEAVER WOMEN. He said something like that, too. That's nothing new around here—people faintin' from hunger. Yes, and who knows what'll happen this winter if this cuttin' of wages keeps on—. And the potatoes bein' so bad this year—. It won't be no different here till we're all of us flat on our backs.

OLD BAUMERT. Ya might just as well put a rope 'round your neck and hang yourself on your loom like the Nentwich weaver did. Here, take a pinch of snuff—I was in Neurode, where my brother-in-law works in the snuff factory. He gave me a few grains. You carryin' anything nice in your kerchief?

AN OLD WEAVER. It's only a little bit of barley. The wagon from the Ullbrich miller was drivin' ahead of me, and there was a little slit in one of the sacks. That comes in handy, believe me.

OLD BAUMERT. There are twenty-two mills in Peterswaldau, and still there's nothin' left over for the likes of us.

AN OLD WEAVER. Ah, we mustn't get discouraged. Something always turns up and helps a little bit.

HEIBER. When we're hungry, we have to pray to the fourteen guardian angels, and if that don't fill ya up, then ya have to put a pebble in your mouth and suck on it. Right, Baumert?

DREISSIGER *and* PFEIFER, *as well as the cashier, return.*

DREISSIGER. It was nothing of any importance. The boy's quite all right again. (*Goes around excited and puffing.*) And yet it is a disgrace. A bit of wind would blow that wisp of a child away. It's really unbelievable how people—how parents can be so irresponsible. To load him down with two bundles of cotton and send him a good seven and a half miles on the road. It's really quite unbelievable. I will simply have to take steps to see to it that goods brought by children will not be accepted. (*He walks silently back and forth.*) In any case, I certainly hope that nothing of this sort happens again. On

whose shoulders does the blame finally rest? The manufacturers, of course. We're blamed for everything. When a poor
little fellow falls asleep in the snow in the wintertime, one of
these reporter chaps comes running up, and in two days the
gruesome story is in all the papers. The father, the parents, the
ones who send the child out . . . oh, no . . . they aren't
guilty, certainly not! It must be the manufacturer; the manufacturer is the goat. The weaver is always let off easy, the
manufacturer is the one who catches it; he's a man without a
heart, dangerous fellow who can be bitten in the leg by
every mad dog of a reporter. He lives in splendor and in comfort and pays the poor weavers starvation wages. These scrib-
blers are absolutely silent about the fact that such a man has
troubles, too, and sleepless nights; that he runs great risks
such as the weaver never dreams of; that often he does nothing
but calculate—dividing, adding, and multiplying, calculating
and recalculating until he's nearly out of his mind; that he has
to consider and weigh a hundred different kinds of things, and
always has to fight and compete, you might say, as a matter
of life and death; that not a single day goes by without an-
noyances and losses. All the people who're dependent on the
manufacturer, who suck him dry and want to live off of him—
think of that! No, no! You ought to be in my shoes for a while,
then you'd get fed up with it soon enough, I tell you. (*After
a little reflection.*) How that fellow, that scoundrel there, that
Baecker, behaved! Now he'll go around and tell everybody
how hard-hearted I am. That at the slightest opportunity I
throw the weavers out. Is that true? Am I so hard-hearted?

MANY VOICES. No, Mr. Dreissiger!

DREISSIGER. Well, it doesn't look like that to me, either.
And yet these rascals go around here and sing nasty songs

about us manufacturers. They talk of hunger and yet they have so much money to spend that they can consume their liquor by the quart. They ought to look around in other places, and see how things are among the linen weavers. They can really talk of hard times. But you here, you cotton weavers, you can quietly thank God that things are as they are. And I ask the old, industrious, skilled weavers who are here: Tell me, can a worker, who does a good job, earn his living, working for me or can't he?

VERY MANY VOICES. Yes, Mr. Dreissiger!

DREISSIGER. There, you see! A fellow like Baecker can't, of course. But I advise you, keep those fellows in check; if this goes too far, I'll just quit. Then I'll give up the whole business, and you'll see where you are. You'll see who'll give you work. Certainly not your fine Mr. Baecker.

FIRST WEAVER WOMAN. (*Has come up close to* DREISSIGER *and with fawning humility brushes some dust from his coat.*) You've gone and rubbed against something, Mr. Dreissiger, sir, you have.

DREISSIGER. Business is terrible, you know that yourselves. Instead of earning money, I'm actually losing it. If, in spite of this, I see to it that my weavers always have work, I expect them to appreciate it. The goods lie stocked up here in thousands of yards, and I don't know today if I'll ever sell them. Well, I've heard that a great number of weavers around here have no work at all, and so . . . well, Pfeifer can give you the details. The fact of the matter is this: so you'll see my good intentions—naturally, I can't just hand out charity. I'm not rich enough for that. But I can, up to a certain point, give the unemployed a chance to earn at least a little something.

16

That I'm running a tremendous risk in doing that, well, that's my own affair. I think it's always better if a man can earn a piece of bread and cheese for himself every day rather than starve. Don't you think I'm right?

MANY VOICES. Yes, yes, Mr. Dreissiger.

DREISSIGER. I am therefore willing to put an additional two hundred weavers to work. Pfeifer will explain to you, under what conditions. (*He is about to leave.*)

FIRST WEAVER WOMAN. (*Steps in his path, speaks quickly, imploringly, urgently.*) Mr. Dreissiger, sir, I wanted to ask ya real kindly, if perhaps you . . . I've been laid up twice. . . .

DREISSIGER. (*In haste.*) Speak to Pfeifer, my good woman, I'm late as it is. (*He turns away from her.*)

REIMANN. (*Stops him. In the tone of an injured and accusing man.*) Mr. Dreissiger, I really have a complaint to make. Mr. Pfeifer has . . . I always get 12½ groschen for a web, and. . . .

DREISSIGER. (*Interrupts him.*) There's the manager. Talk to him: he's the person to see.

HEIBER. (*Stops* DREISSIGER.) Mr. Dreissiger, sir, (*Stuttering, in confusion and haste.*) I wanted to ask ya if perhaps ya could . . . if maybe Mr. Pfeifer could . . . if he could. . . .

DREISSIGER. What is it you want?

HEIBER. The advance pay that I got last time. I mean that I. . . .

DREISSIGER. I really do not understand you.

HEIBER. I was pretty hard up, because. . . .

DREISSIGER. Pfeifer's business, that's Pfeifer's business. I really can't . . . take it up with Pfeifer. (*He escapes into the office.*)

17

The supplicants look helplessly at one another. One after the other, they step back, sighing.

PFEIFER. (*Starts the inspection again.*) Well, Annie, and what are you bringing us?

OLD BAUMERT. How much for a web, then, Mr. Pfeifer?

PFEIFER. Ten groschen for each web.

OLD BAUMERT. Ain't that something!

Excitement among the weavers, whispers and grumblings.

Curtain

ACT TWO

SCENE: *A small room in the cottage of* WILHELM ANSORGE *in Kaschbach in the mountains called Eulengebirge.*

The narrow room measures less than six feet from the dilapidated floor to the smoke-blackened rafters. Two young girls, EMMA *and* BERTHA BAUMERT, *sit at looms.* MOTHER BAUMERT, *a crippled old woman, sits on a stool by the bed, at her spooling wheel. Her son,* AUGUST, *twenty years old, an idiot with small body and head and long spiderlike limbs, sits on a footstool, also reeling yarn.*

The weak, rosy light of the setting sun shines through two small window openings in the left wall. These are partly pasted over with paper and partly filled up with straw. The light falls on the pale, blond, loose hair of the girls, on their bare, bony shoulders and thin waxen necks, on the folds of their coarse chemises, which, with a short skirt of the roughest linen, constitute their entire clothing. The warm glow lights up the entire face, neck, and chest of the old woman. Her face is emaciated to a skeleton, with folds and wrinkles in the anemic skin. The sunken eyes are reddened and watery from the lint and smoke and from working by lamplight. She has a long goiter neck with sinews standing out. Her narrow chest is covered with faded shawls and rags. Part of the right wall, with the stove, stove bench, bedstead, and several gaudily tinted pictures of saints, is also lighted up. There are rags hanging on the bar of the stove to dry, and behind the stove, old worthless rubbish is piled up. On the bench are a few old pots and kitchen utensils; a heap of potato peelings is laid out to dry on a piece of paper. Skeins of yarn and reels hang from the rafters. Small baskets with bobbins stand beside the looms. In the back there is a low door without a lock; next to it, a bundle of willow switches leans against the wall. Several broken peck baskets lie about. The room is filled with the noise of the looms: the rhythmic movement of the lathe which shakes the walls and the floor, the shuffle and clicking of the shuttle moving rapidly back and forth. This blends with the low constant humming of the spooling wheels that sounds like the buzzing of bumble bees.

MOTHER BAUMERT. (*In a pitiful, exhausted voice, as the girls stop their weaving and bend over their webs.*) Do ya have to make knots again?

EMMA. (*The elder of the girls, twenty-two years old, is tying up the torn threads.*) This is the worst yarn!

BERTHA. (*Fifteen years old.*) The warp sure causes a lot of trouble.

EMMA. Where's he been so long? He's been gone since nine o'clock.

MOTHER BAUMERT. I should say so! Where can he be, girls?

BERTHA. Don't ya worry, mother!

MOTHER BAUMERT. I can't help it!

EMMA *continues weaving.*

BERTHA. Wait a minute, Emma!

EMMA. What is it?

BERTHA. I thought I heard somebody comin'.

EMMA. That'll be Ansorge comin' home.

FRITZ. (*A small four-year old boy, barefoot and dressed in rags, comes in crying.*) Mother, I'm hungry.

EMMA. Wait, Fritzi, just you wait a bit. Grandfather's comin' soon. He's bringin' bread and grain.

FRITZ. But I'm so hungry, Mama.

EMMA. I just told ya. Don't be so silly. He's comin' right away. He'll bring some nice bread and some coffee grain. When we stop workin', Mamma'll take the potato peelin's to the farmer, and he'll give her a bit of buttermilk for her boy.

FRITZ. But where's grandfather gone?

EMMA. He's at the manufacturer's, deliverin' a web.

FRITZ. At the manufacturer's?

EMMA. Yes, Fritzi! Down at Dreissiger's, in Peterswaldau.

FRITZ. Will he get some bread there?

EMMA. Yes, yes, they'll give him some money, and then he can buy some bread.

FRITZ. Will they give grandfather lots a money?

EMMA. Oh, stop talkin', boy. (*She continues weaving, as does* BERTHA. *Then both stop again.*)

BERTHA. August, go and ask Ansorge if he won't give us a light.

AUGUST *leaves together with* FRITZ.

MOTHER BAUMERT. (*With ever-increasing childlike fear, almost whining.*) Children, children! Where can the man be?

BERTHA. Maybe he dropped in to see Hauffen.

20

MOTHER BAUMERT. (*Crying.*) If he just ain't gone to the tavern.

EMMA. I hope not, Mother! But our father ain't that kind.

MOTHER BAUMERT. (*Quite beside herself with a host of fears.*) Well . . . well . . . well, tell me what'll happen if he . . . if he comes home . . . if he drinks it all up and don't bring nothin' home? There ain't a handful of salt in the house, not a piece of bread . . . we need a shovelful of fuel. . . .

BERTHA. Don't ya worry, Mother! The moon's shining. We'll go to the woods. We'll take August along and bring back some firewood.

MOTHER BAUMERT. Sure, so the forester can catch ya?

ANSORGE. (*An old weaver, with a gigantic frame, who has to bend low in order to enter the room, sticks his head and the upper part of his body through the door. His hair and beard are unkempt.*) Well, what do ya want?

BERTHA. Ya could give us a light!

ANSORGE. (*Muffled, as if speaking in the presence of a sick person.*) It's still light enough.

MOTHER BAUMERT. Now ya'll even make us sit in the dark.

ANSORGE. I've got to do the best I can. (*He goes out.*)

BERTHA. Now ya see how stingy he is.

EMMA. Yeah, we got to sit here till he gets good and ready.

MRS. HEINRICH. (*Enters. She is thirty years old, pregnant. Her face is worn from sorrow and anxious waiting.*) Good evenin' to ya all.

MOTHER BAUMERT. Well, Mother Heinrich, what's the news?

MRS. HEINRICH. (*Limping.*) I've stepped on a piece of glass.

BERTHA. Come over here and set down. I'll see if I can't get it out.

MRS. HEINRICH. (*Sits down;* BERTHA *kneels in front of her and busies herself with* MRS. HEINRICH'S foot.)

MOTHER BAUMERT. How's things at home, Mother Heinrich?

MRS. HEINRICH. (*Breaks out in despair.*) Soon I won't be able to stand it no more. (*She fights in vain against a flood of tears. Then she weeps silently.*)

MOTHER BAUMERT. It'd be the best for the likes of us, Mother Heinrich, if the dear Lord would have pity on us and take us out of this world.

MRS. HEINRICH. (*Losing her self-control, weeps and cries out.*) My poor children are starvin'! (*She sobs and moans.*) I just don't know what to do. Ya try as hard as ya can, ya wear yourself out till ya drop. I'm more dead than alive, and still it ain't no different. Nine hungry mouths to feed and not enough to feed them. Where am I to get the food, huh? Last night I had a little bit of bread—it wasn't enough for the two littlest ones. Who was I supposed to give it to, huh? They all cried: Mama, me, Mama, me. . . . No, no! And all this while I'm still up and about. What'll it be when I have to take to my bed? The few potatoes we had was washed away. We ain't got a bite to eat.

BERTHA. (*Has removed the splinter and washed out the wound.*) We'll put a piece of cloth around it. (*To* EMMA.) Look and see if ya can find one.

MOTHER BAUMERT. We ain't no better off, Mother Heinrich.

MRS. HEINRICH. At least ya've still got your girls. Ya've got a husband who can work for ya, but mine—he fell down again this past week. He's had another spell, and I was that scared to death—I didn't know what to do. And after he's had one of them fits, he's laid up for at least a week.

MOTHER BAUMERT. Mine ain't no better. He's ready to collapse, too. He's got trouble with his chest and his back. And there ain't a single pfennig in the house either. If he don't bring some money home today, I don't know what we're goin' to do either.

EMMA. That's so, Mother Heinrich. We're so bad off, Father had to take little Ami with him . . . we had to have him butchered so we can get something real in our stomachs again.

MRS. HEINRICH. Ain't ya even got a handful of flour left over?

MOTHER BAUMERT. Not even that much, Mother Heinrich; there ain't a pinch of salt left in the house.

MRS. HEINRICH. Well, then I don't know what to do! (*Gets up, stands brooding.*) I really don't know what to do! (*Crying out in anger and panic.*) I'd be satisfied if it was nothin' but pig swill!—but I just can't go home empty-handed again. That just won't do. God forgive me. I don't know nothin' else to do. (*She limps out quickly, stepping only on the heel of her left foot.*)

MOTHER BAUMERT. (*Calls after her, warning.*) Mother Heinrich, don't ya go an' do nothin' foolish.

BERTHA. She won't do no harm to herself. Don't ya worry.

EMMA. She always acts like that. (*She sits at the loom again and weaves for a few seconds.*)

AUGUST *enters with a candle, lighting the way for his father,* OLD BAUMERT, *who drags in a bundle of yarn.*

MOTHER BAUMERT. My God, man, where in the world have ya been so long?

OLD BAUMERT. Ya don't have to snap at me like that, right away. Just let me catch my breath first. Better look an' see who's come in with me.

MORITZ JAEGER. (*Enters, stooping, through the door. He is a well-built, average-sized, red-cheeked soldier. His Hussar's cap sits jauntily on the side of his head; he wears good clothes and shoes and a clean shirt without a collar. He stands erect and gives a military salute. In a hearty voice.*) Good evening, Auntie Baumert.

MOTHER BAUMERT. Well, well, now! So you've come home again? And ya didn't forget us? Why, set down. Come here, set down.

EMMA. (*With her skirt cleans off a wooden stool and shoves it toward JAEGER.*) Good evenin', Moritz! Did ya come back to have another look at how poor folks is living?

JAEGER. Well, now, say, Emma! I never really could believe it! Why, you've got a boy who'll soon be big enough to be a soldier. Where did ya get him?

BERTHA. (*Takes the small amount of food that her father brought in, puts the meat in a pan, and shoves it in the oven while AUGUST builds a fire.*) Ya know the Weaver Finger, don't ya?

MOTHER BAUMERT. He used to live here in the cottage with us. He would have married her, but his lungs was almost completely gone then. I warned the girl often enough. But would she listen to me? Now, he's dead and gone and forgotten a long time and she'll have to see how she can support the boy. But now, you tell me, Moritz, how's things been goin' with you?

OLD BAUMERT. You be quiet, Mother, can't ya see he's had plenty to eat; he's laughin' at all of us; he's got clothes like a prince and a silver pocket watch, and on top of all that, ten silver thalers in cash.

JAEGER. (*Stands with his legs apart, showing off, a boastful*

24

smile on his face.) I can't complain. I didn't have a bad time in the army.

OLD BAUMERT. He was an orderly to a captain. Just listen to him—he talks like elegant folks.

JAEGER. I've got so used to fine talk that I can't help it.

MOTHER BAUMERT. No, no, well, I never! Such a good-for-nothin' as you was, and comin' into such money. You never was good for nothin' much; ya couldn't unwind two spools in a row. But you was always off and away, settin' wrenboxes and robin snares. You'd rather do that. Well, ain't that the truth?

JAEGER. It's true, Auntie Baumert. And I didn't catch just robins, I caught swallows, too.

EMMA. No matter how often we used to say swallows was poison.

JAEGER. It was all the same to me. But how have all of you been getting along, Auntie Baumert?

MOTHER BAUMERT. O dear Lord Jesus, it's been awful hard these last four years. I've been havin' bad pains. Just look at my fingers. I really don't know if it's the rheumatiz or what. I'm in such misery! I can hardly move a muscle. Nobody knows the kind of pain I have to put up with.

OLD BAUMERT. She really has it bad now. She won't be with us long.

BERTHA. In the mornin' we got to dress her, in the evenin' we got to undress her. We got to feed her like a little baby.

MOTHER BAUMERT. (*Continuing in a complaining, tearful voice.*) I got to be waited on, hand and foot. I ain't just sick. I'm also a burden. How often I've prayed to the good Lord if he'd only call me away. O Lord, O Lord, my life's too hard, it really is. I don't know . . . people might think . . . but I've

25

been used to working hard from the time I was a child. I've always been able to do my share and now, all at once—(*She tries, in vain, to get up.*)—I just can't do nothin', no more! I've got a good husband and good children, but if I've got to sit by and see. . . . See how those girls look! They ain't got hardly no blood in 'em. They got as much color as a sheet. They keep workin' away at the treadle if they get anything for it or not. What kind of a life is that? They ain't been away from the treadle all year long. They ain't even earned enough so they could buy just a few clothes so they could be seen in public, or could step into church and get some comfort. They look like skeletons, they do, young girls of fifteen and twenty.

BERTHA. (*At the stove.*) It's smokin' again.

OLD BAUMERT. Yeah, just look at that smoke. Do ya think something can be done about it? It'll damn soon collapse, that stove. We'll have to let it collapse, and we'll just have to swallow the soot. All of us cough, one worse than the other. Anyone as coughs, coughs, and if it chokes us, and if our lungs are coughed up with it, nobody cares a bit.

JAEGER. Why, that's Ansorge's business, he has to fix it, doesn't he?

BERTHA. A lot he cares. He does enough complainin'.

MOTHER BAUMERT. He thinks we're takin' up too much room, as it is.

OLD BAUMERT. And if we make a fuss, out we go. He ain't seen a bit of rent from us for almost half a year.

MOTHER BAUMERT. A man like that livin' alone could at least be civil.

OLD BAUMERT. He ain't got nothin' neither, Mother. Things is hard enough with him, too, even if he don't make a fuss about his troubles.

26

MOTHER BAUMERT. He's still got his house.

OLD BAUMERT. Oh, no, Mother, what are ya talkin' about? There ain't hardly a stick of wood in this house he can call his own.

JAEGER. (*Has sat down. He takes a short pipe with a decorative tassel out of one coat pocket and a flask of whiskey out of the other.*) This can't go on much longer. I'm amazed at how things are with you people around here. Why, dogs in the city live better than you live.

OLD BAUMERT. (*Eagerly.*) That's the truth, ain't it? You know it, too? And if ya complain, they tell ya it's just hard times.

ANSORGE. (*Enters with an earthen bowl full of soup in one hand, a half-finished basket in the other.*) Welcome home, Moritz! So you're here again?

JAEGER. Thank you, Father Ansorge.

ANSORGE. (*Shoving his bowl into the oven.*) Say, if you don't look like a count!

OLD BAUMERT. Show him your fine watch. He's brought back a new suit, too, and ten silver thalers in cash.

ANSORGE. (*Shaking his head.*) Well, well! Well, well!

EMMA. (*Putting the potato peelings into a little sack.*) I'll take the peelin's over now. Maybe it'll be enough for a little skimmed milk. (*She goes out.*)

JAEGER. (*While all pay close and eager attention to him.*) Well, now, just think how often you've made it hot as hell for me. They'll teach you manners, Moritz, you always said, just you wait, when they take you into the army. Well, now you see, it's gone pretty well with me. In half a year, I had my stripes. You have to be willing, that's the main thing. I polished the sergeant's boots; I curried his horse, I brought him his beer.

I was as quick as a weasel. And I was always on my toes; damn it, my gear was always clean and sparkling. I was the first one in the stable, the first one at roll call, the first one in the saddle; and when it came to the attack—forward! Hell and damnation! I was as keen as a hunting dog. I always said to myself, nobody'll help you here, you can't get out of this job; and I'd pull myself together and do it; and then, finally, the captain said about me, in front of the whole squadron: That's the way a Hussar ought to be. (*Silence. He lights his pipe.*)

ANSORGE. (*Shaking his head.*) My, and such luck you had! Well, well! Well, well! (*He sits down on the floor, with the willow switches beside him. Holding the basket between his legs, he continues mending it.*)

OLD BAUMERT. Let's just hope that ya brought us some of your good luck along with ya. Now maybe we could have a drink with ya, huh?

JAEGER. Why, sure, Father Baumert, and when this is gone, there'll be more. (*He throws a coin down on the table.*)

ANSORGE. (*With foolish, grinning amazement.*) O Lord, such goin's on . . . over there, there's a roast sizzlin' and here's a quart of whiskey—(*He drinks from the bottle.*)—to your health, Moritz. Well, well! Well, well! (*From now on, the whiskey bottle is passed around.*)

OLD BAUMERT. If we could only have a little roast on holidays, instead of not seein' no meat at all, year in and year out. This way, ya've got to wait till a little dog crosses your path like this one did four weeks ago. And that don't happen often these days.

ANSORGE. Did ya have Ami killed?

OLD BAUMERT. He would've starved to death. . . .

ANSORGE. Well, well! Well, well!

MOTHER BAUMERT. And he was such a nice, friendly little dog.

JAEGER. Are you still so eager 'round here for roast dog?

OLD BAUMERT. O Lord, Lord, if we could only get our fill of it.

MOTHER BAUMERT. Yes, a piece of meat like that is sure rare around here.

OLD BAUMERT. Ain't ya got no appetite for such things no more? Well, just stay here with us, Moritz, and ya'll soon get it back.

ANSORGE. (Sniffing.) Well, well! Well, well! That's something that tastes good, and it sure gives off a nice smell.

OLD BAUMERT. (Sniffing.) The real thing, ya might say.

ANSORGE. Now tell us what you think, Moritz. You know how things go, out there in the world. Will things ever be different here with us weavers, or what?

JAEGER. I should hope so.

ANSORGE. We can't live and we can't die up here. Things is really bad with us, believe me. We fight to the last, but in the end we have to give in. The wolf is always at the door. In the old days, when I could still work at the looms, I could half-way get along, in spite of hunger and hardship. It's been a long time since I've been able to get some real work. I can hardly make a livin' weavin' baskets. I work till late into the night and when I fall worn out into bed, I've slaved for just a few pfennigs. You got a' education, now you tell me—can anyone really make out in such hard times? I got to lay out three thalers for taxes on the house, one thaler for land taxes, three thalers for interest. I can figure on makin' fourteen thalers. That leaves me seven thalers to live on all year. Out of that, I have to buy food, firewood, clothes, shoes, and patches and thread for mendin', and ya have to have a place to live, and goodness knows what else. Is it any wonder a man can't pay the interest?

OLD BAUMERT. Somebody sure ought to go to Berlin and explain to the King how things is with us.

JAEGER. That won't do much good, either, Father Baumert. There's already been plenty said about it in the newspapers. But the rich, they turn and twist the whole thing so . . . they out-devil the very best Christians.

OLD BAUMERT. (*Shaking his head.*) To think that in Berlin they ain't got no more sense than that.

ANSORGE. Tell me, Moritz, do you think that can really be? Ain't there a law against it? When I go and pinch and scrape and work my fingers to the bone weaving baskets and still can't pay the interest, can the farmer take my cottage away from me? There ain't a farmer who don't want his money. I just don't know what's to become of me if I've got to get out of my cottage. . . . (*Speaking with a choked voice, through tears.*) Here I was born, here my father sat at his loom, for more than forty years. How often he said to Mother: Mother, he said, when my time comes, you hold on to the cottage. This cottage I've worked for, he told her. Here, every single nail stands for a night's work, every board, a year's dry bread. Ya'd really think. . . .

JAEGER. They'll take your last pfennig, they're capable of it.

ANSORGE. Well, well! Well, well! But if it comes to that, I'd rather they carried me out than have to walk out in my old age. Dyin' ain't nothin'! My father was glad enough to die— only at the end, the very end, he was a bit scared. But when I crawled into the bed with him, he quieted down again. When ya think about it, at the time I was a boy of thirteen. I was

30

tired, and I fell asleep by the sick man. I didn't know no better—and when I woke up, he was stone cold.

MOTHER BAUMERT. (*After a pause.*) Reach into the stove, Bertha, and hand Ansorge his soup.

BERTHA. Here it is, Father Ansorge.

ANSORGE. (*Weeping, while he eats.*) Well, well! Well, well!

OLD BAUMERT *has begun to eat meat out of the pan.*

MOTHER BAUMERT. Why, Father—Father, you wait. Let Bertha set it out on the table, proper.

OLD BAUMERT. (*Chewing.*) It was two years ago that I took the sacrament last. I sold my Sunday suit right afterward. We bought a little piece of pork with the money. I ain't had no meat to eat since then till this very evenin'.

JAEGER. We don't need meat; the manufacturers eat it for us. They wade around in fat way up to here. If anybody doesn't believe that, he only needs to go down to Bielau or Peterswaldau. They'd be amazed—one manufacturer's mansion right after the other—one palace right after the other. With plate glass windows and little towers and fine iron fences. No, no, that doesn't look anything like hard times. There's plenty there for roasts and pastries, for carriages and coaches, for governesses, and who knows what all. They're so puffed up they don't really know what to do with all their high and mighty riches.

ANSORGE. In the old days, it was all different. In those days the manufacturers gave the weavers enough to get along on. Today, they squander it all themselves. I say that's because them people in high places don't believe in God no more, or in the devil, neither. They don't know nothin' about commandments and punishment. So they steal our last bite of bread, and weaken and undermine us wherever they can. Them people are the ones that's causin' all the trouble. If our manufacturers was good men, there wouldn't be no hard times for us.

JAEGER. You listen here, and I'll read you something nice. (*He takes a few sheets of paper from his pocket.*) Come on, August, run to the tavern and get another bottle. Why, August, you're always laughing.

MOTHER BAUMERT. I don't know what's the matter with the boy, he's always happy. No matter what happens, he laughs till his sides are ready to split. Now, quick! (AUGUST *goes out with the empty whiskey flask.*) Huh, Father, you know what tastes good, don't ya?

OLD BAUMERT. (*Chewing, his spirits rising from the food and the whiskey.*) Moritz, you're our man. You can read and write. You know how things is with the weavers. You have a heart for us poor weaver folk. You ought to take up our cause around here.

JAEGER. If that's all. That'd be fine with me. I'd be glad to give those devils of manufacturers something to think about. I wouldn't mind a bit. I'm an easy-going fellow, but when I once get my dander up and get mad, I'd take Dreissiger in one hand and Dittrich in the other and I'd knock their heads together so hard sparks would shoot out of their eyes. If we could manage to stick together, we could start such an uproar against the manufacturers. . . . We wouldn't need the King for that, or the government, either; we could simply say, we want this and that, and we do not want this or that, and they'd soon whistle a different tune. If they once see we've got spunk, they'd soon pull in their horns. I know their kind! They're cowardly bastards.

MOTHER BAUMERT. And that's really the truth. I certainly ain't bad. I was always one to say, there has to be rich people, too. But when it comes to this. . . .

JAEGER. For my part, the devil can take them all. That's what the whole bunch deserves.

BERTHA. Where's father? (OLD BAUMERT *has quietly left.*)

MOTHER BAUMERT. I don't know where he could've gone.

BERTHA. Could it be he ain't used to meat no more?

MOTHER BAUMERT. (*Beside herself, crying.*) Now, ya see, now ya see! He can't even keep it down. He's had to throw it up, all that nice little bit of good food.

OLD BAUMERT. (*Re-enters, crying with rage.*) No, no! It'll soon be all over with me. I'm too far gone. Ya finally get ahold of something good, and ya can't even keep it down. (*He sits down on the stove bench, weeping.*)

JAEGER. (*In a sudden fanatic outburst.*) And, at the same time, there are people, judges, not far from here—pot-bellies— who haven't a thing to do all year long except idle away their time. And they'll say the weavers could get along fine, if only they weren't so lazy.

ANSORGE. They ain't men, they're monsters.

JAEGER. Never mind, he's got what's coming to him. Baecker and I, we've given him a piece of our mind, and before we left, we sang "Bloody Justice."

ANSORGE. O Lord, O Lord, is that the song?

JAEGER. Yes, yes, and I have it here.

ANSORGE. I think it's called "Dreissiger's Song," ain't it?

JAEGER. I'll read it to you.

MOTHER BAUMERT. Who made up the song?

JAEGER. That, nobody knows. Now listen.

He reads, spelling it out like a schoolboy, accenting it badly, but with unmistakably strong feeling. Despair, pain, courage, hate, thirst for revenge—are all expressed.

33

JAEGER. Here a bloody justice thrives
More terrible than lynching
Here sentence isn't even passed
To quickly end a poor man's life.

Men are slowly tortured here,
Here is the torture chamber,
Here every heavy sigh that's heard
Bears witness to man's misery.

OLD BAUMERT. (*Is deeply moved by the words of the song. He frequently has difficulty in resisting the temptation to interrupt* JAEGER. *Now he can no longer contain himself; stammering amid laughter and tears, to his wife.*) "Here is the torture chamber." Whoever wrote that, Mother, spoke the truth. You can bear witness to that . . . how does it go? "Here every sigh that's heard. . . ." What's the rest? . . . "bear witness . . ."

JAEGER. "Bears witness to man's misery."

OLD BAUMERT. Ya know, standin' or sittin', we sigh with misery day after day.

ANSORGE *has stopped working, his body bent over in deep emotion.* MOTHER BAUMERT *and* BERTHA *are continuously wiping their eyes.*

JAEGER. (*Continues reading.*)

The Dreissigers are hangmen all,
Their servants are the henchmen
All of them oppressing us
And never showing mercy.

You scoundrels all, you devil's brood

34

OLD BAUMERT. (*Trembling with rage, stamps the floor.*) Yes, devil's brood!!!

JAEGER. (*Reads.*)

> You demons from the pit of hell
> Who steal the poor man's house and home
> A curse will be your payment.

ANSORGE. Well, well, and that deserves a curse.

OLD BAUMERT. (*Doubling his fist, threatening.*) "Who steal the poor man's house and home. . . !"

JAEGER. (*Reads.*)

> Begging, pleading doesn't help,
> In vain is all complaining,
> "If you don't like it you can go,
> And starve until you're dead."

OLD BAUMERT. What does it say? "In vain is all complaining"? Every word, every single word. . . . It's all as true as the Bible. "Begging, pleading doesn't help."

ANSORGE. Well, well! Well, well! Then nothin' will help.

JAEGER. (*Reads.*)

> Now think about the misery
> And pain of these poor wretches
> Without a bite of bread at home
> Are they not to be pitied?
>
> Pitied! Ha! Such human feeling
> Is unknown to you savages.
> Your goal is known to everyone,
> To bleed us poor men dry.

OLD BAUMERT. (*Springs up, in mad frenzy.*) "Bleed us poor men dry." That's right, bleed a poor man dry. Here I stand, Robert Baumert, master weaver from Kaschbach. Who can step up and say . . . I've been a good man all my life, and now look at me. What good's it done me? How do I look? What have they made of me? "Men are slowly tortured here." (*He stretches out his arms.*) Here, feel these, nothin' but skin and bones. "You scoundrels all, you devil's brood!!" (*He collapses onto a chair, weeping with anger and despair.*)

ANSORGE. (*Flings the basket into the corner, gets up, his entire body trembling with rage, stammers.*) There must be a change, I tell ya, here and now. We won't stand for it no more! We won't stand for it no more, come what may.

Curtain

ACT THREE

SCENE: *The tap room in the principal tavern in Peterswaldau. It is a large room, the raftered ceiling of which is supported at the center by a wooden pillar, around which there is a table. To the right of the pillar—one of its jambs hidden by the pillar —is a door in the back wall leading to another large room in which barrels and brewing utensils can be seen. In the corner to the right of the door is the bar—a high wooden counter with shelves for mugs, glasses, and the like; behind the bar is a cupboard with rows of liquor bottles; between the counter and the liquor cabinet there is a narrow space for the bartender. In front of the bar there is a table covered with a brightly colored cloth. A decorative lamp hangs above the table, around which there are a number of cane-chairs. Not far off in the right wall, a door leads to a room used for special occasions. Nearer the front, to the right, an old grandfather's clock is ticking. To the left of the entrance, against the rear wall, stands a table with bottles and glasses, and beyond it, in the corner, a large tile stove. There are three small windows in the left wall, under them a bench. In front of each window there is a large wooden table with its narrow end toward the wall. On the broad side of the tables are benches with backs and at the other narrow end, a single wooden chair. The walls are painted blue and are hung with placards, posters, and oil prints, among them the portrait of the King of Prussia, William IV.*

Innkeeper WELZEL, *a good-natured giant of around fifty, is drawing beer into a glass from a barrel behind the counter.* MRS. WELZEL *is ironing at the stove. She is a dignified-looking woman, neatly dressed, not quite thirty-five years old.* ANNA WELZEL, *a well-dressed pretty girl of seventeen with magnificent reddish-blonde hair, sits behind the table, embroidering. For a moment she looks up from her work and listens to the sounds of children's voices singing a funeral hymn, off in the distance.* WIEGAND, *the carpenter, in his work clothes, sits at the same table with a glass of Bavarian beer in front of him. He gives the appearance of being the sort of man who knows what is needed to get ahead in the world: cunning, speed, and ruthless determination.* A TRAVELING SALESMAN *sits at the pillar table, busily devouring a chopped steak. He is of medium height, well-fed, rather puffy, disposed to heartiness, lively and impudent. He is dressed in the latest fashion. His baggage, consisting of traveling bag, sample case, umbrella, overcoat, and steamer rug—lie on chairs beside him.*

WELZEL. (*Carrying a glass of beer to the* SALESMAN, *aside to* WIEGAND.) The devil's loose in Peterswaldau today.

37

WIEGAND. (*In a sharp, trumpeting voice.*) Well, of course, it's delivery day up at Dreissiger's.

MRS. WELZEL. Yes, but they weren't always so noisy.

WIEGAND. Well, it might be on account of the two hundred additional weavers that Dreissiger's gettin' ready to take on.

MRS. WELZEL. (*At her ironing.*) Yes, yes, that's it. If he wanted two hundred, probably six hundred will have showed up. We've got more'n enough of that sort.

WIEGAND. Lord, yes, there's plenty of them. And no matter how hard it goes with them, they don't die out. They bring more children into the world than we can ever use. (*For a moment, the hymn can be more clearly heard.*) And to add to it, there's a funeral today, too. Weaver Fabich died.

WELZEL. It took him long enough. He's been goin' around for years lookin' like a ghost.

WIEGAND. I tell ya, Welzel, never in all my life have I glued together such a tiny, shabby coffin. It was such a measly little corpse, it didn't even weigh ninety pounds.

SALESMAN. (*Chewing.*) I really don't understand . . . wherever you look, in all the newspapers, you read the most horrible stories about conditions among the weavers, and you get the impression that all the people here are half-starved. And then you see such a funeral! Just as I came into the village, there were brass bands, schoolteachers, children, the Pastor, and a whole string of people; my God, you'd think the Emperor of China was being buried. If these people can pay for that. . . ! (*He drinks his beer. Then he puts the glass down and suddenly speaks in a frivolous tone.*) Isn't that so, Miss? Don't you agree with me?

ANNA *smiles, embarrassed, and continues busily with her embroidery.*

38

SALESMAN. Those must be slippers for Papa.

WELZEL. Oh, I don't like to wear them things.

SALESMAN. Just listen to that! I'd give half my fortune if those slippers were for me.

MRS. WELZEL. He just don't appreciate such things.

WIEGAND. (*After he has coughed several times and moved his chair about, as if he wanted to speak.*) The gentleman has expressed himself mighty well about the funeral. Now tell us, young lady, isn't that just a small funeral?

SALESMAN. Yes, I must say. . . . That must cost a tremendous amount of money. Where do these people get the money for it?

WIEGAND. You'll forgive me for sayin' it, sir, there is so much folly among the poorer classes hereabouts. If you don't mind my sayin' so, they have such exaggerated ideas of the dutiful respect and the obligations that's due the deceased and the blessed dead. And when it's a matter of deceased parents, they are so superstitious that the descendants and the next of kin scrape together their last penny. And what the children can't raise, they borrow from the nearest money lender. And then they're in debts up to their necks; they'll be owing His Reverence the Pastor, the sexton, and everybody else in the neighborhood. And drinks and victuals and all the other necessary things. Oh yes, I approve of respectful duty on the part of children toward their parents, but not so that the mourners are burdened down the rest of their lives by such obligations.

SALESMAN. I beg your pardon, but I should think the Pastor would talk them out of it.

WIEGAND. Beggin' your pardon, sir, but here I would like to interpose that every little congregation has its ecclesiastical house of worship and must support its reverend pastor. The high clergy get a wonderful revenue and profit from such a big funeral. The more elaborate such a funeral can be arranged, the more profitable is the offertory that flows from it. Whoever knows the conditions of the workers hereabouts can, with unauthoritative certainty, affirm that the pastors only with reluctance tolerate small and quiet funerals.

HORNIG. (*Enters. A small, bow-legged old man with a strap over his shoulders and chest. He is a rag picker.*) Good mornin'. I'd like a drink. Well, young lady, any rags? Miss Anna, in my cart I've got beautiful hair ribbons, lingerie, ribbons, garters, pins and hairpins, hooks and eyes. I'll give them all to ya for a few rags. (*Changing his tone.*) Then, out of the rags, they'll make fine white paper, and your sweetheart'll write ya a lovely letter on it.

ANNA. Oh no, thank you, I don't want a sweetheart.

MRS. WELZEL. (*Puts a hot bolt in the iron.*) That's the way the girl is. She don't want to think of gettin' married.

SALESMAN. (*Jumps up, apparently surprised and pleased, steps up to the table, and holds out his hand to ANNA.*) That's sensible, Miss. You're just like me. O.K., let's shake on it! We'll both stay single.

ANNA. (*Blushing, gives him her hand.*) But surely you are married?

SALESMAN. God forbid, I just make believe I am. You think, perhaps, because I wear this ring? I just put it on my finger to prevent people from taking unfair advantage of my charming personality. Of you, I'm not afraid. (*He puts the ring in his pocket.*) Seriously, Miss, tell me, don't you ever want to get just the least bit married?

ANNA. (*Shaking her head.*) And why should I?

MRS. WELZEL. She'll stay single unless something very special turns up.

SALESMAN. Well, why not? One wealthy Silesian business-man married his mother's maid, and that rich manufacturer, Dreissiger, took an innkeeper's daughter, too. She isn't half as pretty as you, Miss, and now she rides in a carriage with liv-eried servants. Why not, indeed? (*He walks around, stretching his legs.*) I'll have a cup of coffee.

ANSORGE *and* OLD BAUMERT *enter, each with a bundle, and quietly and humbly join* HORNIG *at the front table to the left.*

WELZEL. Welcome, Father Ansorge. Is it you we're seein' again?

HORNIG. Did ya finally crawl out of your smoky nest?

ANSORGE. (*Awkwardly and visibly embarrassed.*) I went and got myself another web.

OLD BAUMERT. He's ready to work for 10 groschen.

ANSORGE. I never would've done it, but there's been an end to my basket weavin'.

WIEGAND. It's always better than nothin'. Ya know he's doin' it so ya'll have work. I'm very well acquainted with Dreissiger. A week ago I took out the storm windows for him. We were talkin' about it. He just does it out of pity.

ANSORGE. Well, well—well, well.

WELZEL. (*Setting a glass of whiskey in front of each of the weavers.*) Your health! Now tell me, Ansorge, how long has it been since ya stopped shavin'? The gentleman would like to know.

SALESMAN. (*Calls across.*) Now, Mr. Welzel, you know I didn't say that. I just noticed the master weaver because of his venerable appearance. One doesn't often run across such a powerful figure.

ANSORGE. (*Scratches his head, embarrassed.*) Well, well—well, well.

SALESMAN. Such extremely powerful, primitive men are seldom seen these days. We are so softened by civilization . . . but I find I still get pleasure out of such natural, unspoiled strength. What bushy eyebrows! Such a heavy beard. . . .

HORNIG. Well, look here, now I'll tell ya, sir—the people hereabouts are too poor to go to the barber, and they haven't been able to afford a razor in many a day. What grows, grows. They haven't anything to spend on the outer man.

SALESMAN. But I ask you, my good man, where would I. . . . (*Softly, to the tavern keeper.*) Would it be proper to offer the hairy one a glass of beer?

WELZEL. God forbid. He'll take nothin'. He's got queer notions.

SALESMAN. Well, then I won't. With your permission, Miss? (*He takes a seat at the table with her.*) I can assure you, from the time I came in, I've been so struck by your hair, such luster, such softness, such a mass of it! (*Delighted, he kisses his finger tips.*) And what color . . . like ripe wheat. What a furor you would cause if you came to Berlin with hair like that. *Parole d'honneur*, with such hair you could be presented at Court. (*Leaning back, looking at her hair.*) Exquisite, really exquisite.

WIEGAND. It's on account of her hair that she's got such a pretty nickname.

SALESMAN. What do they call her?

ANNA. (*Keeps on laughing to herself.*) Oh, don't you listen to them.

HORNIG. They call you Red Fox, don't they?

WELZEL. Now stop that! Stop turnin' the girl's head altogether. They've already put enough high and mighty ideas in her head. Today she wants a count, tomorrow it'll have to be a prince.

MRS. WELZEL. Don't ya run the girl down, man. It's no crime for a person to want to get ahead. Not everybody thinks the way you do. That wouldn't be good, either. Then nobody'd get ahead, then everybody'd always stay in the same old place. If Dreissiger's grandfather had thought the way you do, he'd still be a poor weaver. Now they're rich as can be. Old Tromtra, too, was no more than a poor weaver, now he owns twelve big estates and on top of that, he's got a title.

WIEGAND. You must admit, Welzel, on that score, your wife's right. I can vouch for that. If I'd thought like you, would I have seven journeymen today?

HORNIG. You sure know how to bide your time, we'll have to give ya credit for that. Even before the weaver's off his feet, you're already gettin' his coffin ready.

WIEGAND. You've got to tend to business if you want to get ahead.

HORNIG. Yes, you tend to yours, all right. You know better than the doctor does, when a weaver's child is goin' to die.

WIEGAND. (*No longer smiling, suddenly furious.*) And you know better than the police does where the thieves sit among the weavers, the ones who hold out a few bobbins every week. Ya come after rags and ya get a bobbin of yarn, too, if there's a chance.

HORNIG. And your livin' lays in the graveyard. The more that go to rest on your wood shavings, the better it is for you. When ya look at all the children's graves, ya pat your belly and ya say, this year's been a good one again; the little rascals dropped like June bugs from the trees. So I can afford a bottle of whiskey again this week.

43

WIEGAND. Anyhow, at least I don't trade in stolen goods.

HORNIG. At the most, you bill some rich cotton manufacturer twice, or you take a few extra boards from Dreissiger's barn if the moon ain't shinin'.

WIEGAND. (*Turning his back on* HORNIG.) Oh, go on talkin' to anyone you please, but leave me alone. (*Suddenly.*) Hornig, the liar!

HORNIG. Coffin-maker!

WIEGAND. (*To the others.*) He knows how to bewitch cattle.

HORNIG. Look out, let me tell ya, or I'll put the sign on you. (WIEGAND *turns pale.*)

MRS. WELZEL. (*Had gone out, and now sets a cup of coffee down in front of the* SALESMAN.) Would you perhaps rather have your coffee in the other room?

SALESMAN. Whatever put that idea in your head? (*With a longing look at* ANNA.) I'll stay here until I die.

A YOUNG FORESTER *and a* FARMER *enter, the latter carrying a whip.* (*Together.*) Good morning! (*They stop at the bar.*)

FARMER. We'll have two ginger beers.

WELZEL. Welcome to both of you! (*He pours the drinks; they both take their glasses, touch them to each other, take a sip, and place them back on the bar.*)

SALESMAN. Well, Forester, have you had a long trip?

FORESTER. Pretty far. I've come from Steinseiffersdorf.

FIRST *and* SECOND OLD WEAVERS *enter and sit down next to* ANSORGE, BAUMERT, *and* HORNIG.

SALESMAN. Pardon me, sir, are you one of Count Hochheim's foresters?

FORESTER. No, I'm one of Count Kailsch's.

SALESMAN. Oh, of course, of course—that's what I meant to say. It's most confusing here with all the counts and barons and other people of rank. You've got to have a good memory. What are you carrying the ax for?

FORESTER. I took it away from some thieves I caught stealing wood.

OLD BAUMERT. His Lordship is sure strict about a few sticks of firewood.

SALESMAN. I beg your pardon, it would scarcely do if everybody were to take. . . .

OLD BAUMERT. Beggin' your pardon, it's the same here as everywhere else with the big and the little thieves; there are those that carry on a wholesale lumber business and get rich from stolen wood, but if a poor weaver so much as. . . .

FIRST OLD WEAVER. (*Interrupts* BAUMERT.) We don't dare pick up a single twig, but the lords, they skin us alive. There's insurance money to pay, spinnin' money, payments in kind; then we have to run errands for nothin' and work on the estate, whether we want to or not.

ANSORGE. And that's the truth: what the manufacturers leave us, the noblemen take away.

SECOND OLD WEAVER. (*Has taken a seat at the next table.*) I've said it to the gentleman hisself. Beggin' your pardon, sir, I says to him, I can't do so many days' work on the estate this year. I just can't do it! And why not? Forgive me, but the water has ruined everything. My little bit of ground's been all washed away. I've got to slave night and day if I'm to keep alive. Such a flood . . . I tell ya, I just stood there and wrung my hands. That good soil washed right down the hill and straight into my cottage; and that fine, expensive seed. . . ! Oh my Lord, I just howled into the wind. I cried for a week, till I couldn't see no more. . . . And after that I wore myself out pushin' eighty wheelbarrows of dirt up the hill.

45

FARMER. (*Roughly.*) You do set up an awful howl, I must say. We all have to put up with what Heaven sends us. And if it don't go good in other ways with ya, who's to blame but yourselves? When times was good, what did ya do then? Ya gambled and drank it all up, that's what ya did. If ya had put something aside at that time, ya'd have had something saved for now, and ya wouldn't have had to steal wood and yarn.

FIRST YOUNG WEAVER. (*Standing with several friends in the other room, shouts through the door.*) A farmer's always a farmer, even if he sleeps till nine every mornin'.

FIRST OLD WEAVER. That's a fact; the farmer and the nobleman, they're two of a kind. If a weaver wants a place to live, the farmer says I'll give ya a little hole to live in. You pay me a nice rent, and help me bring in my hay and my grain, and if ya don't like it, ya'll see what happens. Every one of them's just like the next one.

OLD BAUMERT. (*Fiercely.*) We're just like an old apple that everybody takes a bite out of.

FARMER. (*Irritated.*) Oh, you starved wretches, what are you good for, anyway? Can ya handle a plow? Can ya even plow a straight furrow, or pitch fifteen shocks of oats onto a wagon? You're good for nothin' but loafin', and lyin' abed with your women. You're no good at all. You're no-account bums. No use at all.

(*He pays and leaves. The* FORESTER *follows him, laughing.* WELZEL, *the* CARPENTER, *and* MRS WELZEL *laugh out loud, the* SALESMAN *chuckles. Then the laughter quiets down, and there is silence.*)

HORNIG. A farmer like that's just like a bull. As if I didn't know how bad things was around here. All the things ya get to see up here in the villages. Four and five people layin' naked on a single straw ticking.

SALESMAN. (*In a gently, rebuking tone.*) Permit me, my good man, to observe that there is a wide difference of opinion in regard to the distress in this region. If you can read. . . .

HORNIG. Oh, I read everything in the papers as well as you do. No, no, I know these things from goin' around and mixin' with the people. When a man's lugged a pack around for forty years, he learns a thing or two. What happened at the Fullers? The children, they scratched around in the dung heap with the neighbors' geese. Those people died there—naked—on the cold stone floor. They had to eat stinkin' weaver's glue, they was so hungry. Hunger killed them off by the hundreds.

SALESMAN. If you can read, you must be aware that the government has had a thorough investigation made and that. . . .

HORNIG. We know all that. We know all that. The government sends a gentleman who before he sets out knows everything better than if he'd seen it himself. He walks around the village a little where the brook widens and where the best houses are. He won't dirty his good, shiny shoes goin' any farther. He thinks everything is probably just as beautiful everywhere else, and climbs into his carriage, and drives home again. And then he writes to Berlin that he saw no hardships at all. If he'd had a little bit of patience, though, and had climbed around in the village up to where the brook comes in and across it or, even better, off to the side where the little shacks are scattered, the old straw huts on the hills that are sometimes so black and broken-down they wouldn't be worth the match it'd take to set 'em afire, then he'd have made an altogether different report to Berlin. Those gentlemen from

47

the government ought to have come to me, them that didn't want to believe that there was no hardship here. I would've showed them something, I would've opened their eyes to all the hunger-holes around here.

(*The singing of the "Weavers' Song" is heard outside.*)

WELZEL. They're singin' that devil's song again.

WIEGAND. Yes, they're turnin' the whole village upside down.

MRS. WELZEL. It's like there's something in the air.

JAEGER *and* BAECKER, *arm in arm, at the head of a band of young weavers, noisily enter the other room, and then come into the bar.*

JAEGER. Squadron halt! Dismount!

The new arrivals seat themselves at the various tables at which weavers are already sitting, and start conversations with them.

HORNIG. (*Calling to* BAECKER.) Say, tell me, what's up that ya've got such a big crowd together?

BAECKER. (*Significantly.*) Maybe something's goin' to happen. Right, Moritz?

HORNIG. You don't say! Don't do nothin' foolish.

BAECKER. Blood's flowed already. Do ya want to see?

He pushes back his sleeve, stretches out his arm and shows him bleeding tattoo marks on his upper arm. Many of the young weavers at the other tables do the same.

BAECKER. We were at Barber Schmidt's havin' ourselves tattooed,

HORNIG. Well, now that's clear. No wonder there's so much noise in the streets, with such rascals tearin' around. . . !

JAEGER. (*Showing off, in a loud voice.*) Two quarts, right away, Welzel! I'll pay for it. Maybe you think I don't have the dough? Well, just you wait! If we wanted to, we could drink beer and lap up coffee till tomorrow morning as well as a traveling salesman. (*Laughter among the young weavers.*)

SALESMAN. (*With comic surprise.*) Who or whom are you talking about—me?

The tavern keeper, his wife, their daughter, WIEGAND, *and the* SALESMAN, *all laugh.*)

JAEGER. Always him who asks.

SALESMAN. Allow me to say, young man, that things seem to be going right well with you.

JAEGER. I can't complain, I'm a salesman for ready-made clothing. I go fifty-fifty with the manufacturers. The hungrier the weavers grow, the fatter I get. The greater their poverty, the fuller my cupboard.

BAECKER. Well done. Your health, Moritz!

WELZEL. (*Has brought the whiskey; on the way back to the bar, he stops and, in his usual phlegmatic and even manner, turns slowly to the weavers. Quietly and emphatically.*) You let the gentleman alone. He ain't done nothin' to you.

YOUNG WEAVERS' VOICES. We ain't done nothin' to him, either.

MRS. WELZEL *has exchanged a few words with the* SALESMAN. *She takes the cup and the rest of the coffee into the next room. The* SALESMAN *follows her amidst the laughter of the weavers.*

YOUNG WEAVERS' VOICES. (*Singing.*) The Dreissigers are hangmen all, Their servants are the henchmen. . . .

WELZEL. Sh, Sh! Sing that song wherever else ya want to, but I won't allow it here.

FIRST OLD WEAVER. He's quite right. Stop that singin'.

BAECKER. (*Shouts.*) But we've got to march past Dreissiger's again. He's got to hear our song once more.

WIEGAND. Don't go too far, or he might take it the wrong way.

Laughter and cries of "Ho-ho."

OLD WITTIG. (*A gray-haired blacksmith, bareheaded, wearing a leather apron and wooden shoes, and covered with soot, as if he had just come from the smithy, enters and stands at the bar, waiting for a glass of brandy.*) Let 'em make a little noise. Barkin' dogs don't bite.

OLD WEAVERS' VOICES. Wittig, Wittig!

WITTIG. Here he is. What do ya want?

OLD WEAVERS' VOICES. Wittig is here.—Wittig, Wittig!—Come here, Wittig, set with us!—Come over here, Wittig!

WITTIG. I'm awful careful about settin' with such blockheads.

JAEGER. Come on, have a drink on me.

WITTIG. Oh, you keep your liquor. When I drink, I'll pay for my own.

(*He takes his glass of brandy and sits down at the table with* BAUMERT *and* ANSORGE. *He pats the latter on the belly.*) What do the weavers eat nowadays? Sauerkraut and plenty of lice.

OLD BAUMERT. (*Ecstatically.*) But what if they wasn't to put up with it no more?

WITTIG. (*With feigned surprise, staring stupidly at the weaver.*) Well, well, well, Heinerle, tell me, is that really you? (*Laughs without restraint.*) I laugh myself sick at you people. Old Baumert wants to start a rebellion. Now we're in for it: now the tailors'll start, too, then the baa-lambs'll be rising up, then the mice and the rats. Good Lord, what a time that'll be!

He holds his sides with laughter.

OLD BAUMERT. Look here, Wittig, I'm the same man I used to be. And I tell ya even now if things could be settled peaceable, it'd be better.

50

WITTIG. Like hell it'll be settled peaceable. Where has anything like this ever been settled peaceable? Maybe things was settled peaceable in France? Maybe Robespierre patted the hands of the rich? There it was just "allay," go ahead! Always up to the guillotine! Let's go. It had to be "along songfong." Roast geese just don't fly into your mouth.

OLD BAUMERT. If I could just halfway earn my livin'. . . .

FIRST OLD WEAVER. We're fed up, up to here, Wittig.

SECOND OLD WEAVER. We don't even want to go home, no more. . . . Whether we work or whether we lay down and sleep, we starve either way.

FIRST OLD WEAVER. At home ya go completely crazy.

ANSORGE. It's all the same to me now, no matter what happens.

OLD WEAVERS' VOICES. (*With mounting excitement.*) There's no peace left nowhere.—We ain't even got the spirit to work no more.—Up our way in Steinkunzendorf there's a man settin' by the brook all day long and washin' hisself, naked as God made him. . . . He's gone completely out of his head.

THIRD OLD WEAVER. (*Rises, moved by the spirit, and begins to "speak with tongues," raising his finger threateningly.*) Judgment Day is comin'! Don't join with the rich and the gentry. Judgment Day is comin'! Lord God of Sabaoth. . . .

Several laugh. He is pushed down into his chair.

WELZEL. All he has to do is drink just one glass of liquor and his head's in a whirl.

THIRD OLD WEAVER. (*Continues.*) Hearken, they don't believe in God nor hell nor heaven. They just mock at religion.

FIRST OLD WEAVER. That's enough, now, that's enough.

BAECKER. You let the man say his prayers. Many a man could take it to heart.

MANY VOICES. (*In a tumult.*) Let him talk—let him!

THIRD OLD WEAVER. (*Raising his voice.*) Hell has opened wide and its jaws are gaping open, wide open, crashing down all those who do harm to the poor and violence to the cause of the afflicted, saith the Lord.

Tumult. Suddenly reciting like a schoolboy.

> And then how strange it is.
> If you will carefully observe
> How they the linen weavers' work despise.

BAECKER. But we're cotton weavers. (*Laughter.*)

HORNIG. The linen weavers are even worse off. They wander like ghosts around the mountains. Here you at least have the courage to rebel.

WITTIG. Do ya think, maybe, that here the worst is over? That little bit of courage that they still have left in their bodies the manufacturers will knock right out of them.

BAECKER. Why, he said that the weavers will get so they'll work for just a slice of bread and cheese. (*Tumult.*)

VARIOUS OLD *and* YOUNG WEAVERS. Who said that?

BAECKER. That's what Dreissiger said about the weavers.

A YOUNG WEAVER. That son of a bitch ought to be strung up.

JAEGER. Listen to me, Wittig, you've always talked so much about the French Revolution. You always bragged so much. Now maybe the chance'll soon come for everybody to show how much of a man he is . . . whether he is a loud-mouth or a man of honor.

WITTIG. (*Starting up in a rage.*) Say one more word, boy! Did you ever hear the whistle of bullets? Did you ever stand at an outpost in enemy territory?

JAEGER. Now don't get mad. You know we're all comrades I didn't mean any harm.

WITTIG. I don't give a rap for your comradeship. You puffed up fool!

POLICEMAN KUTSCHE *enters.*

SEVERAL VOICES. Sh! Sh! The Police!

There is a relatively long period of sh-ing before complete silence reigns.

KUTSCHE. (*Sits down by the center pillar amid the deep silence of all the others.*) I'd like a shot of whiskey, please. (*Again complete silence.*)

WITTIG. Well, Kutsche, you here to see that everything's all right with us?

KUTSCHE. (*Not listening to* WITTIG.) Good mornin', Mr. Wiegand.

WIEGAND. (*Still in the corner of the bar.*) Good mornin', Kutsche.

KUTSCHE. How's business?

WIEGAND. Fine, thanks for askin'.

BAECKER. The Chief of Police is afraid we might spoil our stomachs on all the wages we get. (*Laughter.*)

JAEGER. Isn't that so, Welzel, we've all had pork roast and gravy and dumplings and sauerkraut, and now we're getting ready to drink our champagne. (*Laughter.*)

WELZEL. Everything's the other way 'round.

KUTSCHE. And if ya did have champagne and roast, ya'd still not be satisfied. I don't have no champagne, neither, and I manage to get along.

BAECKER. (*Referring to* KUTSCHE'S *nose.*) He waters his red beet with brandy and beer. That's how it got so nice and ripe. (*Laughter.*)

53

WITTIG. A cop like him's got a hard life. Now, he's got to throw a starvin' little boy in jail for beggin', then he has to seduce a weaver's pretty daughter, then he has to get dead drunk and beat his wife so she goes runnin' to the neighbors for fear of her life. Ridin' about on his horse, lyin' in his featherbed . . . till nine, I tell ya, ain't that easy.

KUTSCHE. Always a'talkin'! You'll talk yourself into a big mess one of these days. It's been known for a long time what sort of a fellow you are. Even as high as the judge they've known about your rebellious tongue for a long time. I know someone who'll bring his wife and children to the poorhouse with his drinkin' and hangin' around taverns, and hisself into jail. He'll agitate and agitate until he comes to a terrible end.

WITTIG. (*Laughs bitterly.*) Who know what's ahead? You might be right after all. (*Breaking out angrily.*) But if it comes to that, then I'll know who I can thank, who has blabbed to the manufacturers and to the nobles, and reviled and slandered me so I don't get a lick of work no more.—Who set the farmers and the millers against me so that, for a whole week, I haven't had a single horse to shoe or a wheel to put a rim on. I know who that is. I once yanked the damned scoundrel off his horse because he was thrashing a poor little nitwit boy with a horsewhip for stealin' a few green pears. I tell ya, and ya know me, put me in jail, and ya'd better be makin' out your will at the same time. If I get the slightest warnin', I'll take whatever I can get my hands on, whether it's a horseshoe or a hammer, a wagon spoke or a bucket, and I'll go lookin' for ya, and if I have to pull ya out of bed, away from your woman, I'll do it and I'll cave your skull in, as sure as my name is Wittig.

He has jumped up and is about to attack KUTSCHE.

54

OLD *and* YOUNG WEAVERS. (*Holding him back.*) Wittig, Wittig, don't lose your head.

KUTSCHE. (*Has stood up involuntarily; his face is pale. During what follows he keeps moving backward. The nearer he gets to the door, the braver he becomes. He speaks the last few words at the very threshold, and then immediately disappears.*) What do ya want with me? I've got nothin' to do with you. I've got to talk to one of the weavers here. I've done nothin' to you and I've got no business with you. But I'm to tell you weavers this: the Chief of Police forbids ya to sing that song—"Dreissiger's Song," or whatever it's called. And if that singin' in the streets don't stop right away, he'll see to it that you get plenty of time and rest in jail. Then ya can sing on bread and water as long as ya like.

Leaves.

WITTIG. (*Shouts after him.*) He ain't got no right to forbid us anything, and if we roar till the windows rattle and they can hear us way off in Reichenbach, and if we sing so the houses tumble down on all the manufacturers and all the policemen's helmets dance on their heads, it's nobody's business.

BAECKER. (*In the meantime has stood up, and has given the signal for the singing to begin. He begins to sing, together with the others.*)

> Here a bloody justice thrives
> More terrible than lynching
> Here sentence isn't even passed
> To quickly end a poor man's life.

WELZEL *tries to quiet them, but no one listens to him.* WIEGAND *holds his hands over his ears and runs away. The weavers*

get up and, singing the following verses, march after WITTIG
and BAECKER, *who, by nods, gestures, have signaled for everyone to leave.*

> Men are slowly tortured here,
> Here is the torture chamber,
> Here every heavy sigh that's heard
> Bears witness to the misery.

*Most of the weavers sing the following verse when they are in
the street; only a few young fellows are still inside the tap-
room, paying for their drinks. At the end of the next verse the
room is empty except for* WELZEL, *his wife, his daughter,*
HORNIG, *and* OLD BAUMERT.

> You scoundrels all, you devil's brood
> You demons from the pit of hell
> Who steal the poor man's house and home
> A curse will be your payment.

WELZEL. (*Calmly gathers up the glasses.*) Why, they're
completely out of their heads today.

OLD BAUMERT *is about to leave.*

HORNIG. Tell me, Baumert, what's afoot?

OLD BAUMERT. They'll be goin' to Dreissiger's to see if he'll
add to their wages.

WELZEL. Are you goin' to join up with such madness?

OLD BAUMERT. Well, you see, Welzel, it ain't up to me. A
young man sometimes may, and an old man must. (*A trifle
embarrassed, leaves.*)

HORNIG. (*Rises.*) It'll sure surprise me if things don't come
to a bad end here.

WELZEL. Who'd think the old fellows would completely lose their heads?

HORNIG. Well, every man has his dream.

Curtain

ACT FOUR

SCENE: *Peterswaldau—A living room in the house of the cotton manufacturer, DREISSIGER. It is luxuriously furnished in the cold style of the first half of the nineteenth century. The ceiling, stove, and doors are white; the wallpaper is a cold grayish blue, with straight lines and little flowers. The room is filled with red upholstered mahogany furniture, including chairs and cupboards, richly decorated and carved. The furniture is placed as follows: on the right, between two windows with cherry-red damask curtains, is a secretary with a drop leaf that folds down to form a desk; directly opposite it, the sofa, with an iron safe nearby; in front of the sofa a table, armchairs, and straight chairs; against the back wall, a gun case. Pictures reflecting poor taste hang in gilt frames on the walls. Above the sofa hangs a mirror with a heavily gilded rococo frame. A door on the left leads to the vestibule; an open double door in the back wall leads into the drawing room, also overloaded with uncomfortable, showy furnishings. In the drawing room, MRS. DREISSIGER and MRS. KITTELHAUS, the pastor's wife, can be seen looking at pictures while Pastor KITTELHAUS converses with the tutor, WEINHOLD, a student of theology.*

KITTELHAUS. (*A small, friendly man, enters the front room, smoking and chatting amiably with the tutor, who is also smoking.* KITTELHAUS *looks around and, when he sees no one is in the room, shakes his head in amazement.*) Of course it is not at all surprising, Weinhold; you are young. At your age, we old fellows had—I won't say the same views—but yet, similar ones. Similar ones, at any rate. And there is, after all, something wonderful about youth—and all its beautiful ideals. Unfortunately, however, they are fleeting—fleeting as April sunshine. Just wait till you are my age. When once a man has said his say to the people from the pulpit for thirty years, fifty-two times a year, not counting holidays—then he, of necessity, becomes quieter. Think of me, Weinhold, when that time comes for you.

WEINHOLD. (*Nineteen years old, pale, emaciated, tall and thin, with long, straight, blond hair. He is very restless and nervous in his movements.*) With all respect, sir . . . I really don't know . . . there certainly is a great difference in temperaments.

KITTELHAUS. My dear Weinhold, you may be ever so restless a soul—(*In a tone of reproof.*) and that you are—you may be ever so violent—and rudely attack existing conditions, but that will subside. Yes, yes, I certainly do admit that we have colleagues who, though rather advanced in years, still play rather childish and foolish tricks. One preaches against drinking and founds temperance societies; another writes appeals which, undeniably, are most touching to read. But what does he accomplish with it? The distress among the weavers, where it exists, is not relieved thereby. And yet the peace of society is undermined by it. No, no, in such a case one might almost say, cobbler, stick to your last! A keeper of souls should not concern himself with bellies. Preach the pure word of God and, for the rest, let Him take care who provides shelter and food for the birds and sees that the lily in the field does not perish.—But now I would really like to know where our worthy host went so suddenly.

MRS. DREISSIGER. (*Comes into the front room with the Pastor's wife. She is a pretty woman, thirty years old, a robust, healthy type. A certain discrepancy is noticeable between her manner of speaking or moving and her elegant attire.*) You're quite right, Pastor. Wilhelm's always that way. When something strikes him, he runs off and leaves me alone. I've talked to him about it plenty, but you can say what you will, that's the way it is.

KITTELHAUS. That's the way with businessmen, Madam.

WEINHOLD. If I'm not mistaken, something's been happening downstairs.

DREISSIGER. (*Enters, out of breath and excited.*) Well, Rosa, has the coffee been served?

MRS. DREISSIGER. (*Pouting.*) Oh, why do you always have to run away?

DREISSIGER. (*Lightly.*) Oh, what do you know about it?

KITTELHAUS. I beg your pardon! Have you had trouble, Mr. Dreissiger?

DREISSIGER. God knows, that I have every single day, my dear Pastor. I'm used to that. Well, Rosa? I guess you're taking care of it?

MRS. DREISSIGER *in a bad temper pulls violently several times at the broad, embroidered bell pull.*

DREISSIGER. Just now—(*After walking up and down a few times.*)—Mr. Weinhold, I would have liked you to have been there. You would have had an experience. At any rate . . . come, let's have a game of whist.

59

KITTELHAUS. Yes, yes, by all means. Shake the dust and trouble of the day from your shoulders, and come and be one of us.

DREISSIGER. (*Has stepped to the window, pushes the drapery aside, and looks out. Involuntarily.*) Rabble!—come here, Rosa! (*She comes.*) Tell me . . . that tall, red-headed fellow there. . . .

KITTELHAUS. That is the one they call Red Baecker.

DREISSIGER. Tell me, is he by any chance the one who insulted you, two days ago? You know, what you told me, when Johann helped you into the carriage.

MRS. DREISSIGER. (*Makes a wry face, drawls.*) I don't remember.

DREISSIGER. Now don't be that way. I've got to know. I'm fed up with this impudence. If he's the one, I'll make him answer for it. (*The "Weavers' Song" is heard.*) Just listen to it! Just listen to it!

KITTELHAUS. (*Extremely indignant.*) Won't this nonsense ever come to an end? Now, really, I too must say, it's time the police took a hand. Permit me. (*He steps to the window.*) Look at that, Weinhold! Those aren't only young people; the old, steady weavers are running with the crowd. Men whom for years I have considered to be respectable and pious are in with them. They're taking part in this unheard-of nonsense. They are trampling God's law under their feet. Perhaps you would still like to defend these people, even now?

WEINHOLD. Certainly not, sir. That is, sir, *cum grano salis.* You must realize they are just hungry, ignorant men. They are expressing their dissatisfaction in the only way they know how. I don't expect such people. . . .

MRS. KITTELHAUS. (*Small, thin, faded, more like an old maid*

60

than a married woman.) Mr. Weinhold, Mr. Weinhold! I must beg of you!

DREISSIGER. Mr. Weinhold, I regret very much. . . . I did not take you into my house so that you should give me lectures on humanitarianism. I must request that you restrict yourself to the education of my sons, and for the rest, leave my affairs to me—completely—to me alone! Do you understand?

WEINHOLD. (*Stands a moment, motionless and deathly pale, and then bows with a strange smile, softly.*) Of course, of course, I understand. I have seen it coming: that is why I wish to leave.

Exit.

DREISSIGER. (*Brutally.*) Then, as soon as possible. We need the room.

MRS. DREISSIGER. Please, Wilhelm, Wilhelm!

DREISSIGER. Are you out of your mind? Are you defending a man that takes sides with such vulgarity and rowdyism as this insulting song?

MRS. DREISSIGER. But hubby, hubby, he really didn't. . . .

DREISSIGER. Reverend Kittelhaus, did he or did he not defend it?

KITTELHAUS. Mr. Dreissiger, one must ascribe it to his youth.

MRS. KITTELHAUS. I don't know—the young man comes from such a good and respectable family. His father was a civil servant for forty years and never allowed the slightest reproach to fall on himself. His mother was so overjoyed that he had found such an excellent position here. And now . . . now he shows so little appreciation of it.

PFEIFER. (*Tears open the vestibule door, shouts in.*) Mr. Dreissiger, Mr. Dreissiger! They've caught him. You ought to come. They've caught one of them.

61

DREISSIGER. (*Hastily.*) Has someone gone for the police?

PFEIFER. The Chief of Police is comin' up the stairs right now.

DREISSIGER. (*At the door.*) Your humble servant, sir! I am very glad that you have come.

KITTELHAUS *gestures to the ladies that it would be better if they withdrew. He, his wife, and Mrs. Dreissiger disappear into the drawing room.*

DREISSIGER. (*Very excited, to the* CHIEF OF POLICE, *who has entered in the meantime.*) I have finally had my dyers catch one of the ringleaders. I couldn't put up with it any longer. This impudence simply goes beyond all bounds. It's shocking. I have guests, and these rascals dare . . . they insult my wife when she shows herself; my children aren't sure of their lives. Chances are my guests will be beaten up. I assure you—if blameless people—such as me and my family—in a law-abiding community—can be openly and continuously insulted . . . without proper punishment, really . . . then I regret that I have different ideas of law and order.

POLICE CHIEF. (*A man of perhaps fifty, of medium height, fat, red-faced. He is wearing a cavalry uniform, saber and spurs.*) Certainly not . . . no . . . certainly not, Mr. Dreissiger!—I am at your service. Calm yourself, I am completely at your service. It is quite all right. . . . I am, in fact, very glad that you had one of the ringleaders caught. I am glad that this thing has finally come to a head. There are a few troublemakers around here that I've had it in for, for quite a long time.

DREISSIGER. You are right, a few young fellows, thoroughly shiftless rabble, lazy rascals, who lead a dissolute life, day after day, sitting around in the taverns till the last penny has trickled down their throats. But now I am determined, I will put an end to these professional slanderers, once and for all. It's in the common interest, not merely in my own.

POLICE CHIEF. By all means! Certainly—by all means, Mr. Dreissiger. Nobody could find fault with you there. And as far as it's within my power. . . .

DREISSIGER. The whip should be used on these ruffians.

POLICE CHIEF. Quite right, quite right. We must set an example.

KUTSCHE. (*Enters and salutes. As the vestibule door opens, the noise of heavy feet stumbling up the steps is heard.*) Chief, it's my duty to inform you that we have caught a man.

DREISSIGER. Would you like to see him, Chief?

POLICE CHIEF. Why, of course, of course. First of all, let's have a close look at him. Please do me the favor, Mr. Dreissiger, of not interfering. I'll see to it that you're given satisfaction, or my name isn't Heide.

DREISSIGER. I won't be satisfied—not until that man is brought before the state's attorney.

JAEGER. (*Is led in by five dyers. They have come directly from work. Their faces, hands, and clothes are stained with dye. The captured man has his cap cocked on the side of his head and displays a cheerful impudence. A few drinks of whiskey have put him in high spirits.*) You miserable wretches, you! You want to be workers, huh? You want to be comrades, huh? Why, before I'd do a thing like this—before I'd lay hands on a fellow worker of mine, I think I'd let my hand rot off first.

At a signal from the POLICE CHIEF, KUTSCHE *orders the dyers to take their hands off the victim and to guard the doors.* JAEGER, *now free, stands there impudently.*

POLICE CHIEF. (*Shouts at* JAEGER.) Take your cap off, you! (JAEGER *removes it, but very slowly. He continues to smile ironically.*) What's your name? *

JAEGER. (*Simply and quietly.*) That's none of your business! *The impact of the words creates a stir among the others.*

DREISSIGER. This is too much.

POLICE CHIEF. (*Changes color, is about to burst out, but conquers his anger.*) We'll see about this later. I'm asking you what your name is! (*When there is no reply, in rage.*) Speak up, you scoundrel, or I'll have you whipped.

JAEGER. (*Perfectly cheerful and without batting an eye at the furious outburst, calls over the heads of the spectators to a pretty servant girl about to serve coffee. She is perplexed at the unexpected sight and stands still, open-mouthed.*) Why, tell me, Emily, are you in service in high society now? Well, then, see to it that you get out of here. The wind might start blowing around here one of these days, and it'll blow everything away—overnight.

The girl stares at JAEGER. *When she realizes that the speech is meant for her, she blushes with shame, covers her eyes with her hands and runs out, leaving the dishes in confusion on the table. Again there is a commotion among the spectators.*

POLICE CHIEF. (*Almost losing control of himself, to* DREISSIGER.) As old as I am . . . I've never encountered such unheard-of impudence. . . .

JAEGER *spits on the floor.*

DREISSIGER. See here, you! You're not in a stable—understand?

---

* In the original, the chief of police uses the familiar "Du," whereupon Jaeger makes the remark that the two had never gone "tending swine together," i.e., they had not been on familiar terms.

POLICE CHIEF. Now, I'm at the end of my patience. For the last time—what is your name?

KITTELHAUS. (*During this past scene has been peeking out from behind the partly open door of the drawing room and listening. Now, carried away by the incident and trembling with excitement, he comes forward to intervene.*) His name's Jaeger, Chief. Moritz . . . isn't it? Moritz Jaeger. (*To* JAEGER.) Why, Jaeger, don't you remember me?

JAEGER. (*Seriously.*) You are Reverend Kittelhaus.

KITTELHAUS. Yes, your pastor, Jaeger! If I'm the one who received you as an infant into the Communion of the Saints. The one—from whose hands you first received Holy Communion. Do you remember? There—I've worked and worked and brought the Word of God to your heart. Is this the thanks I get?

JAEGER. (*Gloomily, like a schoolboy who has been scolded.*) I've paid my thaler.

KITTELHAUS. Money, money—do you really believe that that vile, miserable money will. . . . Keep your money . . . I'd much rather you did. What nonsense that is! Behave yourself —be a good Christian! Think of what you've promised. Keep God's commandments—be good and pious. Money, money. . . .

JAEGER. I'm a Quaker now, Reverend. I don't believe in anything any more.

KITTELHAUS. What? A Quaker? Don't talk that way! Try to reform and leave words that you don't understand out of this! They're pious folk, not heathens like you. Quaker! What do you mean, Quaker?

POLICE CHIEF. With your permission, Reverend. (*He steps between him and* JAEGER.) Kutsche! Tie his hands!

Wild shouting outside: "Jaeger! Let Jaeger come on out!"

DREISSIGER. (*A little bit frightened, as are the others, has stepped instinctively to the window.*) Now, what does this mean?

POLICE CHIEF. I know. It means that they want this ruffian back. But that favor we won't do them this time. Understand, Kutsche? He goes to jail.

KUTSCHE. (*The rope in his hand, hesitating.*) With all respect, I'd like to say, Chief, we'll be havin' trouble. That's a damn big crowd. A regular gang of cutthroats, Chief. Baecker is among them, and the blacksmith. . . .

KITTELHAUS. With your kind permission—in order not to create more ill-feeling, wouldn't it be more appropriate, Chief, if we tried to settle this peaceably? Perhaps Jaeger will promise that he'll go along quietly or. . . .

POLICE CHIEF. What are you thinking? This is my responsibility. I can't possibly agree to a thing like that. Come on, Kutsche! Don't lose any time!

JAEGER. (*Putting his hands together and holding them out, laughing.*) Tie them tight—as tight as you can. It won't be for long.

KUTSCHE, *with the help of the dyers, ties his hands.*

POLICE CHIEF. Now, come on, march! (*To* DREISSIGER.) If you're worried about this, have six of the dyers go along. They can put him in the middle. I'll ride ahead—Kutsche will follow. Whoever gets in our way—will be cut down.

Cries from outside: "Cock-a-doodle-doo!! Woof, woof, woof!"

POLICE CHIEF. (*Threatening, toward the window.*) Rabble! I'll cock-a-doodle-doo and woof-woof you. Get going! Forward! March!

He marches out ahead, with drawn saber; the others follow with JAEGER.

JAEGER. (*Shouts as he leaves.*) And even if Milady Dreissiger acts so proud—she's no better than the likes of us. She's served my father his bit of whiskey a hundred times. Squadron, left wheel, ma-a-arch!

Leaves, laughing.

DREISSIGER. (*After a pause, apparently composed.*) What do you think, Pastor? Shall we begin our game of whist now? I don't think anything else will interfere now. (*He lights a cigar, gives several short laughs. As soon as the cigar is lit, he laughs out loud.*) Now I'm beginning to find this business funny. That fellow! (*In a nervous burst of laughter.*) It really is indescribably funny. First the dispute at dinner with the tutor. Five minutes later, he leaves. Good riddance! Then this business. And now—let's get on with our whist.

KITTELHAUS. Yes, but. . . . (*Roars from downstairs.*) Yes, but . . . you know, those people are making a terrible row.

DREISSIGER. We'll simply retire to the other room. We'll be quite undisturbed there.

KITTELHAUS. (*Shaking his head.*) If I only knew what has happened to these people. I must admit that the tutor was right in this respect. At least—until a short time ago—I, too, was of the opinion that the weavers were humble, patient, compliant people. Don't you think so too, Mr. Dreissiger?

DREISSIGER. Certainly they used to be patient and easily managed—certainly they used to be a civilized and orderly people—as long as the so-called "humanitarians" kept their hands out of it. Then for the longest time the terrible misery of their lives was pointed out to them. Think of all the societies and committees for the relief of distress among the weavers. Finally the weaver himself believes it—and now he's all mixed up. Let some one come in and set him straight again. He won't be stopped now. Now he complains endlessly. This doesn't please him and that doesn't please him. Now, everything has to be just so.

Suddenly a swelling roar of "Hurrah!" is heard from the crowd.

KITTELHAUS. So—with all their humanitarianism, they have accomplished nothing more than literally making wolves out of lambs, overnight.

DREISSIGER. No, Reverend, by the use of cool logic we might even be able to see the good side of this affair. Perhaps such happenings won't pass unnoticed in leading circles. Possibly at last they will come to the conclusion that such things can not go on any longer—that something must be done—if our home industries are not to collapse completely.

KITTELHAUS. Yes, but what would you say was the cause of this enormous falling off of trade?

DREISSIGER. Foreign countries have put up high tariff walls against our goods. Our best markets are thus cut off, and at home we've got to compete for our very lives. We have no protection—absolutely no protection.

PFEIFER. (*Staggers in, breathless and pale.*) Mr. Dreissiger! Oh, Mr. Dreissiger!

DREISSIGER. (*Standing in the doorway, about to enter the drawing room, turns, angrily.*) Well, Pfeifer, what is it this time?

PFEIFER. No . . . no. . . . This is the limit.

DREISSIGER. What's wrong now?

KITTELHAUS. You're alarming us—speak up!

PFEIFER. (*Hasn't recovered himself yet.*) This is the limit! I never saw anything like it! The authorities . . . they'll make them pay for it.

DREISSIGER. What the devil's got into you? Has anyone been —killed?

PFEIFER. (*Almost weeping with fear, cries out.*) They've set Moritz Jaeger free, they've beaten up the Chief of Police, and chased him away, they've beaten up the policeman—and chased him away, too—without his helmet—his saber broken. . . . Oh, I never. . . .

DREISSIGER. Pfeifer, you've lost your mind.

KITTELHAUS. Why, that would be revolution.

PFEIFER. (*Sitting down in a chair, his whole body trembling, moaning.*) It's gettin' serious, Mr. Dreissiger! It's gettin' serious, Mr. Dreissiger.

DREISSIGER. Well, then, the entire police force isn't. . . .

PFEIFER. It's gettin' serious, Mr. Dreissiger!

DREISSIGER. Damn it all, Pfeifer, shut up!

MRS. DREISSIGER. (*Comes from the drawing room with* MRS. KITTELHAUS.) Oh, but this is really shocking, Wilhelm. Our lovely evening is being ruined. There you are, now Mrs. Kittelhaus wants to go home.

KITTELHAUS. My dear Mrs. Dreissiger, perhaps it would be best today. . . .

MRS. DREISSIGER. Wilhelm, you should put a stop to this.

DREISSIGER. You go and talk to them. You go! Go on! (*Stopping in front of the Pastor, bursts out.*) Am I really a tyrant? Am I really a slave-driver?

JOHANN, THE COACHMAN. (*Enters.*) If you please, ma'am, I've harnessed the horses. The tutor has already put Georgie and Carl in the carriage. If things get worse we'll drive off.

MRS. DREISSIGER. If what gets worse?

JOHANN. Well, I don't know, either. I'm just thinkin'—the crowds are gettin' bigger all the time. After all, they have chased off the Chief of Police along with Kutsche.

PFEIFER. I'm tellin' ya, it's gettin' serious, Mr. Dreissiger! It's gettin' serious!

MRS. DREISSIGER. (*With mounting fear.*) What's going to happen? What do these people want? They couldn't attack us, Johann, could they?

JOHANN. There are some mangey dogs among them, ma'am.

PFEIFER. It's gettin' serious—deadly serious.

DREISSIGER. Shut up, you ass! Are the doors barred?

KITTELHAUS. Do me a favor . . . do me a favor . . . I have decided to . . . please do me a favor. . . . (*To* JOHANN.) What is it that the people really want?

JOHANN. (*Embarrassed.*) The stupid good-for-nothin's, they want more pay, that's what they want.

KITTELHAUS. Good, fine! I will go out and do my duty. I will have a serious talk with them.

JOHANN. Reverend, don't do that. Words won't do no good, here.

KITTELHAUS. My dear Mr. Dreissiger, just one word more. I would like to ask you to post some men behind the door and lock it immediately after I've gone.

MRS. KITTELHAUS. Oh, Joseph, are you really going to do this?

KITTELHAUS. I'll do it, of course . . . I'll do it! I know what I'm doing. Have no fear, the Lord will protect me.

MRS. KITTELHAUS *presses his hand, steps back, and wipes tears from her eyes.*

KITTELHAUS. (*All the time the muffled noise of a large*

crowd is heard from below.) I'll act . . . I'll act as if I were just quietly going home. I want to see whether my holy office . . . whether I still command the respect of these people . . . I want to see . . . (*He takes his hat and stick.*) Forward then, in God's name. (*Leaves, accompanied by* DREISSIGER, PFEIFER, *and* JOHANN.)

MRS. KITTELHAUS. Dear Mrs. Dreissiger,—(*She bursts into tears and puts her arms around* MRS. DREISSIGER'S *neck.*)—if only nothing happens to him!

MRS. DREISSIGER. (*Absently.*) I really don't know, Mrs. Kittelhaus—I am so . . . I really don't know how I feel. Such a thing can't hardly be humanly possible. If that's how it is . . . then it's like it was a sin to be rich. You know, if somebody had told me, I don't know but what, in the long run, I would rather have stayed in—in my humble circumstances.

MRS. KITTELHAUS. Dear Mrs. Dreissiger, believe me, there are disappointments and troubles enough in all walks of life.

MRS. DREISSIGER. Yes, of course—of course. I believe that, too. And if we've got more than other people . . . Lord knows, we certainly didn't steal it. Every single pfennig's been honestly earned. Surely it can't be that the people are going to attack us. Is it my husband's fault if business is bad?

From below comes tumultuous shouting. While the two women stare at each other, pale and terrified, DREISSIGER *bursts in.*

DREISSIGER. Rosa, throw on a coat and get into the carriage. I'll follow right after you!

He hurries to the safe, opens it, and takes out various valuables.

JOHANN. (*Enters.*) Everything's ready! But hurry, before they get to the back gate!

MRS. DREISSIGER. (*Panic-stricken, throws her arms around the coachman's neck.*) Johann, dear—good Johann! Save us, dearest Johann! Save my children, oh, oh. . . .

DREISSIGER. Be reasonable! Let go of Johann!

JOHANN. Madam, madam! Aw, don't be scared. Our horses are in good shape. Nobody can catch up with them. If they don't get out of the way, they'll get run over.

Exit.

MRS. KITTELHAUS. (*In helpless anxiety.*) But my husband? What about my husband? What will become of him, Mr. Dreissiger?

DREISSIGER. He is all right, Mrs. Kittelhaus. Just calm down, he is all right.

MRS. KITTELHAUS. I know something terrible's happened to him. You just won't tell me. You just won't say.

DREISSIGER. They'll be sorry for this, you mark my words. I know exactly who is responsible for it. Such unheard of, shameless impudence will not go unpunished. A community that does harm to its pastor—it's terrible! Mad dogs, that's what they are —beasts gone mad. And they should be treated accordingly. (*To* MRS. DREISSIGER, *who stands there, as if stunned.*) Now go, and hurry up! (*Sounds of beating against the entrance door are heard.*) Don't you hear me? The mob's gone mad. (*The smashing of the downstairs windows is heard.*) They've gone absolutely insane. There's nothing left to do but to get out.

A chorus of shouts is heard, "We want Pfeifer!" "Pfeifer come out!"

MRS. DREISSIGER. Pfeifer, Pfeifer! They want Pfeifer outside.

PFEIFER. (*Rushes in.*) They're at at the back gate, too. The front door won't hold out another minute. Wittig is beating it in with a stable bucket—like—like a mad man.

72

From downstairs, the shouts become louder and clearer,
"Pfeifer come out!" "Pfeifer come out!"

MRS. DREISSIGER *rushes off, as if pursued.* MRS. KITTELHAUS
follows.

PFEIFER. (*Listens. His face changes color. Once he makes*
out the cries, he is seized with an insane fear. He speaks the
following words frantically, crying, whimpering, pleading,
whining all at the same time. He overwhelms DREISSIGER *with*
childish caresses, strokes his cheeks and arms, kisses his hands,
and, finally, like a drowning man, put his arms around him,
clutching him and not letting him go.) Oh, good, kind, merci-
ful Mr. Dreissiger! Don't leave me behind. I have always served
you loyally—I always treated the people well. Wages were
fixed—I couldn't give them more. Don't leave me in the lurch.
Don't! I beg you. They'll kill me. If they find me—they'll strike
me dead. O, God in heaven, God in heaven, my wife, my
children. . . .

DREISSIGER. (*As he leaves, vainly trying to free himself from*
PFEIFER.) Let go of me, man! We'll see, we'll see!

Leaves with PFEIFER.

The room remains empty for a few seconds. In the drawing
room, window panes are being smashed. A loud crash resounds
through the house, followed by a roar of "Hurray," then
silence. A few seconds pass, then soft and cautious footsteps of
people coming upstairs to the second floor are heard; then,
timid and shy cries: "To the left!—Get upstairs!—Sh!—Slow!
—Don't shove!—Help push!—Smash!—Here we are!—Move
on! We're goin' to a weddin'—You go in first!—No, you go!"

Young weavers and weaver girls appear in the vestibule door.
They don't dare to enter, and each one tries to push the other
one in. After a few moments, they overcome their timidity, and

73

the poor, thin figures, some of them sickly, some ragged or patched, disperse throughout DREISSIGER'S *room and the drawing room. At first they look around curiously and shyly, then they touch everything. The girls try out the sofas; they form groups that admire their reflections in the mirror. A few climb up on chairs to look at pictures and to take them down, and in the meantime a steady stream of wretched-looking figures moves in from the vestibule.*

FIRST OLD WEAVER. (*Enters.*) No, no, this is goin' too far. Downstairs they're already startin' to break things up. It's crazy. There ain't no rhyme nor reason to it. In the end, that'll be a bad thing. Nobody with a clear head . . . would go along. I'll be careful and won't take part in such goin's on!

JAEGER, BAECKER, WITTIG *with a wooden bucket,* BAUMERT *and a number of young and old weavers come storming in as if they were chasing something, yelling back and forth in hoarse voices.*

JAEGER. Where is he?

BAECKER. Where is that dirty slave-driver?

OLD BAUMERT. If we're to eat grass, let him eat sawdust.

WITTIG. When we catch him, we'll string him up.

FIRST OLD WEAVER. We'll take him by the legs and throw him out of the window so he'll never get up again.

SECOND YOUNG WEAVER. (*Enters.*) He's flown the coop.

ALL. Who?

SECOND YOUNG WEAVER. Dreissiger.

BAECKER. Pfeifer, too?

VOICES. Let's look for Pfeifer! Look for Pfeifer!

OLD BAUMERT. Look for him, Little Pfeifer—there's a weaver for ya to starve! (*Laughter.*)

74

JAEGER. If we can't get this beast Dreissiger—we'll make him poor.

OLD BAUMERT. He'll be as poor as a churchmouse—just as poor.

All rush to the door of the drawing room, ready to destroy everything.

BAECKER. (*Runs ahead, turns around, and stops the others.*) Stop—listen to me! Once we're through here, we'll really get goin'. From here we'll go over to Bielau—to Dittrich's—he's the one who's got the steam power looms. . . . All the trouble comes from those factories.

ANSORGE. (*Comes in from the vestibule. After he has taken a few steps, he stands still, looks unbelievingly about, shakes his head, strikes his forehead, and says.*) Who am I? The Weaver Anton Ansorge? Has he gone crazy, Ansorge? It's true—things are buzzin' around in my head like a gadfly. What's he doin' here? He'll do whatever he wants to. Where is he, Ansorge? (*He strikes himself on the forehead.*) I ain't myself! I don't understand, I ain't quite right. Go away—you go away! Go away, you rebels! Heads off—legs off—hands off! You take my cottage, I'll take yours. Go to it!

With a yell, he goes into the drawing room. The rest follow him amid yells and laughter.

Curtain

ACT FIVE

SCENE:—*The tiny weaver's room at* OLD HILSE'S. *To the left is a small window, in front of it a loom; to the right, a bed with a table pushed up close to it. In the corner, to the right is the*

75

stove with a bench. Around the table, on the foot bench, on the edge of the bed, and on a wooden stool, the following persons are seated: OLD HILSE; *his old, blind, and almost deaf wife; his son,* GOTTLIEB; *and* GOTTLIEB'S *wife,* LUISE. *They are at morning prayers. A winding wheel with bobbins stands between table and loom. On top of the smoky, brown rafters, all kinds of old spinning, winding, and weaving implements are stored. Long hanks of yarn hang down; all sorts of rubbish are strewn about the room. The very low, narrow room has a door leading to the hall in the back wall. Opposite it, another door in the entrance hall stands open and affords a view into a second weaver's room similar to the first. The hall is paved with stones, the plaster is crumbling, and a dilapidated wooden stair leads to the attic. A washtub on a wooden stool is partly visible; shabby bits of laundry and household goods of the poor are scattered about. The light falls from the left into all the rooms.*

OLD HILSE. (*A bearded, heavy-boned man, now bent and worn with age, hard work, sickness, and exertion. An ex-soldier, he has lost one arm. He has a sharp nose, livid coloring. His hands tremble, and his body seems to be just skin, bones, and sinews. He has the deep-set, sore eyes characteristic of the weavers. He stands up, together with his son and daughter-in-law, and begins to pray.*) O Lord, we cannot be grateful enough that Thou this night, in Thy grace and goodness . . . hast taken pity upon us. That we have come to no harm this night. "Lord, Thy mercy reaches so far," and we are but poor, evil and sinful human beings not worthy to be trampled under Thy feet, so sinful and corrupted are we. But Thou, dear Father, willst look upon us and accept us for the sake of Thy beloved Son, our Lord and Savior, Jesus Christ. "Jesus' blood and righteousness, they are my jewels and my robe of glory. . . ." And if sometimes we despair under Thy scourge —when the fire of purification burns too raging hot, then do not count it too highly against us—forgive us our trespasses. Give us patience, O Heavenly Father, that after this suffering we may become part of Thy eternal blessedness. Amen.

MOTHER HILSE. (*Who has been bending forward in a great effort to hear, weeping.*) Father, you always say such a beautiful prayer.

LUISE *goes to the washtub,* GOTTLIEB *into the room on the other side of the hall.*

OLD HILSE. Wherever is the girl?

LUISE. She went over to Peterswaldau—to Dreissiger's. She finished windin' a few hanks of yarn again last night.

OLD HILSE. (*Speaking in a very loud voice.*) Well, Mother, now I'll bring ya the wheel.

MOTHER HILSE. Yes, bring it, bring it to me, Father.

OLD HILSE. (*Placing the wheel in front of her.*) I'd be glad to do it for ya. . . .

MOTHER HILSE. No . . . no. . . . What would I be doin' then with all that time?

OLD HILSE. I'll wipe your fingers off for ya a bit, so the yarn won't get greasy—do ya hear? (*He wipes her hands with a rag.*)

LUISE. (*At the washtub.*) When did we have anything fat to eat?

OLD HILSE. If we don't have fat, we'll eat dry bread—if we don't have bread, we'll eat potatoes—and if we don't have potatoes neither, then we'll eat dry bran.

LUISE. (*Insolently.*) And if we ain't got rye flour, we'll do like the Wenglers—we'll find out where the flayer has buried an old dead horse. We'll dig it up and live off the rotten beast

77

—for a couple of weeks—that's what we'll do, won't we?

GOTTLIEB. (*From the back room.*) What kind of damn nonsense are ya spoutin'?

OLD HILSE. Ya ought to be more careful with such godless talk! (*He goes to the loom, calls.*) Won't ya help me, Gottlieb —there's a few threads to pull through.

LUISE. (*From her work at the washtub.*) Gottlieb, you're to lend a hand to your father.

GOTTLIEB *enters. The old man and his son begin the tiresome job of reeding. They have hardly begun when* HORNIG *appears in the entrance hall.*

HORNIG. (*In the doorway.*) Good luck to your work!

OLD HILSE AND HIS SON. Thank ya, Hornig!

OLD HILSE. Tell me, when do ya sleep, anyhow? In the daytime ya go about tradin'—in the night ya stand watch.

HORNIG. Why, I don't get no sleep at all no more!

LUISE. Glad to see ya, Hornig!

OLD HILSE. Any good news?

HORNIG. A pretty piece of news. The people in Peterswaldau have risked their necks and have chased out Dreissiger and his whole family.

LUISE. (*With signs of excitement.*) Hornig's lyin' his head off again.

HORNIG. Not this time, young woman! Not this time—I have some pretty pinafores in the cart.—No, no, I'm tellin' the honest-to-God truth. They've up and chased him out. Yesterday evenin' he got to Reichenbach. By God! They didn't dare keep him there—for fear of the weavers—so he had to hurry off to Schweidnitz.

OLD HILSE. (*Picks up the thread of the warp carefully and*

78

pulls it close to the reed. His son catches the thread with a hook and pulls it through.) Now, it's time for ya to stop, Hornig!

HORNIG. If I'm lyin', I don't want to leave this place alive, I swear. There ain't a child that don't know the story.

OLD HILSE. Now tell me, am I all mixed up, or are you?

HORNIG. Well, now. What I'm tellin' ya is as true as Amen in the church. I wouldn't of said nothin' if I hadn't been standin' right there, but that's the way I saw it. With my own eyes, just like I see you here, Gottlieb. They've smashed up the manufacturer's house, from cellar to attic. They threw the fine china from the attic window and smashed it—right down over the roof. Hundreds of pieces of cotton are layin' in the bottom of the brook! Believe me, the water can't even flow on no more; it swelled up over the banks; it turned real blue from all the indigo they poured out of the windows. The air itself was filled with all them blue clouds. No, no, they did a terrible job there. Not just in the house, mind you, . . . in the dye plant . . . in the warehouse. . . ! Banisters smashed, the floors torn up —mirrors broken—sofas, arm chairs—everything—torn and slashed—cut to pieces and smashed—trampled and hacked to pieces—damn it! believe me, it was worse than war!

OLD HILSE. And you say those were weavers from around here?

Slowly and incredulously, he shakes his head. A group of tenants of the house has gathered at the door, listening intently.

HORNIG. Well, who else? I could mention all of them by name. I led the Commissioner through the house. I talked with plenty of them. They were just as friendly as usual. They went about the whole business quietly—but they were thorough. The Commissioner talked with a lot of them. They were just as polite as usual. But they wouldn't stop. They hacked at the elegant furniture, just like they were workin' for wages.

OLD HILSE. You led the Commissioner through the house?

HORNIG. Well, I sure wasn't afraid. The people all know me, always turnin' up like a bad penny. I never had trouble with nobody. I'm in good with all of them. As sure as my name is Hornig, I went through the house. Yes—and ya can really believe it—I was sore at heart—and I can tell ya about the Commissioner—he took it to heart, too. And why? Ya couldn't hear a single word the whole time, it was that quiet. It gave ya a real solemn feelin'—the way them poor hungry devils was takin' their revenge.

LUISE. (*Bursting out with excitement, trembling and wiping her eyes with her apron.*) That's only right—that had to happen!

VOICES OF THE TENANTS. There's enough slave-drivers 'round here. There's one livin' right over there.—He's got four horses and six coaches in his stable, and he lets his weavers starve!

OLD HILSE. (*Still incredulous.*) How could that have started over there?

HORNIG. Who knows? Who knows? One says this—another that.

OLD HILSE. What do they say?

HORNIG. By God, Dreissiger is supposed to have said the weavers could eat grass if they got hungry. I don't know no more.

Commotion among the tenants, who repeat it to each other with signs of indignation.

OLD HILSE. Now just listen to me, Hornig. For all I care, ya might say to me, Father Hilse, tomorrow you've got to die. That's likely, I'd answer, why not?—You might say, Father

Hilse, tomorrow the King of Prussia will come to visit ya—but that weavers, men like me and my son—should be up to such things, never in the world, never, never will I believe that.

MIELCHEN. (*A pretty girl of seven, with long, loose, flaxen hair. She runs in with a basket on her arm. She holds out a silver spoon to her mother.*) Mamma, Mamma, look what I've got! Ya can buy me a dress with it!

LUISE. Why are ya in such a hurry, child? (*With mounting excitement and curiosity.*) Tell me, what did ya come draggin' in this time? You're all out of breath. And the bobbins are still in the basket. What's the meanin' of all this, child?

OLD HILSE. Where did ya get the spoon?

LUISE. Could be she found it.

HORNIG. It's worth at least two or three thalers.

OLD HILSE. (*Beside himself.*) Get out, girl! Hurry up and get out! Will ya do what I say, or do I have to get a stick to ya! And take the spoon back where ya got it. Out with you! Do ya want to make thieves out of all of us, huh? You—I'll knock the thievin' out of ya—(*He looks for something with which to hit her.*)

MIELCHEN. (*Clinging to her mother's skirt, cries.*) Grand-papa, don't hit me—we, we—really found it. The bob-bobbin girls—they all—got—one, too.

LUISE. (*Bursts out, torn between fear and anxiety.*) There now—ya see. She found it. That's what she did. Where did ya find it?

MIELCHEN. (*Sobbing.*) In Peters—waldau—we—found 'em —in front of—Dreissiger's house.

OLD HILSE. Well, now we're in a fine mess. Hurry up, now, or I'll help ya to get goin'.

MOTHER HILSE. What's goin' on?

HORNIG. I'll tell ya what, Father Hilse. Let Gottlieb put on his coat and take the spoon to the police.

OLD HILSE. Gottlieb, put your coat on.

GOTTLIEB. (*Already doing so, eagerly.*) And then I'll go on up to the office and I'll say, they shouldn't blame us, a child like that just don't understand such things. And so I'm bringin' the spoon back. Stop that cryin', girl!

The mother takes the crying child into the back room and shuts the door on her. LUISE *returns.*

HORNIG. That might well be worth all of three thalers.

GOTTLIEB. Come, give me a piece of cloth so it don't get hurt, Luise. My, my—what an expensive thing. (*He has tears in his eyes while he wraps up the spoon.*)

LUISE. If it was ours, we could live on it for weeks.

OLD HILSE. Hurry up! Get a move on. Go as fast as ya can. That would be something! That would just about finish me. Hurry up, so we get rid of that devil's spoon. (GOTTLIEB *leaves with the spoon.*)

HORNIG. Well, I'd better be goin'. (*He talks to some of the tenants for a few seconds on his way out, then leaves.*)

PHYSICIAN SCHMIDT. (*A fidgety fat little man, with a cunning face, red from drinking, enters the house through the entrance hall.*) Good morning, people! Well, that's a fine business, that is. You can't fool me! (*Raising a warning finger.*) I know what you're up to. (*In the doorway, without coming into the room.*) Good morning, Father Hilse! (*To a woman in the hall.*) Well, Mother, how's the rheumatism? Better, eh? There you are! Now, let me see how things are with you, Father Hilse. What the devil's wrong with Mama Hilse?

LUISE. Doctor, the veins in her eyes are all dried up and she can't see at all no more.

SCHMIDT. That comes from the dust and the weaving by candlelight. Now tell me, do you know what it all means? All of Peterswaldau is on its feet, heading this way. I started out this morning in my buggy, thinking nothing was wrong, nothing at all. Then, I keep hearing the most amazing things. What in the devil's gotten into these people, Hilse? Raging like a pack of wolves. Starting a revolution, a rebellion; starting to riot; plundering and marauding. . . . Mielchen! Why, where is Mielchen? (MIELCHEN, *her eyes still red from weeping, is pushed in by her mother.*) There, Mielchen, you just reach into my coat pocket. (MIELCHEN *does so.*) Those ginger snaps are for you. Well, well, not all at once, you rascal. First, a little song! "Fox, you stole the . . ." well? "Fox, you stole . . . the goose. . . ." Just you wait, what you did—you called the sparrows on the church fence dirty names. They reported you to the teacher. Now, what do you say to that! Close to fifteen hundred people are on the march. (*Ringing of bells in the distance.*) Listen—they're ringing the alarm bells in Reichenbach. Fifteen hundred people. It's really the end of the world. Uncanny!

OLD HILSE. Are they really comin' over her to Bielau?

SCHMIDT. Yes, of course, of course.—I drove right through. Right through the whole crowd. I wanted to get out and give each one of them a pill. They trudged along, one behind the other—like misery itself—and sang a song—it really turned your stomach—you actually began to gag. My driver, Friedrich, he trembled like an old woman. We had to have some strong bitters right afterwards. I wouldn't want to be a manufacturer —not even if I could afford to have fine rubber tires on my carriage. (*Distant singing.*) Just listen! As if you beat on an old cracked boiler with your knuckles. I tell you, they'll be here on top of us in less than five minutes. Goodbye, people. Don't do anything foolish. The soldiers'll be right behind them. Don't lose your heads. The people from Peterswaldau have lost theirs. (*Bells ring close by.*) Heavens, now our bells are beginning to ring, too. It'll drive the people completely crazy. (*Goes upstairs.*)

GOTTLIEB. (*Enters again. Still in the entrance hall, panting.*) I've seen them—I've seen them. (*To a woman in the hall.*) They're here, Auntie, they're here! (*In the doorway.*) They're here, Father, they're here! They've got beanpoles and spikes and axes. They're stoppin' at Dittrich's and kickin' up a terrible row. I think he's givin' them money. Oh, my God, whatever is goin' to happen here? I won't look. So many people! So many people! If once they get goin' and make an attack—oh, damn it, damn it! Then our manufacturers'll have a bad time of it.

OLD HILSE. Why did you run so? You'll run like that till ya get your old trouble back, till you're flat on your back again, kickin' and hittin' all around ya.

GOTTLIEB. (*With increasing excitement and joy.*) I had to run, or else they would've caught me and kept me there. They were all yellin' I should hold out my hand, too. Godfather Baumert was one of them. He said to me—Come and get your two bits, you're a poor starvin' creature too. He even said —Tell your Father . . . he said I should tell ya, Father, you should come and help make the manufacturers pay back for all the terrible drudgery. (*Passionately.*) Now times've changed, he said. Now it'd be different with us weavers. We should all of us come and help bring it about. Now we'd all have our half pound of meat on Sundays and blood sausage and cabbage on Holy Days. Now everything would be changed, he said to me.

OLD HILSE. (*With repressed indignation.*) And he calls himself your godfather! And asked ya to take part in such criminal doin's? Don't ya have nothin' to do with such things, Gottlieb. The devil's got his hand in such carryin's on. That's Satan's work, what they're doin'.

LUISE. (*Overcome by passionate feeling, vehemently.*) Yes, yes, Gottlieb, just you hide behind the stove—crawl into the chimney corner—take a ladle in your hand and put a dish of buttermilk on your knee—put on a petticoat and say nice little prayers so you'll please Father!—And ya call that a man?

Laughter from the people in the entrance hall.

OLD HILSE. (*Trembling, with suppressed rage.*) And ya call that a proper wife, huh? Let me tell ya straight out—you call yourself a mother and have a vile tongue like that? Ya think ya can tell your daughter what she should do, and stir up your husband to crime and wickedness?

LUISE. (*Completely uncontrolled.*) You with your bigoted talk! It never filled one of my babies' bellies. All four of 'em laid in filth and rags on account of it. That didn't so much as dry one single diaper. I do call myself a mother, now you know it! And ya know that's why I wish all the manufacturers was in hell and damnation! It's because I am a mother—Can I keep a little worm like that alive? I've cried more than I've breathed, from the moment one of them tender, little creatures first came into the world, until death took pity on it, and took it away. You—you didn't give a damn. Ya prayed and ya sang, and I walked my feet bloody, for just a drop of skim milk. How many hundreds of nights I've racked my brains, just once to

85

cheat the graveyard of a baby of mine. And tell me, what's the wrong that a little baby like that has done, huh? That he has to come to such a miserable end—and over there—at Dittrich's they're bathed in wine and washed in milk. No, no, I tell ya, if it starts here, ten horses won't hold me back. And this I'll say, too, if they was to attack Dittrich's, I'll be the first one—and God help them that tries to stop me. I'm fed up—and that's the truth.

OLD HILSE. You're lost—you're past helpin'.

LUISE. (*In a frenzy*) You're the ones that's past helpin'! You're dishrags—not men! Fools to be spit at. Milksops who'd run away in fright if they so much as heard a child's rattle. Ya'd say "Thank ya kindly" three times for every thrashin' ya get. They haven't left enough blood in your veins so ya can get red in the face. Somebody ought to take a whip to ya, and beat some courage into your rotten bones! (*Leaves hurriedly.*)

A moment of embarrassment.

MOTHER HILSE. What's wrong with Luise, Father?

OLD HILSE. Nothin', Mama. What would be wrong with her?

MOTHER HILSE. Tell me, Father, am I just imagin' it, or are the bells ringin'?

OLD HILSE. I guess they're buryin' somebody, Mother.

MOTHER HILSE. And for me the end never seems to come. Tell me, Father, why don't I ever die? (*Pause.*)

OLD HILSE. (*Leaves his work, draws himself up, solemnly.*) Gottlieb! Your wife has said such things to us. Gottlieb, look here! (*He bares his breast.*) Here laid a bullet as big as a thimble. And the King himself knows where I lost my arm. It wasn't the mice that ate it. (*He walks back and forth.*) Your wife—before she was even thought of, I shed my blood by the quart for the Fatherland. So let her rave on as much as

she wants to.—That's all right with me. I don't give a damn.—
Afraid? Me, afraid? What would I be afraid of, I'd like to
know. Of the few soldiers who'll be rushin' after the rioters,
maybe? Oh, Lord, if that was it—that wouldn't be nothin'!
If I'm a bit brittle in my bones, when it comes to action, they're
like iron. I wouldn't be scared to stand up against a few miserable bayonets—and, if it comes to the worst? Oh, how glad
I'd be to take a rest. I certainly ain't afraid to die. Better today
than tomorrow. No. No. And it'd be a good thing. For what
would we be leavin'? Nobody'd weep for our poor old tortured bodies. That little heap of fear and pain and drudgery
that we call life—we'd be glad enough to leave behind. But
afterward, Gottlieb, afterward there's something—and if ya
throw that away, too—then everything's really gone.

GOTTLIEB. Who knows what happens when you're dead?
Ain't nobody seen it.

OLD HILSE. I'm tellin' ya, Gottlieb! Don't go and doubt the
only thing poor folks have got. Why would I have set here
—and worked the treadle like a slave for forty years and more?
And watched quietly how that fellow over there lives in pride
and gluttony—and makes money out of my hunger and hardship. And for what? Because I've got hope. I've got something,
in all this misery. (*Pointing out the window.*) You've got your
share here—me, in the world beyond. That's what I've been
thinkin'. And I'd let myself be drawn and quartered—I'm
that sure. It has been promised to us. Judgment Day is comin',
but we are not the judges, no, on the contrary, "Vengeance is
mine, saith the Lord."

A VOICE. (*Through the window.*) Weavers, come on out!

OLD HILSE. I don't care—do what ya want. (*He sits down
at the loom.*) You'll have to leave me in here.

87

GOTTLIEB. (*After a short struggle.*) I'll go and work, come what will.

Leaves.

Many hundreds of voices are heard near-by singing the "Weavers' Song"; it sounds like a dull, monotonous lament.

VOICES OF THE TENANTS. (*In the entrance hall.*) My God! My God! Now they're comin' like ants.—Where'd so many weavers come from?—Don't push—I want to see, too.—Look at that lanky fellow who's walkin' out front. Oh! Oh!—They're comin' in swarms!

HORNIG. (*Joins the people in the entrance hall.*) It's quite a show, ain't it? Ya don't see the likes of that every day. Ya ought to come around to Dittrich's. What they've done up there is really something. He ain't got no house, no more—no factory, no wine cellar—no nothin' at all. The wine bottles, they're drinkin' them all up . . . they don't even take the time to pull out the corks. One, two, three—the necks come off; nobody cares if they cut their mouths on the broken glass or not. Lots of 'em are runnin' around bleedin' like stuck pigs.— Now they're lookin' for the other Dittrich, the one here.

The singing of the crowd has stopped.

VOICES OF THE TENANTS. They really don't look so mad.

HORNIG. Don't ya worry. You just wait. Now they're takin' a good look at everything. See how they're lookin' over the place from all sides. Watch that little fat man—him with the stable bucket. That's the blacksmith from Peterswaldau, and a quick worker he is, too. He breaks down doors like they was pretzels—ya can believe me. If that man ever gets a manufacturer in his claws—he'll be done for!

VOICES OF THE TENANTS. Smash! Something happened! That was a stone flyin' through the window!—Now old Dittrich's

gettin' scared.—He's hangin' out a sign!—What's on it?—
Can't ya read? Where'd I be if I couldn't read?—Well, read
it! "Your demands will be met." "Your demands will be met."

HORNIG. He could've spared hisself that. It won't help much.
The weavers have their own ideas. Here it's the factory they're
after. They want to put an end to the power looms. They're
the things that are ruinin' the handweavers—even a blind
man can see that. No, no! Those fellows won't stop now. They
don't pay no attention to the judge, or to the chief of police
—and certainly not to a sign. Anybody who's seen them kick
up a riot, knows what it means.

VOICES OF THE TENANTS. All them people! What do they
want? (*Hastily.*) They're comin' across the bridge! (*Anxiously.*) Are they comin' over on this side? (*In great surprise
and fear.*) They're comin' this way, they're comin' this way.—
They're pullin' the weavers out of their houses!

*Everybody flees; the entrance hall is empty. A disorderly
crowd of rioters, dirty, dusty, their faces red with liquor and
exertion, wild-looking, exhausted, as if they had been up all
night, tattered, pushes its way in, with the cry, "Come on out,
weavers!" The crowd disperses through the various rooms.*
BAECKER *and a few* YOUNG WEAVERS, *armed with cudgels and
poles, enter* OLD HILSE'S *room. When they recognize* OLD HILSE,
they are taken aback and calm down a little.

BAECKER. Father Hilse, stop that slavin'! Let whoever wants
to work the treadle. Ya don't need to work till ya've harmed
yourself. We'll see to that.

FIRST YOUNG WEAVER. Ya won't have to go to bed hungry
another day.

SECOND YOUNG WEAVER. Weavers'll have a roof over their
heads and a shirt on their backs once more.

OLD HILSE. What's the devil makin' ya come in here for, with poles and axes?

BAECKER. These we're goin' to break in pieces on Dittrich's back.

SECOND YOUNG WEAVER. We'll get 'em red-hot and shove 'em down the manufacturers' throats, so they'll know how hunger burns.

THIRD YOUNG WEAVER. Come along, Father Hilse. We don't give no quarter.

SECOND YOUNG WEAVER. They took no pity on us. Neither God nor man. Now we're makin' our own justice.

OLD BAUMERT. (*Comes in, somewhat unsteady on his feet, with a newly killed chicken under his arm. He stretches out his arm.*) My dear—dear—br-brother—we are all brothers! Come to my heart, brother! *Laughter.*

OLD HILSE. Is that you, Willem?

OLD BAUMERT. Gustav!—Gustav, poor, old wretch, come to my heart. (*Moved.*)

OLD HILSE. (*Growls.*) Let me alone.

OLD BAUMERT. Gustav, that's the way it is. A man's got to have luck! Gustav, just look at me. How do I look? A man's got to have luck. Don't I look like a count? (*Patting his belly.*) Guess what's in my belly. Food fit for a prince is in my belly. A man's got to have luck. Then he gets champagne and roast hare. I'll tell ya something—we've been makin' a mistake— we've got to help ourselves.

ALL. (*Speaking at once.*) We've got to help ourselves. Hurray!

OLD BAUMERT. And once ya've had your first good bite to eat, ya feel like a different man. Jesus! Then ya get to feelin' strong like a bull. Then the strength goes through your limbs so ya don't even see no more what ya're strikin' at. Damn it, that's fun!

JAEGER. (*In the door, armed with an old cavalry saber.*) We've made a few excellent attacks.

BAECKER. Yes, we've got the hang of it, now. One, two, three, and we're inside the house. Then it goes like wild fire —cracklin' and shiverin'—like sparks flyin' in a forge.

FIRST YOUNG WEAVER. We ought to make a little fire.

SECOND YOUNG WEAVER. We're marchin' on to Reichenbach and burnin' the houses of the rich right over their heads.

JAEGER. I bet they'd like that. Then they'd get a lot of insurance money. (*Laughter.*)

BAECKER. From here we'll march to Freiburg, to Tromtra's.

JAEGER. We ought to string up some of the officials. I've read all the trouble comes from the bureaucrats.

SECOND YOUNG WEAVER. Soon we'll be marchin' to Breslau. The crowd keeps gettin' bigger.

OLD BAUMERT. (*To* HILSE.) Have a drink, Gustav! Come on!

OLD HILSE. I never drink.

OLD BAUMERT. That was in the old times—today things is different, Gustav.

FIRST YOUNG WEAVER. Everyday ain't a holiday. (*Laughter.*)

OLD HILSE. (*Impatiently.*) You infernal firebrands, what do ya want here in my house?

OLD BAUMERT. (*Somewhat intimidated, overly friendly.*) Now look, I wanted to bring ya a little chicken—so's you can cook some soup for Mother.

OLD HILSE. (*Perplexed, half-friendly.*) Oh, go and tell Mother.

MOTHER HILSE. (*Her hand to her ear, has been listening*

with difficulty. Now she wards BAUMERT *off.*) You let me alone. I don't want no chicken soup.

OLD HILSE. You're right, Mother. Me, neither. Not that kind, anyway. And you, Baumert! I'll tell ya one thing. When old men talk like little children, then the devil claps his hands with joy. And let me tell ya this: you and me, we have nothin' in common. You're not here because I want ya here. Accordin' to law and justice and righteousness, you ain't got no business here!

A VOICE. Who ain't with us, is against us.

JAEGER. (*Threatens brutally.*) You've got the whole thing wrong. Listen here, old man, we aren't thieves.

A VOICE. We're hungry, that's all.

FIRST YOUNG WEAVER. We want to live, and that's all. And that's why we've cut the rope 'round our necks.

JAEGER. And that was right! (*Holding his fist in front of* OLD HILSE'S *face.*) Just say another word! Ya'll get a punch— right between the eyes.

BAECKER. Be quiet, be quiet! Let the old man alone.—Father Hilse, this is the way we look at it. Better dead than start the old life again.

OLD HILSE. Haven't I lived that kind of a life for sixty years or more?

BAECKER. That don't matter. There's got to be a change, anyway.

OLD HILSE. That day'll never come.

BAECKER. What they don't give us willingly, we'll take by force.

OLD HILSE. By force? (*Laughs.*) Ya might as well go and dig your own graves. They'll show you where the force is. Just wait, young man!

JAEGER. Maybe—because of the soldiers? I've been a soldier, too. We can handle a few companies of soldiers.

OLD HILSE. With your loud mouths, that I'll believe. And if ya chase a couple of them out, a dozen more'll come back.

VOICES. (*Through the window.*) The soldiers are comin'! Look out! (*Suddenly everyone is silent. For a moment, the faint sound of fifes and drums can be heard. In the stillness a short, involuntary cry.*) Damn it, I'm gettin' out! (*General laughter.*)

BAECKER. Who's talkin' of gettin' out? Who was it?

JAEGER. Who's afraid of a few lousy soldiers? I'll give the commands. I've been in the army. I know the tricks.

OLD HILSE. What'll ya shoot 'em with? With clubs, maybe, huh?

FIRST YOUNG WEAVER. Never mind that old man—he ain't quite right in the head.

SECOND YOUNG WEAVER. Yes, he is a bit crazy.

GOTTLIEB. (*Has come into the room, unnoticed, and grabs hold of the speaker.*) Ought ya to be so impudent to an old man?

FIRST YOUNG WEAVER. Let me alone. I ain't said nothin' bad.

OLD HILSE. (*Meditating.*) Oh, let him talk. Don't meddle, Gottlieb. He'll see soon enough who's crazy—me or him.

BAECKER. You goin' with us, Gottlieb?

OLD HILSE. He'll have nothin' to do with it.

LUISE. (*Comes into the entrance hall, calls in.*) Don't keep hangin' around here. Don't lose no time with such prayer-book hypocrites. Come on out to the square! Ya ought to come on to the square! Uncle Baumert is comin' as fast as he can. The Major's speakin' to the people from horseback. He's tellin' 'em to go home. If ya don't come quick, we're through.

JAEGER. (*As he leaves.*) A fine, brave man you have for a husband!

LUISE. A man for a husband? I ain't got no man for a husband.

Several in the entrance hall sing.

> Once there was a man so small,
> Heigh ho!
> He would have a wife so tall,
> Heigh diddle diddle dum, dum, dum, hurrah!

WITTIG. (*Has entered from upstairs, a stable bucket in his hand. As he is about to go out, he stops for a minute in the entrance hall.*) Forward! Those that ain't cowards, hurray! (*He rushes out. A crowd, among them* LUISE *and* JAEGER, *follow him amid shouts of "hurray."*)

BAECKER. Good luck to ya, Father Hilse, we'll be seein' each other again. (*Is about to leave.*)

OLD HILSE. I doubt that. I won't last another five years. And you won't be out before that.

BAECKER. (*Surprised, standing still.*) Get out of where, Father Hilse?

OLD HILSE. Out of jail—where else?

BAECKER. (*Laughing wildly.*) That wouldn't be so bad. At least I'd get enough to eat there, Father Hilse.

Leaves.

OLD BAUMERT. (*Has been sitting slumped on a stool, moodily meditating; now he gets up.*) It's true, Gustav—I am sorta drunk. But even so, my head's clear enough. You've got your opinion in this matter—I've got mine. I say Baecker's right —if it ends in chains and ropes—it's better in prison than at home. There, they at least take care of ya; there, ya don't have

94

to starve. I didn't want to join 'em. But ya see, Gustav, there comes a time when a man has to have a breath of air. (*Going slowly toward the door.*) Good luck to ya, Gustav. If something was to happen, say a prayer for me, will ya?

Leaves.

The mob of rioters has now left the stage. The entrance hall gradually fills up with curious tenants. OLD HILSE *goes about tying knots in his web.* GOTTLIEB *has taken an ax from behind the stove and instinctively is testing its edge. Both* OLD HILSE *and* GOTTLIEB *are agitated, but remain silent. From outside come the buzz and roar of a large crowd.*

MOTHER HILSE. Tell me, Father, the boards is shakin' so—what's goin' on here? What's goin' to happen? (*Pause.*)

OLD HILSE. Gottlieb!

GOTTLIEB. What do ya want?

OLD HILSE. Put down that ax.

GOTTLIEB. And who'll chop the wood? (*He leans the ax against the stove.—Pause.*)

MOTHER HILSE. Gottlieb, listen to what your father says.

A VOICE. (*Singing outside the window.*)

> The little man at home will stay
> Heigh-ho!
> And wash the dishes all the day
> Heigh diddle diddle, dum, dum, dum, hurrah!

It fades out.

GOTTLIEB. (*Leaps up, shakes his fist at the window.*) You son of a bitch, don't make me mad!

A volley is fired.

MOTHER HILSE. (*Starts up in alarm.*) Oh, dear Lord, is it thunderin' again?

95

OLD HILSE. (*Instinctively folding his hands.*) Dear God in heaven, protect the poor weavers, protect my poor brothers!

There is a short silence.

OLD HILSE. (*To himself, deeply moved.*) Now the blood'll flow.

GOTTLIEB. (*When the shots were heard, jumped up and held the ax tight in his hand. He is pale and scarcely able to control his great excitement.*) Well, are we to take it layin' down, even now?

GIRL. (*Calling into the room from the entrance hall.*) Father Hilse, Father Hilse, get away from that window. A bullet came right through our window upstairs. (*Disappears.*)

MIELCHEN. (*Puts her head in through the window, laughing.*) Grandpa, Grandpa, they're shootin' with guns. A couple of 'em fell down. One of 'em turned 'round in a circle—'round and 'round like a top. One's all floppin' like a sparrow with its head tore off. Oh, and so much blood spurtin' out—! (*She disappears.*)

A WOMAN WEAVER. They've killed some of 'em.

AN OLD WEAVER. (*In the entrance hall.*) Watch out! They're goin' at the soldiers.

A SECOND WEAVER. (*Beside himself.*) Look at the women! Just look at the women! If they aren't liftin' up their skirts, and spittin' at the soldiers!

A WOMAN WEAVER. (*Calls in.*) Gottlieb, look at your wife. She's got more courage than you. She's jumpin' around in front of the bayonets like she was dancin' to music.

FOUR MEN *carry a wounded man through the entrance hall. Silence. A voice is clearly heard saying, "It's Weaver Ullbrich." After a few seconds, the voice says again, "He's done for, I guess—a bullet got him in the ear." The men are heard walk-*

ing up the wooden stairs. Sudden shouts from outside, "Hur-ray, hurray!"

VOICES IN THE HOUSE. Where'd they get the stones? Ya'd bet-ter run for it! From the road construction—So long, soldiers! —Now it's rainin' pavin' stones.

Shrieks of terror and yelling are heard outside and con-tinuing in the entrance hall. There is a cry of fear, and the entrance door is banged shut.

VOICES IN THE ENTRANCE HALL. They're loadin' again.— They're goin' to shoot again.—Father Hilse, get away from that window.

GOTTLIEB. (*Runs for the ax.*) What! Are we mad dogs? Are we to eat powder and shot instead of bread? (*Hesitating a minute with the ax in his hand. To the old man.*) Am I to stand by and let my wife get shot? No, that mustn't happen! (*As he rushes out.*) Watch out—here I come!

Leaves.

OLD HILSE. Gottlieb, Gottlieb!

MOTHER HILSE. Where's Gottlieb?

OLD HILSE. He's gone to the devil.

VOICES. (*From the entrance hall.*) Get away from the win-dow, Father Hilse!

OLD HILSE. Not me! Not if ya all go crazy. (*To* MOTHER HILSE *with mounting excitement.*) Here my Heavenly Father put me. Right, Mother? Here we'll stay sittin' and doin' what's our duty—even if the snow was to catch fire.

He begins to weave. A volley is fired. Fatally hit, OLD HILSE *rises from his stool and then falls forward over the loom. At the same time loud cries of "Hurray" are heard. Shouting "Hur-ray" the people who have been standing in the entrance hall rush outside. The old woman asks several times: Father—*

97

Father—What's wrong with ya?" The steady shouting grows more and more distant. Suddenly MIELCHEN *comes running into the room.*

MIELCHEN. Grandpa, Grandpa, they're drivin' the soldiers out of town. They've attacked Dittrich's house. They did like at Dreissiger's, Grandpa! (*Frightened, the child sees that something is wrong—sticks her finger in her mouth and cautiously steps close to the dead man.*) Grandpa!

MOTHER HILSE. Come now, Father—say something! You're scarin' me!

Curtain

HANNELE

A Dream Poem in Two Acts

DRAMATIS PERSONAE

HANNELE
GOTTWALD, a teacher
SISTER MARTHA, a deaconesss [1]
TULPE ⎱ inmates of a
HEDWIG ⎰ poorhouse

PLESCHKE ⎱ inmates of a
HANKE ⎰ poorhouse
SEIDEL, a woodcutter
BERGER, a judge
SCHMIDT, a police official
DR. WACHLER

APPARITIONS: *Mattern, a mason, Hannele's father – Hannele's dead mother – A large dark angel – Three angels of light – The deaconess – The teacher Gottwald and his pupils – Pleschke, Hanke, and other inmates of the poorhouse – The village tailor – Seidel – Four youths clad in white – The Stranger – Numerous small and large angels – Mourners, women, etc.*

ACT ONE

SCENE: *A room in the poorhouse of a mountain village. The walls are bare, a door in the middle, a small window, like a peephole, to the left. In front of the window are a rickety table and a bench. To the right, a bedstead with a straw ticking. At the back, a stove with its bench and another bedstead, also with a straw ticking and a few rags on it.*

---

[1] Deaconess—a member of a German Protestant order devoted to the care of the poor and the nursing of the sick. She is addressed as *Schwester*, the German equivalent of "Sister."

It is a stormy December night. At the table TULPE, *an old ragged beggarwoman, is sitting singing from a hymnbook by the light of a tallow candle.*

TULPE. (*Sings.*)

> Abide, O dearest Jesus,
> Among us with thy grace
> That Satan may not harm us,
> Nor we to sin give place. . . .

HEDWIG, *nicknamed* HETE, *a dissolute woman, about thirty years old, with short curly bangs, enters. She wears a thick cloth around her head and carries a bundle under her arm. She is scantily and poorly dressed.*

HETE. (*Blowing into her hands without taking the bundle from under her arm.*) Oh Lord, Lord! Such weather! (*Continuing to blow into her hands, she lets the bundle slip to the table. She stands with one foot on top of the other, alternately. Her shoes are old and torn.*) We ain't had such weather for years.

TULPE. What have ya got there?

HETE. (*Grins and whines with pain, sits by the stove and tries to take off her shoes.*) Oh, Lord, Lord! My toes! they burn like fire.

TULPE. (*Has untied the bundle; it contains a loaf of bread, a package of chicory, a small bag of coffee, a few pairs of stockings, etc.*) I guess there'll be a little bit left for me, too.

HETE. (*Too busy taking off her shoes to have noticed* TULPE. *Now she pounces on her things like a vulture and gathers them together.*) Tulpe! (*Wearing only one shoe, she hobbles with her things to the bed at the back.*) So ya think I'd walk for miles and freeze every bone in my body, for you? Huh?

TULPE. Aah, shut up, you old fool! I don't want none of the

trash—(*She gets up, closes the hymnbook with a bang, and wipes it carefully on her dress.*)—you got together by beggin'.

HETE. (*Putting her things away under the straw ticking.*) Who's done more beggin' in his life, you or me? You've never done nothin' else—and as old as ya are. Everybody knows that.

TULPE. You've done plenty of other things, besides. The Pastor gave ya a piece of his mind. When I was a young girl like you, I sure took better care of myself.

HETE. And I suppose that's why ya ended up in jail.

TULPE. And you'll get there in no time, if you don't look out. Just let me meet a cop. I'll tell him a thing or two. Ya'd better be careful, girlie, I tell ya.

HETE. Go on, send a cop around to me—I'll be telling him plenty, myself.

TULPE. Tell him anything ya want, for all I care.

HETE. Yeh, and who stole the overcoat from Innkeeper Richter's little boy, huh? (TULPE *gets ready as if to spit at* HETE.) Tulpe! Damn it! Now ya sure won't get nothin'.

TULPE. Fer all I care! I don't want no presents from you.

HETE. Sure—'cause you ain't gettin' nothin'.

PLESCHKE *and* HANKE *are literally thrown into the entrance door by the storm which has just struck with furious force against the house.* PLESCHKE, *a ragged, childish old man with a goiter, breaks out into a loud laugh.* HANKE, *a young ne'er-do-well, swears. Both, seen through the open door, shake the snow from their caps and coats onto the stone floor. They each carry a bundle.*

PLESCHKE. Thunder and lightning!—It's blowin' like the very devil—This old shack of a poorhouse—one of—one of these days—it'll fall to pieces.

Catching sight of the pair HETE *hesitates, then drags her*

*bundle from under the straw ticking, and runs past the men,
out of the room and up the stairs.*

PLESCHKE. (*Shouting after* HETE.) What are ya—what are
ya runnin' away for? We—we won't do nothin'—nothin' to ya.
Ain't that so, Hanke? Ain't that so?

TULPE. (*Busy at the stove with a pot.*) That woman ain't
right in her head. She thinks we'll take her things away from
her.

PLESCHKE. (*Entering.*) Jesus! Jesus! You people—That sure
beats everything. That's the limit. Good evenin'. Good evenin'.
Hell, it's terrible out—terrible. I fell flat—flat on my face, all
o' me, as big as I am.

*He limps to the table, puts down his bundle, and turns his
head toward* TULPE. *He is shaking; his hair is white, his eyes
are bleary. He is still gasping for breath from the exertion,
coughing, and flapping his arms to warm himself. In the meantime,* HANKE *has entered the room, too. He puts his beggar's
bundle down against the door and immediately, shivering from
the cold, begins to stuff dry twigs in the stove.*

TULPE. Where do you come from?

PLESCHKE. Me? Me? Where do I come from? A long ways—
a long ways off. Up on the hill—up on the hill. . . . I've hit
every house.

TULPE. Did ya bring something along?

PLESCHKE. Yeah, yeah, fine stuff. I got fine stuff. From the
organist, I got a nickel, yeah—and from the innkeeper—up
there—I got—I got a pot full— yeah—a pot full—pot full of
soup.

TULPE. I'll put it right on to warm. Give it to me. (*She takes
the pot out of the bundle, sets it on the table, and continues to
rummage.*)

PLESCHKE. A tail end o'—sausage—yeah, that's there, too. The butcher—Seipelt, the butcher give it to me.

TULPE. How much money did ya get?

PLESCHKE. Three groschen—yeah,—three groschen—I think.

TULPE. Well, give it to me. I'll keep it for ya.

HETE. (*Entering again.*) You're really dumb to be givin' everythin' away. (*She goes to the stove.*)

TULPE. Mind your own business!

HANKE. He's her sweetheart.

HETE. Oh, my God!

HANKE. So he's got to bring his sweetheart somethin'. That's the way it's done.

PLESCHKE. Ya can make a fool—a fool of—of anybody ya want to—an old man—an old man, ya'd better let alone.

HETE. (*Imitating* PLESCHKE.) Old Pleschke—old Pleschke—pretty soon he won't—he won't even be able to—to talk. Soon—soon—he won't even be able to—to say one, one, one, one word.

PLESCHKE. (*Threatening her with his stick.*) Now ya—ya'd better get out—get out—

HETE. Says who?

PLESCHKE. Ya'd better—get out!

TULPE. Let her have it.

PLESCHKE. Ya'd better—get out!

HANKE. Stop the nonsense.

TULPE. You be quiet!

HETE, *behind* HANKE's *back, takes advantage of the moment when he is busy with* PLESCHKE, *defending her, to snatch something from* HANKE's *bundle and run away with it.* TULPE, *who has noticed it, shakes with laughter.*

HANKE. That ain't nothin' to laugh about.

TULPE. (*Continuing to laugh.*) My, my! He don't see nothin' to laugh about.

PLESCHKE. Jesus, Jesus, just look at that.

TULPE. Better look after your own things. Could be there ain't as many as there was.

HANKE. (*Turns and notices that he has been tricked.*) Bitch! —(*He rushes after* HETE.) If I get ya! (*Noises are heard outside as* HANKE *chases up the steps. There are muffled cries.*)

PLESCHKE. A real she-devil! A real she-devil! (*He laughs wildly.* TULPE *almost bursts with laughter. Suddenly the sound of the abrupt opening of the door is heard. The laughter stops.*) Now what's that?

A powerful gust of wind strikes the house. Great flakes of snow and hail strike against the window. A moment of silence. Then the teacher, GOTTWALD, *appears. He is about thirty-two years old and has a black beard. He is carrying* HANNELE MATTERN, *about fourteen, in his arms. The girl whimpers. Her long, red hair hangs down over the teacher's shoulder. Her face is buried in the teacher's neck; her arms are hanging down, limp and lifeless. She is scantily dressed and wrapped in shawls. With great care,* GOTTWALD *lets his burden slip to the bed that stands along the right wall, without paying any attention to the others. A man, the forester named* SEIDEL, *enters with a lantern. He carries, besides his saw and ax, a bundle of wet rags. He wears an old hunter's cap rather jauntily on his graying head.*

PLESCHKE. (*Staring stupidly and perplexed.*) Hey! Hey! What's—goin' on here? What's—goin' on here?

GOTTWALD. (*Spreading some covers and his own coat over the girl.*) Seidel, heat some stones! Quick!

SEIDEL. Hurry up, hurry up—a couple of bricks. Hey, there, be quick about it.

TULPE. What's the matter with her?

SEIDEL. Stop askin' questions! (*Hurries off with* TULPE.)

GOTTWALD. (*Calming* HANNELE.) It's all right. It's all right. Don't be afraid. Nothing will happen to you.

HANNELE. (*Her teeth chattering.*) I'm so afraid! I'm so afraid!

GOTTWALD. But you have nothing at all to be afraid of. No one will do anything to you.

HANNELE. My father, my father. . . .

GOTTWALD. Why, he isn't here.

HANNELE. I'm so afraid that my father will come.

GOTTWALD. But he's not coming. Please believe me. (*Someone in a great hurry comes down the stairs.*)

HETE. (*Holding a grater in the air.*) Now just look at this. This is the sort of thing they give Hanke.

HANKE *rushes in right behind her, and wants to grab the grater out of her hand, but with a quick motion she throws it into the middle of the room.*

HANNELE. (*Sits up, terrified.*) He's coming! He's coming!

She half rises and stares in the direction of the commotion— her head stretched forward and an expression of terrible fear on her pale, sickly, grief-stricken face. HETE *has eluded* HANKE *and has gone into the back room.* HANKE *comes in to pick up the grater.*

HANKE. I'll get even with ya. You bitch!

GOTTWALD. (*To* HANNELE.) It's all right, Hannele. (*To* HANKE.) What do you want?

HANKE. (*Astonished.*) Me? What do I want?

HETE. (*Sticks her head in and calls.*) Thief! Thief!

HANKE. (*Threatening.*) Take it easy. I'll get even with ya.

GOTTWALD. Please, be quiet. The girl's sick.

HANKE. (*Picks up the grater and puts it into his pocket. Withdraws, a little ashamed.*) What's wrong?

SEIDEL. (*Re-enters with two bricks.*) I've got two for now.

GOTTWALD. (*Examines the bricks.*) Are they warm enough?

SEIDEL. They'll warm her a bit. (*He puts one of the bricks under the covers at the girl's feet.*)

GOTTWALD. (*Points to another place.*) Put the other one here.

SEIDEL. She don't seem to be gettin' warmer.

GOTTWALD. Her whole body is shaking.

TULPE *enters behind* SEIDEL. HETE *and* PLESCHKE *follow. A few other rather questionable inmates of the poorhouse appear at the door. All are curious. They whisper, press closer, their voices becoming louder.*

TULPE. (*Standing next to the bed, her arms akimbo.*) Hot water and brandy, if there's any here.

SEIDEL. (*Produces a flask.* PLESCHKE *and* HANKE *follow suit.*) Here's a drop.

TULPE. (*At the stove.*) Bring it here.

SEIDEL. Is there any hot water?

TULPE. Lord, it's hot enough to scald an ox.

GOTTWALD. And put a little sugar in, if you have any.

HETE. Where would we get any sugar?

TULPE. You've got some. Don't talk so dumb.

HETE. Me? Sugar? Naw. (*She forces a laugh.*)

TULPE. You brought some with ya. I saw it in the bundle. Don't lie.

SEIDEL. Hurry. Bring it here.

HANKE. Run, Hete, run.

SEIDEL. You can see the girl's in a bad way.

HETE. (*Stubbornly.*) What do I care.

PLESCHKE. You get the sugar.

HETE. Ya can get it at the grocer's.

Exit.

SEIDEL. And ya'd better be quick about it, or I'll box your ears. Maybe that'll help. I'm sure ya wouldn't ask for more.

PLESCHKE. (*Who has left for a minute, returns.*) That's what the girl's like—that's what she's like.

SEIDEL. I'd knock the grumblin' out of her. If I was the Judge, I'd take a big, strong stick and—you'd see if she worked or not—a girl like her—who's young and strong—What business has she got in a poorhouse?

PLESCHKE. I got a little bit—a—a little bit—of sugar here.

HANKE. (*Sniffing the grog.*) I wish I was sick.

SCHMIDT. (*Enters with a lantern. He acts pompous and puts on a somewhat familiar air.*) Make room here. The Judge is coming.

JUDGE BERGER *enters. His manner unmistakably stamps him as a reserve officer. He has a mustache and, although he is still young, his hair is getting quite gray. He wears a long overcoat and carries a cane—all with a touch of elegance. His hat sits jauntily on his head. There is something boyish in his manner.*

THE PAUPERS. Good evenin', Judge. Good evenin', Captain.

BERGER. Evening. (*Removing his hat, cane, and coat, he commands with an appropriate gesture.*) Now, everybody get out. (SCHMIDT *herds everyone out and into the back room.*) Good evening, Mr. Gottwald. (*Extends his hand.*) Now then, what goes on here?

GOTTWALD. We've just pulled her out of the water.

SEIDEL. (*Steps forward.*) Pardon me, Judge. (*Gives a military salute.*) I had some things to do at the blacksmith's shop. I wanted a strap made for my ax. As I was stepping out of the smithy—that is down at Jeuncher's smithy—there's a pond, ya know. Ya might say it's almost a lake. (*To* GOTTWALD.) Well, it's true. It's almost that big. And as maybe ya know, Judge, there's a spot in it that don't freeze. It don't never freeze. I can remember when I was a little boy. . . .

BERGER. Yes, yes. But what happened?

SEIDEL. (*Saluting again.*) Well, just as I was steppin' out of the smithy—the moon came through the clouds a little while— I heard someone cryin'. At first I thought somebody was playin' tricks on me. But then I see that somebody's out in the pond. And right in the spot that don't freeze. I yelled—and then she disappeared. Well, without a word, I ran into the smithy and got a board and ran around to the pond. I put the board on the ice, and in no time at all I got ahold of her hair.

BERGER. That's very good, Seidel. One usually hears a different story—fights, bloody heads, broken bones. It's at least something different this time. Did you bring her straight here?

SEIDEL. Mr. Gottwald. . . .

GOTTWALD. I happened to be going past. I was coming home from the teachers' meeting and my wife got a few things together in a hurry, so the girl would have something dry to wear.

BERGER. What's the rest of the story?

SEIDEL. (*Hesitating.*) Well,—she's Mattern's step-daughter.

BERGER. (*Taken back for a moment.*) Whose? His? That scoundrel's?

SEIDEL. The mother died six weeks ago. There ain't much more to tell. The girl scratched and hit at me, just 'cause she thought I was her father.

BERGER. (*Murmurs.*) Such a poor little child.

SEIDEL. And right now he's sittin' at the tavern; he's been drinkin' hard since yesterday. He drinks like a fish.

BERGER. We'll fix him for that. (*He leans over the bed to talk to* HANNELE.) Now! Little girl! You're crying so much. You don't have to be afraid of me. I won't hurt you. What is your name?—What did you say?—I can't understand you.—(*He straightens up.*) I think the girl's stubborn.

GOTTWALD. She's only frightened.—Hannele!

HANNELE. (*Breathes out.*) Yes.

GOTTWALD. You must answer the Judge.

HANNELE. (*Trembling.*) Dear God, I'm freezing.

SEIDEL. (*Brings the grog.*) Here, drink a little of this.

HANNELE. (*As before.*) Dear God, I'm hungry.

GOTTWALD. (*To the* JUDGE.) It's no use, she won't eat.

HANNELE. Dear God, it hurts so much.

GOTTWALD. Where does it hurt you?

HANNELE. I'm so afraid.

BERGER. Who's frightening you?—Who?—Just try to tell me.—I can't understand a word you're saying, child.—I can't help you if you don't tell me.—Listen to me, has your step-father treated you badly? Beaten you, I mean?—Locked you up? Thrown you out of the house?—What? Good heavens, I. . . .

SEIDEL. The girl's awful quiet. Things'll be pretty bad before she talks. She's still—like a lamb, ya might say.

BERGER. I would just like to have something definite. Perhaps then I could get hold of the fellow.

GOTTWALD. She has an unholy fear of the man.

SEIDEL. She sure does. People know—everybody knows—You can ask around if ya want to. I'm just surprised that the girl's still alive. You wouldn't think it was possible.

BERGER. What's he done to her?

SEIDEL. Well—about everything, ya might say. He'd throw

her out in the evenin'—and if the weather's like it is today—then she had to bring back money—just more money for him to drink up. Where would the girl get it? She'd have to stay out half the night in the cold. If she came home without any money . . . why she'd cry so hard people would hear her and come from all over, ya might say.

GOTTWALD. She used to have the mother to fall back on.

BERGER. Well, at any rate, I'll have the fellow locked up. He's been a drunkard too long. Now come, little girl, look at me.

HANNELE. (*Pleading.*) Oh, please, please, please, please.

SEIDEL. Ya won't get nothin' out of her very easy.

GOTTWALD. (*Softly.*) Hannele.

HANNELE. Yes.

GOTTWALD. Do you know me?

HANNELE. Yes.

GOTTWALD. Who am I?

HANNELE. The teacher Gottwald.

GOTTWALD. Fine. Now you see, I've always been good to you. You can tell me everything. . . . You were down at the pond by the smithy—Why didn't you stay at home? Well? Why not?

HANNELE. I'm afraid.

BERGER. We'll leave you alone. You don't have to tell anybody but the teacher.

HANNELE. (*Timidly, mysteriously.*) Somebody called.

GOTTWALD. Who called?

HANNELE. The dear Lord Jesus.

GOTTWALD. Where—did the dear Lord Jesus call you?

HANNELE. In the water.

GOTTWALD. Where?

HANNELE. Way down—in the water.

BERGER. (*Changing his mind, puts on his overcoat.*) First of all, we must get the doctor. I think he'll still be at the inn.

GOTTWALD. I have already sent for a nurse. The child needs special care.

BERGER. I'll go and talk to the doctor at once. (*To* SCHMIDT.) You call the sergeant. I'll wait at the inn. Good night, Mr. Gottwald. We will have that fellow locked up right away. (*Leaves with* SCHMIDT. HANNELE *falls asleep.*)

SEIDEL. (*After a pause.*) I don't think he'll lock him up.

GOTTWALD. Why not?

SEIDEL. He knows why. Don't forget who the girl's father is?

GOTTWALD. Ah, Seidel, that's just idle talk.

SEIDEL. Well, ya know—the man has led quite a life.

GOTTWALD. What lies people tell! You can't believe half of what they say. If only the doctor would come soon.

SEIDEL. (*Softly.*) I don't believe the girl will make it.

DR. WACHLER *enters, a serious-looking man about thirty-four years old.*

DR. WACHLER. Good evening.

GOTTWALD. Good evening.

SEIDEL. (*Helping him with his coat.*) Good evenin', Doctor.

DR. WACHLER. (*Warms his hands at the stove.*) I must have another candle. (*The sound of a barrel organ comes from the next room.*) They seem to be crazy in there.

SEIDEL. (*Already at the open door of the back room.*) Be a little quiet in there. (*The noise stops.* SEIDEL *disappears into the back room.*)

DR. WACHLER. Mr. Gottwald, isn't it?

GOTTWALD. My name is Gottwald.

DR. WACHLER. She tried to drown herself, I hear.

GOTTWALD. I guess she knew no other way out.

A short pause.

DR. WACHLER. (*Stepping to the bed and watching* HANNELE.) Does she talk in her sleep?

HANNELE. Millions of little stars. (DR. WACHLER *and* GOTT-WALD *watch her. Moonlight falls through the window and upon the group.*) Why are you pulling at my bones? Don't. Don't. It hurts so.

DR. WACHLER. (*Carefully loosens her shirt at the neck.*) Her entire body seems covered with bruises.

SEIDEL. Her mother was that way, too, when they laid her in the casket.

DR. WACHLER. Shameful! Shameful!

HANNELE. (*In a different, stubborn tone.*) I won't. I won't. I won't go home. I must go to Lady Holle's—I must go to the well. Please, let me, Father. Such a terrible smell! You've been drinking whiskey again.—Hear, how the wind blows through the woods.—There's a storm brewing in the mountains today. I hope a fire doesn't break out.—If the tailor doesn't carry a stone in his pocket and an iron in his hand, the wind will blow him over the mountains. Listen to the storm! . . .*

SISTER MARTHA, *a deaconess, enters.*

GOTTWALD. Good evening, Sister.

SISTER MARTHA *nods.* GOTTWALD *steps toward the* DEACON-ESS, *who is preparing things, and talks to her in the background.*

HANNELE. Where is my mother? In heaven? Oh, oh, so far!

---

* In her hallucinations, Hannele remembers the traditional comic character of the thin village tailor she has read and heard about and Grimm's fairy tale of "Frau Holle" with its beginning at the well. She wants to escape from reality—to find Lady Holle's house and the green meadow.

(*She opens her eyes, looks strangely around her, passes her hands over her eyes, and speaks in a barely audible tone.*) Where—where am I?

DR. WACHLER. (*Bending over her.*) With good people.

HANNELE. I am thirsty.

DR. WACHLER. Water! (SEIDEL, *who has brought a second candle, goes to get water.*) Do you have any pains anywhere? (HANNELE *shakes her head.*) No? You see, it isn't bad after all.

HANNELE. Are you the doctor?

DR. WACHLER. That's right.

HANNELE. Then—I'm sick?

DR. WACHLER. A little—not very.

HANNELE. Will you make me well?

DR. WACHLER. (*Rapidly examining her.*) Does it hurt here? There? Does it hurt here?—Here? You don't have to be afraid of me. I won't hurt you. How is it here? Does it hurt here?

GOTTWALD. (*Steps to the bed again.*) Answer the doctor, Hannele.

HANNELE. (*Pleading, with trembling voice and tears in her eyes.*) Oh, dear Mr. Gottwald.

GOTTWALD. Just pay attention to what the doctor says and answer him nicely. (HANNELE *shakes her head.*) Why not?

HANNELE. Because—because I want very much to go to my mother.

GOTTWALD. (*Deeply moved, strokes her hair.*) Don't say that.

A short pause. DR. WACHLER *straightens up, holds his breath and meditates for a minute.* SISTER MARTHA *has taken the second light from the table and stands nearby, holding it.*

DR. WACHLER. (*Beckons to* SISTER MARTHA.) Oh, please, Sister Martha.

He steps to the table and softly gives her instructions. GOTT-
WALD *now takes his hat and stands waiting. He glances alternately at* HANNELE, *the* DEACONESS, *and the* DOCTOR.

DR. WACHLER. (*Ends his quiet conversation with* SISTER
MARTHA.) I'll be back after a while. I'll have the medicine sent
around later. (*To* GOTTWALD.) They say the man's been arrested at the tavern.

SISTER MARTHA. At least that's what I was told.

DR. WACHLER. (*Putting on his overcoat. To* SEIDEL.) You'd
better come along with me to get the medicine.

The DOCTOR, GOTTWALD, *and* SEIDEL *quietly say good-bye to*
SISTER MARTHA.

GOTTWALD. (*Urgently.*) What do you think of her con-
dition?

All three then leave. The DEACONESS *is now alone with*
HANNELE. *She pours milk into a small bowl.* HANNELE *opens
her eyes and watches her.*

HANNELE. Do you come from Lord Jesus?

SISTER MARTHA. What did you say?

HANNELE. I asked if you came from Lord Jesus.

SISTER MARTHA. Don't you recognize me, Hannele? I am
Sister Martha. Don't you remember how you stayed with us,
and we prayed together and sang such beautiful songs?

HANNELE. (*Nods happily.*) Such beautiful songs.

SISTER MARTHA. Now I will take care of you in God's name
until you are well again.

HANNELE. I don't want to get well.

SISTER MARTHA. (*Standing by her with a bowl of milk.*) The
doctor says you must drink some milk, so you will get your
strength back.

HANNELE. (*Refuses the milk.*) I don't want to get well.

SISTER MARTHA. You don't want to get well? Now think it over a little—Come, come, I'll tie your hair up. (*She does so.*)

HANNELE. (*Cries softly.*) I don't want to get well.

SISTER MARTHA. But why not?

HANNELE. I want so much—so very much to go to heaven.

SISTER MARTHA. That's not within our power, dear child. We must wait until God calls us. And then if you repent your sins. . . .

HANNELE. (*Eagerly.*) Oh, Sister, I do repent.

SISTER MARTHA. And believe in Lord Jesus.

HANNELE. I believe in my Savior with all my heart.

SISTER MARTHA. Then you can be of good hope and wait patiently.—I'll smooth your pillow now, and you go to sleep.

HANNELE. I can't sleep.

SISTER MARTHA. You try.

HANNELE. Sister Martha!

SISTER MARTHA. Well?

HANNELE. Sister Martha, are there sins—are there sins that will not be forgiven?

SISTER MARTHA. Now go to sleep, Hannele. Don't excite yourself.

HANNELE. Oh, please tell me. Please, pretty please.

SISTER MARTHA. There are such sins. Certainly. The sins against the Holy Ghost.

HANNELE. Oh, if only I haven't committed one of those.

SISTER MARTHA. Nonsense. Only very bad people do that. Like Judas, who betrayed Lord Jesus.

HANNELE. But—but it might be.

SISTER MARTHA. Now you must go to sleep.

HANNELE. I'm so frightened.

SISTER MARTHA. There's no need to be.

HANNELE. Even if I've committed such a terrible sin?

SISTER MARTHA. You have committed no such sin.

HANNELE. (*Clings to the* SISTER *and stares into the darkness.*) Oh, Sister! Sister!

SISTER MARTHA. You must be quiet.

HANNELE. Sister!

SISTER MARTHA. What is it?

HANNELE. He's coming in. Don't you hear him?

SISTER MARTHA. I hear nothing.

HANNELE. It's his voice. Outside. Listen!

SISTER MARTHA. Who do you mean?

HANNELE. My father, my father!—He's standing there.

SISTER MARTHA. Where, child?

HANNELE. Look.

SISTER MARTHA. Where?

HANNELE. At the foot of the bed.

SISTER MARTHA. It's just a hat and coat hanging there. We'll take the nasty things away and give them to Papa Pleschke. I'll bring you back some water and fix a cold compress. Will you stay alone a minute? But be very, very still.

HANNELE. Oh, I am silly. It was only a hat and coat, wasn't it?

SISTER MARTHA. Very, very quiet now, I'm coming right back. (*She goes but has to return, since the entrance hall is pitch dark.*) I'll put the candle out here in the hall. (*She shakes her finger at* HANNELE, *tenderly.*) And be quite, quite still.

Exit.

It is almost completely dark. Immediately the figure of Mattern appears at the foot of HANNELE'*s bed. The face is wasted from drink. His red hair is unkempt. On his head he wears a worn-out military cap, without a peak. He carries a mason's tool in his left hand. There is a leather strap coiled in his right hand. He remains tense the entire time, as if he wanted any minute to strike* HANNELE. *The* APPARITION *emits a pale light which illuminates the area around* HANNELE'S *bed.* HANNELE, *terrified, covers her eyes with her hands, groans, turns, and utters soft, moaning sounds.*

THE APPARITION. (*In a hoarse and very angry voice.*) Where have ya been, girl? What have ya been doin'? I'll teach ya. I'll show ya. What have ya been tellin' people? That I beat ya and treated ya bad? Eh? Is that true? You're no child of mine. Get up. Quick! You don"t mean nothin' to me. I can throw ya into the street. Get up and build a fire. Will ya hurry? It's only out of kindness that you're in the house. Now, you're lazy, too. Well? Will ya hurry up? I'll beat ya until ya—until ya. . . .

HANNELE *wearily rises with her eyes closed and drags herself to the stove. She opens the door and faints.*

At this moment SISTER MARTHA *comes in with the candles and a jug of water, and the hallucination disappears. She stops, notices* HANNELE *lying in the ashes. Frightened, she cries out "Lord Jesus," puts down the candle and the jug, runs to* HANNELE *and lifts her from the floor. The cry brings the other inmates of the poorhouse back into the room.*

SISTER MARTHA. I just went to get some water, and she climbed out of bed. Please, Hedwig, help me!

HANKE. Now ya'd better be careful, Hete, or you'll break every bone in her body.

PLESCHKE. I think—somethin' . . . I think somethin'—has —has happened to the girl.

TULPE. Maybe—the girl—is really hexed.

HANKE. (*Loudly.*) I say she won't last long.

SISTER MARTHA. (*With* HETE'S *help, puts* HANNELE *to bed*

again.) You may be quite right, my good man, but please—you
understand—we must not disturb her any more.

HANKE. We don't make much fuss here.

PLESCHKE. (*To* HANKE.) You're a bad one—you're a bad one
—you are—and ya know it—nothin' else. A sick—a sick child
—has got to have rest.

HETE. (*Imitating him.*) A sick—a sick—

SISTER MARTHA. I must really ask you, please. . . .

TULPE. The Sister's right. Hurry up and get out.

HANKE. We'll go when we're good and ready.

HETE. I guess we should sleep in the henhouse.

PLESCHKE. There'll be a place—there'll be a place for you.—
You won't suffer.

The paupers all leave.

HANNELE. (*Opens her eyes, fearfully.*) Is—is he gone?

SISTER MARTHA. The people are all gone. You weren't
frightened, were you, Hannele?

HANNELE. (*Still frightened.*) Has my father gone?

SISTER MARTHA. He was never here.

HANNELE. Yes, Sister, yes.

SISTER MARTHA. You were only dreaming.

HANNELE. (*With a deep sigh, praying.*) Oh, dear Lord Jesus!
Oh, most beautiful, beautiful Jesus. Take me to you. Please,
take me to you. (*Her tone changes.*)

> Oh, that He would come,
> Oh, that He might take me,
> So that I'd be safe
> From the eyes of the world.

I know it for certain, Sister Martha. . . .

SISTER MARTHA. What do you know?

HANNELE. He promised me I'd go to heaven. He promised me.

SISTER MARTHA. Oh?

HANNELE. Do you know who?

SISTER MARTHA. Who?

HANNELE. (*Whispers mysteriously into* SISTER MARTHA'S *ear.*) Dear Lord—Gottwald.

SISTER MARTHA. Now you know you must go to sleep.

HANNELE. Sister—Mr. Gottwald is a handsome man, isn't he? His name is Henry. Henry is a beautiful name, isn't it? (*Ardently.*) Oh, dear, sweet Henry! Sister, you know what? We're going to be married. Oh, yes, the two of us—Gottwald and me.

> And when they thus were married
> They journeyed off together
> To sleep in a snow-white feather bed
> In a darkened marriage chamber.

He has such a beautiful beard. (*Entranced.*) Blooming clover grows all over his head!—Listen—He is calling me. Don't you hear?

SISTER MARTHA. Go to sleep, Hannele. No one is calling.

HANNELE. That was the Lord—Jesus.—Listen! Listen! Now He's calling me again, "Hannele!"—Quite loud. "Hannele!" very, very clearly. Come, go with me.

SISTER MARTHA. When the Lord calls me, I shall be ready.

HANNELE. (*Bathed in moonlight again, makes a gesture as if she were smelling some sweet perfume.*) Don't you smell anything, Sister?

SISTER MARTHA. No, Hannele.

HANNELE. Lilacs? (*With increasing, ecstatic happiness.*)

Listen! Listen! What is it? (*A sweet voice is heard far in the distance.*) Is that the angels? Can't you hear them?

SISTER MARTHA. Of course I hear them, but you know you must lie very still and sleep quietly until tomorrow morning.

HANNELE. Can you sing that song?

SISTER MARTHA. Sing what song, dear?

HANNELE. "Sleep, darling, sleep."

SISTER MARTHA. Would you really like to hear it?

HANNELE. (*Lies back and strokes the* SISTER'*s hand.*) Sing it to me, Mother dear. Sing it to me.

SISTER MARTHA. (*Puts the candle out, leans over the bed, and speaks softly to the accompaniment of the music.*)

> Sleep, darling, sleep
> In the garden goes a sheep

(*She nows sings, and it becomes completely dark.*)

> In the garden goes a little lamb,
> It walks upon the little dam,
> Sleep, darling, sleep.

A dim light now fills the desolate room. Upon the edge of the bed, bending forward, supporting herself with her pale, thin elbows, sits the ghostly form of a woman. She is barefooted, and her long, white hair falls loosely down to the bed. Her face is wasted and sorrowful. Her sunken eyes, although closed, seem fastened on HANNELE. *She speaks in a monotone, as if talking in her sleep. Before she says a word, she moves her lips, as if to speak. With great effort she seems to utter the sounds from deep in her breast. She is aged before her time, hollow-cheeked, and poorly clothed.*

THE FEMALE APPARITION. Hannele!

HANNELE. (*Also with closed eyes.*) Mother, Mother dear, is it you?

THE FEMALE APPARITION. Yes. I have washed the feet of our dear Savior with my tears and dried them with my hair.

HANNELE. Do you bring me good tidings?

THE FEMALE APPARITION. Yes.

HANNELE. Have you come a long way?

THE FEMALE APPARITION. A hundred thousand miles through the night.

HANNELE. Mother, what do you look like?

THE FEMALE APPARITION. Like the children of the world.

HANNELE. Bluebells must grow in your throat, your voice sounds so sweet.

THE FEMALE APPARITION. It is not a pure voice.

HANNELE. Mother, dear Mother, how you shine in your beauty.

THE FEMALE APPARITION. The angels in heaven are a hundred times more beautiful.

HANNELE. Why aren't you as beautiful as they?

THE FEMALE APPARITION. I suffered for you.

HANNELE. Mother dear, stay with me.

THE FEMALE APPARITION. (*Rises.*) I must go.

HANNELE. Is it beautiful where you are?

THE FEMALE APPARITION. In God's house there are wide, wide meadows, sheltered from the wind and storm and hail.

HANNELE. Do you rest when you are tired?

THE FEMALE APPARITION. Yes.

HANNELE. Do you have food to eat when you are hungry?

THE FEMALE APPARITION. I still my hunger with fruit and

meat. When I am thirsty, I drink golden wine. (*She draws back.*)

HANNELE. Are you going away, Mother?

THE FEMALE APPARITION. God is calling.

HANNELE. Does God call loudly?

THE FEMALE APPARITION. God calls loudly for me.

HANNELE. My heart is in flames, Mother.

THE FEMALE APPARITION. God will cool it with roses and lilies.

HANNELE. Will God redeem me?

THE FEMALE APPARITION. Do you know what flower I am holding in my hand?

HANNELE. It's a primrose.*

THE FEMALE APPARITION. (*Puts it into* HANNELE's *hand.*) You shall keep it as God's pledge. Farewell!

HANNELE. Mother, stay with me!

THE FEMALE APPARITION. (*Draws back.*) A little while, and ye shall not see me and again, a little while, and ye shall see me.

HANNELE. I'm afraid.

THE FEMALE APPARITION. (*Draws back farther.*) As the white snow drifts are blown about on the mountains, so shall God pursue your tormentors.

HANNELE. Don't go away.

THE FEMALE APPARITION. The children of heaven are as the blue lightning in the night.—Sleep!

It gradually becomes dark again. At the same time boys' lovely voices are heard singing the second stanza of "Sleep, darling, sleep."

> Sleep, darling, sleep,
> Strange guests are coming.

---

* Hauptmann uses the German term for primrose, *Himmelsschlüssel,* literally, "key to heaven."

Now the room is filled with a beam of golden-green light. Three bright figures of ANGELS *are seen—beautiful winged youths with wreaths of roses on their heads. They hold music in their hands, and when the singing stops, they take up the song. Both the* DEACONESS *and the* FEMALE APPARITION *are gone.*

> The guests are come now,
> They are beloved angels.
> Sleep, darling, sleep.

HANNELE. (*Opens her eyes and stares enchanted at the figures of the* ANGELS.) Angels? (*With growing surprise and overflowing joy, but not yet free of doubt.*) Angels!! (*Rapturously.*) Angels!!!

A short pause. The ANGELS *now speak the following lines accompanied by music.*

FIRST ANGEL.

> Upon those hills, the sun
> Gave not its gold to you;
> The blowing grass of the valleys
> Spread not itself for you.

SECOND ANGEL.

> The golden grain of the fields
> Would not still your hunger;
> The milk of the grazing cows
> Foamed not in the pail for you.

THIRD ANGEL.

> The flowers and blossoms of the earth,
> Swelling with sweetness and fragrance,
> All purple and heavenly blue,
> Bloomed not along your path.

A short pause.

FIRST ANGEL.

> We bring the first greetings
> Carried through darkness and gloom;
> We bring on our feathered wings
> The first breath of happiness.

SECOND ANGEL.

> We bring on the hems of our robes
> The first sweet fragrance of spring;
> It blooms from our lips,
> The first red hint of the dawn.

THIRD ANGEL.

> There gleams from around our feet,
> The green light of our homeland.
> There flash from the depths of our eyes
> The spires of the heavenly city.

Curtain

ACT TWO

SCENE: *Everything is as it was before the appearance of the* ANGELS. *The* DEACONESS *sits beside the bed on which* HANNELE *lies. She lights the candle again, and* HANNELE *awakens, still filled with rapture. Her face has an expression of heavenly exaltation. As soon as she recognizes the Sister, she begins to talk in breathless joy.*

HANNELE. Sister! Angels! Sister Martha, angels!—Do you know who was here?

SISTER MARTHA. You are wide awake again.

HANNELE. Just think! (*Impulsively.*) Angels, angels! Real angels! Angels from heaven! Sister Martha! You know—angels with long wings.

SISTER MARTHA. Now child, you've just had such a beautiful dream. . . .

HANNELE. Oh dear, she thinks I've been dreaming. Then what is this? Look at it.

She acts as if she has a flower in her hand. She holds out the imaginary flower for the Sister to see.

SISTER MARTHA. What is it?

HANNELE. Can't you see?

SISTER MARTHA. Hm.

HANNELE. Look at it.

SISTER MARTHA. Aha!

HANNELE. Just smell it.

SISTER MARTHA. (*Pretending to smell the flower.*) Hm. Beautiful.

HANNELE. Not so hard—you'll break it.

SISTER MARTHA. I'm so sorry. What kind of flower is it?

HANNELE. Oh, it's a primrose. Can't you tell?

SISTER MARTHA. Yes, of course.

HANNELE. You don't really. . . . Then bring the light closer. Hurry, hurry!

SISTER MARTHA. (*While she holds the light.*) Oh yes, now I see it.

HANNELE. You see?

SISTER MARTHA. But you're really talking far too much. We must be quite still, or else the doctor will be angry with us. He even sent us medicine and we must take it.

HANNELE. Oh, Sister! Why do you trouble so much about me? You don't even know what has happened, do you? Because

125

you would say if you knew. Who gave me this flower? Who do you think gave me the golden primrose? Well? Do you know?

SISTER MARTHA. You can tell me all about it tomorrow morning when you are rested and fresh and well.

HANNELE. But I am well. (*She sits up and puts her feet on the floor.*) You see, I am quite well, Sister.

SISTER MARTHA. No, Hannele! You mustn't do that. You are not allowed to.

HANNELE. (*Waving the* SISTER *aside, gets out of bed and takes a few steps.*) Leave me alone—You must leave me alone. I have to go away. (*She looks at something, startled.*) Oh heavenly Saviour!

An ANGEL *appears with black clothes and wings. Tall, mighty and beautiful, he carries a long, snake-like sword, the hilt of which is wrapped in black crepe. Silently and seriously he sits by the stove, looking calmly and steadily at* HANNELE. *A white dreamlike light fills the room.*

HANNELE. Who are you? (*No answer.*) Are you an angel? (*No answer.*) Have you come to see me? (*No answer.*) I am Hannele Mattern. Have you come to see me? (*Again no answer. Devout and humble,* SISTER MARTHA *has been standing there with folded hands. Now she slowly leaves the room.*)

HANNELE. Has God taken the speech from your tongue? (*No answer.*) Do you come from God? (*No answer.*) Are you my friend? Do you come as an enemy? (*No answer.*) Is that a sword in the fold of your robe? (*No answer.*) Brr. I'm so cold. Cutting frost blows from your wings. Your breath is cold. Who are you? (*No answer. A sudden terror overcomes her. With a cry she turns around as if some one were behind her.*) Mother! Dear Mother!

A figure in the dress of the DEACONESS, *but younger and*

126

more beautiful than she, with long, white wings, enters. HAN-
NELE *rushes toward the figure, grasping its hands.*

HANNELE. Mother! Mother, there is someone here.

DEACONESS. Where?

HANNELE. There—there.

DEACONESS. Why are you trembling?

HANNELE. I'm afraid.

DEACONESS. Don't be afraid. I am with you.

HANNELE. My teeth are chattering. I am so afraid. I can't
help it. He scares me.

DEACONESS. Don't be afraid. He is your friend.

HANNELE. Who is he, Mother?

DEACONESS. Don't you know him?

HANNELE. Who is he?

DEACONESS. Death.

HANNELE. Death. (HANNELE *stares mutely and reverently at
the* BLACK ANGEL.) Must it be?

DEACONESS. Death is like a gate, Hannele.

HANNELE. Must everybody go through the gate?

DEACONESS. Everybody.

HANNELE. Will you seize me harshly, Death?—"He is silent"
—he doesn't answer anything I ask him, Mother.

DEACONESS. The words of God are loud in your heart.

HANNELE. I have often longed for death—from my heart.
Now I am so afraid.

DEACONESS. Get ready, Hannele.

HANNELE. For Death?

DEACONESS. Yes.

HANNELE. (*After a pause, timidly.*) Will I have to lie in the
coffin in these tattered and ragged clothes?

DEACONESS. God will clothe you.

She takes out a tiny silver bell and rings it. Immediately there enters—silently, as all the following figures—a little, hunchback VILLAGE TAILOR, *carrying a wedding gown, a veil, and a wreath over his arm, and in his hand a pair of crystal slippers. He has a strange walk, bows silently before the* ANGEL, *the* DEACONESS, *and finally deepest before* HANNELE.

VILLAGE TAILOR. (*Always with obeisance.*) Miss Johanna Katherina Mattern. (*He clears his throat.*) Your father, his Excellency the Count, has been pleased to allow me to arrange for your bridal robes.

DEACONESS. (*Takes the robe from the* TAILOR *and dresses* HANNELE.) Come, I will help you, Hannele.

HANNELE. (*Joyfully.*) Oh, how it rustles.

DEACONESS. White silk, Hannele.

HANNELE. (*Looking down at herself, enraptured.*) The people will be astonished to see how beautifully dressed I will be, lying in my coffin.

VILLAGE TAILOR. (*Clearing his throat constantly.*) Miss Johanna Katherina Mattern—the entire village is talking—of the good fortune Death is bringing you. Your father—his Excellency the Count—has been to the Mayor. . . .

DEACONESS. (*Putting the wreath on* HANNELE's *head.*) Now bow your head, you heavenly bride!

HANNELE. (*Trembling with childish joy.*) You know what, Sister Martha? I'm glad I'm to die. (*To* SISTER MARTHA, *suddenly doubting.*) Are you really Sister Martha?

DEACONESS. Yes.

HANNELE. You are Sister Martha, aren't you?—No, you're not. You're my Mother, aren't you?

DEACONESS. Yes.

HANNELE. Are you both?

DEACONESS. The children of God are one in Him.

VILLAGE TAILOR. Now if I may be permitted, Princess Hannele—(*Kneeling with the slippers.*) These are the tiniest shoes in the kingdom. Everybody else's feet are too big: Hedwig, Agnes, Liese, Martha, Minna, Anna, Katie, Gretchen! (*He puts on the slippers.*) They fit! They fit! The bride is found! Little Hannele has the tiniest feet.—If there is anything else you need, I am your servant—your servant—(*Bows and leaves.*)

HANNELE. I can hardly wait, Mother.

DEACONESS. You won't have to take any more medicine now.

HANNELE. No.

DEACONESS. Now you will be as healthy and happy as a lark, Hannele.

HANNELE. Yes.

DEACONESS. Now come, dear, and lie down on your death bed. (*She takes* HANNELE *by the hand and leads her to the bed, where* HANNELE *lies down.*)

HANNELE. Now I'll finally know what Death is like.

DEACONESS. You will, Hannele.

HANNELE. (*Lying on her back, pretending to hold the flower.*) I'm holding this pledge in my hands.

DEACONESS. Press it close to your breast, Hannele.

HANNELE. (*Growing fearful again, timidly to the* ANGEL.) Must it be?

DEACONESS. It must.

Far in the distance the sound of a funeral march is heard.

HANNELE. (*Listening.*) Now Master Seyfried and his musicians are announcing the funeral. (*The* ANGEL *arises.*) Now he's getting up. (*The storm outside gets worse. Solemnly and slowly the* ANGEL *approaches* HANNELE.) Now he's coming toward me. Oh, Sister! Mother! I can't see you any more. Where are you? (*Imploringly to the* ANGEL.) Be quick, you dark and silent spirit. (*Speaking as though oppressed by a heavy weight.*) It presses—it presses—like—a stone. (*The* ANGEL *slowly lifts his broad sword.*) He will—he will—destroy me. (*In great fear.*) Help me, Sister!

DEACONESS. (*Steps majestically between the* ANGEL *and* HANNELE *and lays her hands protectively on* HANNELE'S *heart. She speaks loftily, impressively, and with inspiration.*) He does not dare. I place both my consecrated hands upon your heart.

The DARK ANGEL *vanishes. Silence. The* DEACONESS *folds her hands and smiles gently at* HANNELE, *then meditates and moves her lips, praying silently. The funeral march continues. The sound of many feet approaching hesitantly is heard. Immediately the figure of the schoolmaster* GOTTWALD *appears in the center door. The dirge ceases.* GOTTWALD *is dressed in black as for a funeral and carries a bouquet of beautiful bluebells. Reverently he takes off his hat. Still in the doorway, he turns around and makes a gesture for silence. Behind him are his pupils, boys and girls in their best clothes. At his gesture they stop their whispering and remain quite still. They do not dare to cross the threshold. With solemn face,* GOTTWALD *now approaches the* DEACONESS, *who is still praying.*

GOTTWALD. (*Softly.*) Good day, Sister Martha.

DEACONESS. God be with you, Mr. Gottwald.

GOTTWALD. (*Shaking his head sadly as he looks at* HANNELE.) Poor little thing.

DEACONESS. Why are you so sad, Mr. Gottwald?

GOTTWALD. Because she is dead.

DEACONESS. We shouldn't be sad about it. She is at peace now, and I don't begrudge her that.

GOTTWALD. (Sighing.) Yes, she is happy. Now she is free from trouble and sorrow.

DEACONESS. (Looking at HANNELE, engrossed.) She is so beautiful lying there.

GOTTWALD. So beautiful—now that you are dead, you have blossomed forth.

DEACONESS. God has made her beautiful, because she was so pious.

GOTTWALD. Yes, she was pious and good. (Sighs heavily, opens his hymnbook and looks into it sadly.)

DEACONESS. (Looking into the hymnbook with him.) We shouldn't complain. We must be patient.

GOTTWALD. Still, it's hard for me.

DEACONESS. Because she is saved?

GOTTWALD. Because two flowers have withered.

DEACONESS. Where?

GOTTWALD. The two violets I have in my hymnbook. They are like the dead eyes of my beloved Hannele.

DEACONESS. They will bloom more beautifully in heaven.

GOTTWALD. Oh, Lord! How much longer must we journey through this dark valley of sorrows. (Suddenly changing, busy and bustling, hurriedly producing some notes.) What do you think? I thought we might sing "Jesus Christ, My Sure Defense" for the first hymn here at the house.

DEACONESS. Yes, that is a beautiful hymn, and Hannele Mattern was such a faithful child.

GOTTWALD. And then at the churchyard I thought we would sing "Let me go, Let me go." (He sings softly, beating time.)

Let me go, let me go,
Lord, to me thy presence show

(*The children sing along softly.*) Children, are you all dressed warm enough? It will be cold out in the churchyard. Come in and take a last look at our poor Hannele. (*The children file in and stand reverently around the bed.*) See how beautiful death has made the little girl. She was clad in rags—now she has clothes of silk. Once she ran about bare-footed, now she has crystal slippers on her feet. Soon she will live in a golden palace and eat roast beef every day.—Here she lived on cold potatoes—and never had enough to eat. Here you always called her the Ragged Princess. Now she will soon be a real princess. Those of you who have hurt her, ask forgiveness now. Otherwise she will tell Our Heavenly Father everything and it will go hard with you.

A BOY. (*Slipping a little forward.*) Dear little Princess Hannele, don't be angry with me and don't tell God that I called you the Ragged Princess.

ALL THE CHILDREN. (*Together.*) We are all very sorry.

GOTTWALD. I'm sure poor Hannele will forgive you. Now go out and wait for me.

DEACONESS. Come into the back room with me, and I will tell you what you must do if you want to become beautiful angels like Hannele. (*She goes out; the children follow her. The door closes.*)

GOTTWALD. (*Now alone with HANNELE. Deeply moved, he lays the flowers at her feet.*) My dear Hannele, here are the bluebells I have brought you. (*Kneeling at her bed, his voice trembling.*) Do not forget me in your glory. (*He sobs and*

132

presses his forehead against the folds of her dress.) My heart is breaking at the thought of being separated from you.

Voices are heard. GOTTWALD *arises; he puts a cover over* HANNELE. *Two old women, dressed in mourning, handkerchiefs and yellow-edged hymnbooks in their hands, slip in quietly.*

FIRST WOMAN. (*Looking around.*) Are we really the first ones?

SECOND WOMAN. Naw. The teacher's here already. Good day, teacher.

GOTTWALD. Good day.

FIRST WOMAN. You're sure taking it to heart, teacher. She was a good child, really a good child. Always busy as a little bee.

SECOND WOMAN. Is it really true what people say—is it? Did she really take her own life?

A third figure has appeared.

THIRD WOMAN. That'd be a sin.

SECOND WOMAN. A sin against the Holy Ghost.

THIRD WOMAN. Such a terrible sin, it's never forgiven, the preacher says.

GOTTWALD. Don't you remember what Christ said: Suffer little children to come unto me?

A fourth woman has arrived.

FOURTH WOMAN. Mercy, what weather. We'll freeze sure before we're done. I just hope the Pastor don't take too long. There's snow a foot deep in the churchyard.

FIFTH WOMAN. (*Enters.*) Listen, the Pastor won't bless her. He says holy ground ain't no place for her.

PLESCHKE. (*Enters.*) Have ya heard—have ya heard? A fine

gentleman's been to see the preacher—and he said—yep—that Hannele's a—a saint.

HANKE. (*Enters hastily.*) They're bringin' a crystal coffin.

VARIOUS VOICES. A crystal coffin! A crystal coffin!

HANKE. Lord, it musta cost a fortune.

VARIOUS VOICES. A crystal coffin! A crystal coffin!

SEIDEL. (*Enters.*) There's wonderful things goin' on. An angel's walked right through the village—as big as a poplar tree, believe me. And there's a couple of 'em sittin' by the smithy—but they're little ones no bigger 'n babies. That girl's more than a beggar.

VARIOUS VOICES. The girl's more than a beggar.—They're bringin' a crystal coffin. An angel has walked right through the village.

Four white-clad youths enter carrying a crystal coffin which they place not far from HANNELE's *bed. The mourners, inquisitive, curious, and amazed, whisper to each other.*

GOTTWALD. (*Lifts slightly the sheet that covers* HANNELE.) Now you may see the dead child.

FIRST WOMAN. (*Looking under the sheet curiously.*) Look at her hair—why it's like gold.

GOTTWALD. (*Drawing the cloth completely away from* HANNELE. *Her entire body is covered with a pale light.*) And look at her silk clothes and crystal slippers!

All shrink back with cries of astonishment, as if dazzled.

SEVERAL VOICES. Oh, she is beautiful!—Who is it? Is that Hannele? Hannele Mattern? I don't believe it.

PLESCHKE. That girl—that girl's a saint. She's—a saint.

The four youths lift HANNELE *tenderly into the crystal coffin.*

134

HANKE. They say she won't be buried.

FIRST WOMAN. They'll put her in the church.

SECOND WOMAN. I don't think the girl's really dead. She sure looks alive.

PLESCHKE. Give me a—a—a—a feather. I'll just hold a feather over her mouth. Yep. And see—yep—see if she's still breathin'! (*Someone gives him a feather which he holds over* HANNELE's *mouth*.) It ain't movin'! The girl's dead, all right. There ain't a bit of life in her.

THIRD WOMAN. I'll give her this bit of rosemary. (*She puts a sprig into the coffin*.)

FOURTH WOMAN. She can take my lavendar along, too.

FIFTH WOMAN. Where is Mattern?

FIRST WOMAN. Yes, where is Mattern?

SECOND WOMAN. Him! He's sittin' in the tavern.

FIRST WOMAN. He probably don't know what's happened.

SECOND WOMAN. When he's got his whiskey, he don't know nothin'.

PLESCHKE. Ain't nobody—ain't nobody told him that—that there's a corpse in the house?

THIRD WOMAN. He oughta found that out hisself.

FOURTH WOMAN. I don't want to say nothin'—no sir, not me, but it's sure no secret who killed the girl.

SEIDEL. That's what I say, and the whole village knows it, too. She's got a bruise as big as my fist.

FIFTH WOMAN. Where that fellow walks, no grass will grow.

SEIDEL. I helped put her to bed, and I saw plenty. She had a bruise as big as my fist, I tell ya. And that's what fixed her.

FIRST WOMAN. Nobody's to blame but Mattern.

ALL. (*Whispering angrily*.) Nobody else.

SECOND WOMAN. He's a murderer.

ALL. (*Enraged, but still rather mysteriously.*) A murderer, a murderer!

The roaring voice of the drunken Mattern is heard.

MATTERN. (*Outside.*)

> A qui—et consci—ence
> Is like the gentle ki—iss of peace.

(*He appears in the doorway and shouts.*) Girl! Girl! Brat! Where are ya hidin'? (*He staggers about the threshold.*) I'll give ya till I count five. I won't wait no longer. One—two—three—and one makes—. Don't make me mad, I tell ya. If I gotta look for ya, I'll break every bone in your body. (*Suddenly aware of the others, who stand as still as death.*) What are ya doin' here? (*No answer.*) Why did ya come here? (*No answer.*) Maybe the devil sent ya, huh?—Hurry up and get out. And be quick about it. (*He laughs to himself.*) Now let's wait a bit. I know those tricks. I just had a drop too much, that's all. That's when a fellow gets a little dizzy in his head. "A qui—et consci—ence——Is like the gentle ki—iss of peace." (*Startled.*) Are ya still here? (*Looks for something to strike them with.*) I'll take anything I can find. . . .

A man in a brown, threadbare coat has entered. He is about thirty years old, has long black hair and a pale face with the features of GOTTWALD. *He carries a slouch hat and wears sandals. He is dusty and seems weary from traveling. He interrupts* MATTERN, *gently touching his arm.* MATTERN *turns around abruptly.*

THE STRANGER. (*Looks earnestly and calmly into the mason's face and says humbly.*) God be with you, Mason Mattern!

136

MATTERN. What are you doin' here? What do ya want?

THE STRANGER. (*Humbly pleading.*) My feet are bleeding from the long journey; give me water to wash them. The hot sun has parched my throat; give me wine to drink, that I may be refreshed. I have had nothing to eat since I set out in the morning. I am hungry.

MATTERN. What do I care? Who asked ya to go runnin' around the countryside? Why don't ya work for a livin' the way I have to?

THE STRANGER. I am a worker.

MATTERN. You're a tramp. If ya worked for a livin' ya wouldn't have to beg.

THE STRANGER. I don't work for wages.

MATTERN. You're a tramp.

THE STRANGER. (*Shyly and submissively, but insistently.*) I am a doctor—perhaps I can help you.

MATTERN. I ain't sick. I don't need no doctor.

THE STRANGER. (*His voice trembling with emotion.*) Mason Mattern, consider! If you give me no water, still I will heal you. If you give me no bread to eat, nevertheless, I will make you well. As God is my witness.

MATTERN. Get out! On your way! I'm fit as a fiddle. I don't need no doctor. Do ya understand?

THE STRANGER. Mason Mattern, consider! I will wash your feet. I will give you wine to drink. You shall have sweet bread to eat. Set your foot on my head, and yet I shall heal you and make you well—so help me God.

MATTERN. Now, we'll just see if you'll really go. And if ya don't get out, I'll. . . .

THE STRANGER. (*Earnestly warning him.*) Mason Mattern, do you know what you have in this house?

MATTERN. Everything that belongs here. Everything that really belongs here. You don't belong here—. Why don't ya get out?

THE STRANGER. (*Simply.*) Your daughter is sick.

MATTERN. She don't need no doctor for her kind of sickness. There's nothin' wrong with her, but she's lazy. I can cure her of that myself.

THE STRANGER. (*Solemnly.*) Mason Mattern, I come to you as a messenger.

MATTERN. As a messenger from who?

THE STRANGER. I come from the Father, and I go unto the Father. Where is His child?

MATTERN. How do I know where she's gadding about? What are his children to me. He never troubled hisself about them before.

THE STRANGER. (*Firmly.*) You have a dead child in your house.

MATTERN. (*Aware of* HANNELE *lying there, steps stiffly and quietly to the coffin and looks in, murmuring.*) Where did ya get the beautiful clothes? Who bought ya the crystal coffin?

The mourners whisper vehemently and mysteriously. Several times the word "Murderer" can be heard spoken with great bitterness.

MATTERN. (*Softly, trembling.*) I never treated ya bad. I gave ya clothes. I fed ya. (*Insolently to the* STRANGER.) What do ya want? What's that to me?

THE STRANGER. Mason Mattern, have you nothing to tell me?

The whispering among the mourners grows louder, more and more enraged, and often one hears the word "Murderer. Murderer!"

THE STRANGER. Have you nothing to reproach yourself for?

Have you never torn her from her sleep at night? Have you never beaten her with your fists until she fainted?

MATTERN. (*Beside himself.*) Then strike me dead. Here—now—on the spot. May I be struck by lightning, if I am guilty.

Faint blue lightning and a distant roll of thunder.

ALL. (*In confusion.*) A storm's comin'. In the middle of the winter! He's perjured hisself. The murderer's perjured hisself!

THE STRANGER. (*Urgently, yet kindly.*) Have you still nothing to tell me, Mattern?

MATTERN. (*In miserable fear.*) Spare the rod and spoil the child. Everything I've done was for the good of this girl. I kept her like she was my own daughter. I can beat her if she ain't good.

THE WOMEN. (*Move toward him.*) Murderer! Murderer! Murderer! Murderer!

MATTERN. She cheated me and lied to me. She robbed me day after day.

THE STRANGER. Do you speak the truth?

MATTERN. May God punish me. . . .

At this moment a yellowish-green glow beams from the primrose in HANNELE's *hand. The mason* MATTERN, *his entire body trembling, stares at the vision as if mad.*

THE STRANGER. Mason Mattern, you are lying.

ALL. (*Greatly excited.*) A miracle—a miracle!

PLESCHKE. That girl's—she's—a saint. He's damned hisself —body and soul.

MATTERN. (*Roars.*) I'll hang myself. (*Holding his hands to his temples, he runs out.*)

THE STRANGER. (*Steps to* HANNELE's *coffin and speaks to all present. With reverence they all draw back from the majestic figure who now speaks.*) Fear not! (*He bends over her, grasps*

139

her hand, and speaks gently.) The little girl is not dead.—She sleeps. (*With deep inner strength and conviction.*) Johanna Mattern, arise!!!

A bright golden-green light fills the room. HANNELE *opens her eyes and raises herself on the hand of the* STRANGER, *without, however, daring to look into his face. She rises from the coffin and immediately kneels at the feet of the* STRANGER. *The onlookers flee in dread. The* STRANGER *and* HANNELE *remain alone. The gray cloak slides from his shoulders, and he stands there in a golden-white robe.*

THE STRANGER. (*Softly and sincerely.*) Hannele.

HANNELE. (*Overjoyed, bowing her head as low as possible.*) There he is.

THE STRANGER. Who am I?

HANNELE. You.

THE STRANGER. Say my name.

HANNELE. (*Whispers, trembling with reverence.*) Holy! Holy!

THE STRANGER. I know all your sorrows and pain.

HANNELE. You dear, dear. . . .

THE STRANGER. Arise.

HANNELE. Your clothes are immaculate. I am full of shame.

THE STRANGER. (*Lays his right hand on* HANNELE'S *head.*) Then I take all baseness from you. (*With gentle strength he turns her face up, then touches her eyes.*) Thus I fill your eyes with everlasting light. Reflect all sunlight. Reflect eternal day, from sunrise to sunset, from sunset to sunrise. Reflect the light of the blue sea, the azure sky, the green fields of eternity. (*He touches her ear.*) Thus I give your ear the power to hear the jubilations of all the millions of angels in the myriad heavens of God. (*He touches her mouth.*) Thus I free your stammering tongue and place thereon your soul and my soul and the soul of God the Almighty.

HANNELE *attempts to rise, her entire body trembling. As if oppressed by a terrible weight, she is unable to do it. Shaken with terrible sighs and sobs, she buries her head in the* STRANGER'S *breast.*

THE STRANGER. With these tears I wash from your soul the dust and pain of the world. I will raise you above the stars of God.

Now the STRANGER *speaks to the accompaniment of soft music, stroking* HANNELE'S *head. While he speaks, figures of* ANGELS *appear in the doorway, some large, some small, some boys, and some girls. First they act shy, then they venture in, swinging censers, and adorning the room with carpets and flowers.*

THE STRANGER.

> Salvation is a magnificent, wondrous city
> Where peace and joy are unending.

Harps, softly at first, then gradually loud and full.

> Its houses are marble, its roofs are gold,
> Red wine flows from the silver fountains,
> And the white streets are strewn with flowers,
> From the towers ring eternal wedding bells.
> The spires shine green in the morning light,
> Crown with roses, butterflies whirling about.
> Twelve milk-white swans circle far around them
> And ruffle their swelling plumage;

141

Boldly they travel through the blossoming air,
Through the thrilling, clangorous fragrance of the sky.
They circle, in an eternal, festive procession,
Their wings sound like harps in their flight.
They pull streamers of green veil behind them,
They look upon Zion, on garden and sea.
And down below, hand in hand, they wander,
Stately beings, through the heavenly land.
Red wine reddens the wide, wide sea
Into which they plunge with radiant bodies.
They plunge into the foam and splendor,
Where pure crimson covers them.
And when they rise from the flood rejoicing,
They are cleansed through Jesus' blood.

The STRANGER *turns now to the* ANGELS, *who have finished
their work. With timid joy and happiness they step nearer and
form a semicircle around* HANNELE *and the* STRANGER.

THE STRANGER.

Come forward with fine linens, children of heaven,
Come closer, loved ones, turtle doves.
Cover the weak and wasted body,
Shaken with chills, parched with fever,
Softly, that no pain befall her sickly frame;
And lift her gently, refrain from beating your wings,
Carry her, soaring lightly above the leaves of grass,
Through the soft moonshine lovingly thither,
Through the fragrance and mist of Paradise
Till divine coolness blissfully surrounds her.—

A short pause.

There mix, while she rests on her silken bed,
In a white marble bowl, water of the mountain brook
And purple wine and milk of the antelope,
To wash off all her illness in the pure flood.
Break twigs from the bushes loaded with blossoms:
Jessamine and lilac, heavy with night-dew,
And let their clear drops, moist burdens,
Rain fresh and fragrantly down upon her.
Take up soft satin, and limb by limb,
Like lily leaves, carefully dry her.
Refresh her with wine, offer it in a golden chalice,
In which the pulp of fresh fruit has been pressed.—
Strawberries, still warm from the fire of the sun,
Raspberries, swollen with sweet blood,
The velvety peach, the golden pineapple,
Oranges, yellow and bright, carry them to her
In spacious bowls of sparkling metal.
Feast her palate and encompass her heart
With the splendor and abundance of the new morning.
May her eyes be charmed by the magnificent halls.
Let fire-colored butterflies swing high
Over the green malachite pavement.
Upon outstretched satin may she stride
Through tulips and hyacinths. At her side
Let broad branches of green palm trees tremble,
And everything glitter in the brightness of the walls.
Into fields of red poppies let the poor girl glance,
Where children of heaven throw golden balls

In the early rays of the new-born light,
And with lovely music enrapture her heart.

THE ANGELS. (*Singing in chorus.*)

We carry you forth, silently, gently,
Lullaby, to the heavenly land,
Lullaby, to the heavenly land.

During the song of the ANGELS, *the scene grows dark. Out of the darknes, the singing is heard gradually diminishing. It then grows light, and the room of the poorhouse is seen, everything as it was before the first apparition.* HANNELE *lies on the bed, a poor, sick child.* DR. WACHLER *is bent over her with his stethoscope; the* DEACONESS, *who is holding the light, watches him anxiously. Only now does the singing stop completely.*

DR. WACHLER. (*Straightening up.*) You are right.

SISTER MARTHA. Dead?

DR. WACHLER. (*Nods sadly.*) Dead.

Curtain

THE BEAVER COAT

A Comedy of Thieves in Four Acts

DRAMATIS PERSONAE

VON WEHRHAHN, a judge

KRUEGER, a property owner

DR. FLEISCHER

PHILIPP, his son

MOTES

MRS. MOTES

MRS. WOLFF, a washwoman

JULIUS WOLFF, her husband

LEONTINE ⎱ her daughters
ADELHEID ⎰

WULKOW, a boatman

GLASENAPP, a clerk in the court

MITTELDORF, a deputy

The action takes place somewhere in the neighborhood of Berlin in the 1880's.

ACT ONE

SCENE: *A small, plain, blue-tinted kitchen with a low ceiling; a window to the left; to the right, a rough-framed door leading into the open; a door with the wings removed in the middle of the rear wall. To the left, in the corner, the stove; above it, on the wall, the cooking utensils on a wooden frame; in the right corner, oars and ship gear; firewood under the window in a pile. An old kitchen bench, several footstools, etc. Through the empty window frame in the back wall, a second*

145

room can be seen—a high, neatly made bed above which hang
cheap photographs with even cheaper frames, colored prints
in the form of visiting cards, etc. A pine chair is placed with
its back against the bed. It is winter, and the moon is shining.
Upon the stove, in a metal candlestick, a candle is burning.
LEONTINE WOLFF *sits on a stool next to the stove, asleep, with*
her head and arms on the top of the stove. She is seventeen
years old, a pretty blonde girl in the working clothes of a servant
girl. Over a blue cotton jacket, she wears a wool shawl. It re-
mains quiet for several seconds, then someone is heard trying
to unlock the door from the outside. The key is in the lock on
the inside. Then a knock is heard.

MRS. WOLFF. (*Unseen, from outside.*) Adelheid! Adelheid!
(*Silence; then from the other side a knock at the window.*)
Open the door, hurry!

LEONTINE. (*In her sleep.*) No, no, I won't be abused!

MRS. WOLFF. Open up, girl, or I'll come through the window.
(*She bangs harder on the window.*)

LEONTINE. (*Waking up.*) Oh, it's you, Mama! I'm comin'!
(*She unlocks the door.*)

MRS. WOLFF. (*Without putting down the sack which she car-*
ries on her shoulder.) What are ya doin' here?

LEONTINE. (*Sleepily.*) Hello, Mama.

MRS. WOLFF. How did ya get in, huh?

LEONTINE. Well, the key was layin' on the goat shed, wasn't
it?

A short pause.

MRS. WOLFF. What are ya doin' home, girl?

LEONTINE. (*With a foolish pout.*) Can't I come home to see
ya no more?

MRS. WOLFF. Maybe ya'll be so good as not to make so much

fuss. I just like that. (*She lets the sack fall from her shoulder.*) I don't suppose ya know how late it's gettin'? Just so ya get back to your place.

LEONTINE. What do I care if I get there a bit late.

MRS. WOLFF. Now ya just watch out, do ya understand! And see that ya get back or I'm through with ya.

LEONTINE. (*Tearfully, sulking.*) I won't go back to them people, Mama!

MRS. WOLFF. (*Astonished.*) Ya ain't goin'. . . . (*Ironically.*) Well! That's somethin' new, ain't it?

LEONTINE. Well, do I have to let them abuse me?

MRS. WOLFF. (*Busy taking a piece of venison out of the sack.*) Oh, so they abuse ya at the Kruegers? Aw, ya poor child. —Comin' to me with such airs! Such a hussy. . . . Now take a hold of the bottom of that sack there. And don't act so stupid, understand? Ya won't get away with it. Ya won't learn to be lazy in my house. (*Both hang the venison on a doorpost.*) Now I'm tellin' ya for the last time. . . .

LEONTINE. I won't go back to them people no more. I'd rather drown myself than go, Mama!

MRS. WOLFF. Well, don't catch cold doin' it.

LEONTINE. I'll jump in the river!

MRS. WOLFF. Ya call me then, do ya hear, and I'll give ya a shove so ya won't miss it.

LEONTINE. (*Screams loudly.*) I won't let them do this to me —havin' to carry in two loads of wood at night.

MRS. WOLFF. (*Acts astonished.*) Really—it ain't possible! Ya should lug wood in! No! Such people!

LEONTINE. . . . And 20 thalers for the whole year. And for that I'm gettin' my hands all froze up. And not enough potatoes and herring to eat!

MRS. WOLFF. Don't talk so much, ya silly girl. Here's the key. Go cut yourself some bread. And when you're full, get goin', understand? The plum jam's in the top cupboard.

LEONTINE. (*Takes a loaf from the drawer and cuts a large slice.*) Juste gets 40 thalers from the Schulzes and. . . .

MRS. WOLFF. You're in too big a hurry! Ya ain't stayin' with them people forever; ya ain't hired out to them all your life. For all I care ya can pull out the first of April. Ya'll stay right there that long! First ya take the Christmas money, and then ya want to run away, huh? That's no way.—I have to go in and out of them peoples' houses. I don't want that hangin' over me.

LEONTINE. These old rags I got on?

MRS. WOLFF. Ain't ya forgettin' the cash?

LEONTINE. Oh sure! 6 whole marks.

MRS. WOLFF. Money's money! Never ya mind!

LEONTINE. But if I can earn more?

MRS. WOLFF. With your gabble?

LEONTINE. Naw. With the sewing machine. I'll go to Berlin and sew coats. Stechow's Emilie's been there since New Year's.

MRS. WOLFF. Don't talk to me about that slut! If I could only get my hands on her! I'd show the hussy! Wouldn't that be some fun for you? To fool around with some fellow every night. The very thought of it. I'll beat ya till ya can't get up no more. Papa's comin'—now watch yourself!

LEONTINE. If Papa whips me, I'll run away. I'll be able to get along all right.

MRS. WOLFF. Shut up! Go and feed the goats. They haven't been milked this evenin' neither. And give the rabbits some hay.

LEONTINE. (*Tries to leave in a hurry, but meets her father*

148

at the door and says hastily:) Hello. *(She brushes past him.)*

JULIUS WOLFF, *the father, is a ship's carpenter. He is a tall, slow-moving man with dull eyes, perhaps forty-three years old.—He places two long oars, which he has been carrying on his shoulders, in the corner and silently throws down his tools.*

MRS. WOLFF. Did ya meet Emil?

JULIUS. *Grumbles.*

MRS. WOLFF. Can't ya talk? Yes or no? Is he comin' around? Huh?

JULIUS. *(Brusquely.)* Go on! Yell some more!

MRS. WOLFF. You're sure a brave fellow. And ya forgot to shut the door.

JULIUS. *(Shuts the door.)* What's doin' with Leontine again?

MRS. WOLFF. Oh, it's nothin' at all! What sort of a load did Emil have?

JULIUS. Nothin' but bricks again. What else would he have? What's doin' with that girl again?

MRS. WOLFF. Half a load or a whole one?

JULIUS. *(Flaring up suddenly.)* What's the matter with the girl?

MRS. WOLFF. *(Talking him down.)* I want to know what kind of a load Emil's got—a half or a whole boat full?

JULIUS. Oh, go on, go on—a whole boat full.

MRS. WOLFF. *(Becomes frightened and bolts the door.)* Shh, Julius.

JULIUS. *(Silently staring at her, frightened. After a few seconds, softly.)* It's a young ranger from Rixdorf.

MRS. WOLFF. Go on crawl under the bed, Julius. *(After a pause.)* If only ya wasn't so terrible dumb. All at once ya get as scared as a rabbit. You don't understand them things. Ya let me worry about the girl. It's none of your business; it's mine. If it was boys it'd be different—then I'd never say nothin'. Everybody's got their own business.

JULIUS. Then she better not get in my way.

MRS. WOLFF. You'll beat her till she's lame, will ya, Julius? Don't ya get that into your head! Don't ya think I'd let ya. I won't let her be beat black and blue. That girl's goin' to be our good luck. If ya could only understand them things.

JULIUS. Then she better watch herself.

MRS. WOLFF. Don't you worry about that, Julius. Maybe some day you'll see something. Then she'll live in a big mansion, and we'll be happy, if she'll still know us. What did the doctor tell me? Your daughter's a beautiful girl—she'll be a sensation on the stage.

JULIUS. Then she better see that she gets there.

MRS. WOLFF. You're just ignorant, Julius. You've got no education at all. If it hadn't been for me, Julius, what would've become of the girls? I brought 'em up educated, understand? Education's the important thing nowdays. But things don't happen all at once. Always one thing after the other, a little at a time. Now first let's learn her all about housekeepin', then I don't mind if she goes straight to Berlin. She's still much too young for the stage.

There has been a pounding on the door throughout this speech. Now ADELHEID *is heard outside.*

ADELHEID. Mama! Mama! Open up! (MRS. WOLFF *opens the door and* ADELHEID *enters. She is a lanky schoolgirl in her fourteenth year, with a pretty childish face. The expression in her eyes, however, betrays early depravity.*) Why didn't ya let me in, Mama? My hands and feet are froze.

MRS. WOLFF. Don't stand there talkin' nothin' but nonsense. Make a fire in the stove so you'll be warm. Where've ya been so long, anyway?

ADELHEID. I was gettin' the boots for Father.

MRS. WOLFF. You've been gone two hours again.

ADELHEID. Well, I've only been gone since seven.

MRS. WOLFF. So ya went at seven, did ya? And now it's half past ten. Ya didn't know that? That's only been three and a half hours. That isn't too much, I don't suppose? Now ya just listen to what I say. If ya stay out so late again and with that miserable Filitz—then watch out what happens to ya.

ADELHEID. Do ya want me to be bored stiff at home all the time?

MRS. WOLFF. Now be quiet and don't ya say nothin'.

ADELHEID. If I just go to Filitz' a little bit. . . .

MRS. WOLFF. Will ya be still, I'd like to know? And are ya goin' to tell me about Filitz? He better not brag so much neither. He does something else besides fixin' shoes. When a person's been to jail one or two times . . .

ADELHEID. That ain't true. . . . That's all a pack of lies. He told me so hisself, Mama!

MRS. WOLFF. The whole village knows about it, ya silly goose! He's a regular pimp, he is.

ADELHEID. He even goes to see the Judge quite often.

MRS. WOLFF. Why, of course, he spies on people. He's a reformer, on top of it.

ADELHEID. What's a reformer? *

JULIUS. (*From the next room, into which he has gone.*) Now, don't let me hear another word. (ADELHEID *turns pale*

---

* In the original, Adelheid asks Mrs. Wolff what *Tenunziat*—a distorted foreign word for informer—means. She does not receive an answer from her mother.

and immediately goes quietly to build a fire in the stove.
LEONTINE *enters.*)

MRS. WOLFF. (*Has taken the heart, liver, etc., out of the
deer and hands them to* LEONTINE.) Now, hurry and wash
them off. And be quiet about it, or there'll be a row.

LEONTINE, *noticeably intimidated, busies herself at her work.
The girls whisper to each other.*

MRS. WOLFF. Julius! What are ya doin' in there? Did ya forget again about what I told ya this mornin'—about the board
bein' loose?

JULIUS. What board?

MRS. WOLFF. Ya don't know? In the back of the goat shed.
The wind blew it loose last night—see that it gets nailed back,
understand?

JULIUS. Aah, mornin's plenty of time.

MRS. WOLFF. Oh, no. Don't ya get ideas. We won't start
that. (JULIUS, *grumbling, steps into the room.*) Take the hammer! Here are the nails. Now see that ya get it done.

JULIUS. You're crazy.

MRS. WOLFF. (*Calling after him.*) When Wulkow comes,
what'll I make him pay?

JULIUS. Well, at least 12 marks!

Exit.

MRS. WOLFF. (*Disdainfully.*) Bah, 12 marks! (*Pause.*) Now,
just see that Papa gets his dinner. (*A short pause.*)

ADELHEID. (*Looking at the deer.*) What's that, Mama?

MRS. WOLFF. A stork. (*Both girls laugh.*)

ADELHEID. A stork? Have they got horns, too? I know what
that is—it's a deer.

MRS. WOLFF. If ya know, why did ya ask in the first place?

LEONTINE. Did Papa shoot it?

MRS. WOLFF. Now run out and scream it so's the whole village can hear it: Papa shot a deer!

ADELHEID. I'll be careful—'cause the cop'll come.

LEONTINE. I'm not afraid of the cop—he chucked me under the chin once.

MRS. WOLFF. Let'm come. We ain't done nothin' wrong. If a deer gets shot and it's dyin' and no one finds it, the crows eat it. It's me or the crows—it'll get eaten anyhow. (*A short pause.*) Now tell me, were ya to carry the wood in?

LEONTINE. Yes, in this cold! Two loads of wood! And me tired as a dog! As late as nine-thirty!

MRS. WOLFF. And the wood is still out in the street?

LEONTINE. It's layin' in front of the garden gate. That's all I know.

MRS. WOLFF. But if somebody steals the wood—what happens in the mornin'?

LEONTINE. I won't go back no more.

MRS. WOLFF. Are they green logs or dry?

LEONTINE. It's nice dry kindlin'. (*Yawns time after time.*) Oh, Mama, I'm so terrible tired. I've wore myself out something terrible. (*She sits down with all the signs of exhaustion.*)

MRS. WOLFF. (*After a short silence.*) As far as I care, ya can stay with us tonight. I've changed my mind. In the mornin' we'll see what's next.

LEONTINE. I'm just skin and bones, Mama. My things are hangin' like a sack.

MRS. WOLFF. Now hurry up and get to sleep, up in the little room, so there won't be no quarrel with Papa. He don't understand much about such things.

ADELHEID. Papa always talks so uneducated.

MRS. WOLFF. He ain't had no education. It'd be the same with you, if I hadn't brought ya up right. (*Holds the stewpan, at the oven, to* LEONTINE.) Well, come on, put them in here. (LEONTINE *puts the washed meat in the stewpan.*) Now, go to sleep.

LEONTINE. (*Goes into the back room. Still visible, she speaks.*) Mama! Motes has left Kruegers.

MRS. WOLFF. Didn't he pay his rent?

LEONTINE. With no end of trouble, Mr. Krueger says. But he finally threw him out, he was such a lyin', unreliable fellow. And always so high and mighty to Mr. Krueger.

MRS. WOLFF. If I was Mr. Krueger, I wouldn't have taken it this long.

LEONTINE. Motes always looks down on him because Mr. Krueger was a cabinetmaker. He quarreled with Dr. Fleischer, too.

MRS. WOLFF. Now, who'd quarrel with him . . . that I'd like to know. Them people wouldn't harm a fly!

LEONTINE. The Fleischers won't let him come and see them no more.

MRS. WOLFF. If once ya could get in with those people. . . .

LEONTINE. They treat the girls there like their own children.

MRS. WOLFF. And the brother in Berlin is a cashier at a theater.

WULKOW. (*Has been pounding at the door, and calls now in a hoarse voice.*) Would ya please let me in?

MRS. WOLFF. Well, sure. Why not? Come on in.

WULKOW. (*Enters. A shipman on the River Spree, close to sixty years old, bent, with a yellowish-gray full beard that runs under his chin, allowing his weather-beaten face to show.*) A very good evenin' to ya.

154

MRS. WOLFF. Here ya come again to cheat the Wolffs a bit.

WULKOW. Oh, I don't try that no more.

MRS. WOLFF. Oh, it won't be no different this time either.

WULKOW. The shoe'll be on the other foot.

MRS. WOLFF. Hardly!—Here she hangs. Well? A good one, huh?

WULKOW. That Julius better watch his step. They're all pretty much on the lookout.

MRS. WOLFF. What'll ya give me? That's the main thing. What good's such silly talk here?

WULKOW. I'm tellin' ya. I just came from Gruenau. I heard it there for sure. They shot Fritz Weber. They filled his pants with shot.

MRS. WOLFF. What'll ya give me? That's the main thing.

WULKOW. (*Prodding the deer.*) I already got four in the boat.

MRS. WOLFF. Your scow won't sink on that account.

WULKOW. Better not. That'd be something. But what if I have to wait? I have to get them things to Berlin. It's bad enough on the river today, and if it freezes in the night, there'll be no gettin' away tomorrow. Then I'll be sittin' in the ice with my boat and have them things on my neck.

MRS. WOLFF. (*Apparently changing her mind.*) Well, girl, dash down to Schultz. Say hello nice to him, and tell him he should come up—your mother's got something to sell.

WULKOW. Did I say I wouldn't buy it?

MRS. WOLFF. It's all the same to me who buys it.

WULKOW. I'll buy it.

MRS. WOLFF. If ya don't want it, leave it.

WULKOW. I'll buy the animal. How much do you want?

MRS. WOLFF. (*Taking hold of the deer.*) This stag here must weigh thirty pounds. Oh, at least that, I tell ya. Well, Adelheid. You were here. We could hardly lift it up on the nail.

ADELHEID. (*Who was not present at all.*) I almost dislocated something.

WULKOW. I'll give ya 13 marks. I won't even make 10 pfennigs on it.

MRS. WOLFF. (*Acts quite astonished; then takes up something else. As if she had forgotten* WULKOW's *presence, she speaks, seemingly noticing him for the first time.*) I wish ya a good trip.

WULKOW. I can't give ya more than 13 marks.

MRS. WOLFF. Oh, forget it.

WULKOW. I can't give ya no more than I said. I do it only to keep my customers. God help me! It's as true as I'm standing here. I don't make much on the whole business. And even if I wanted to say 14, then I lose and I'm out one mark. It's all the same to me. Just so you all see the good will, I'll pay ya fourteen.

MRS. WOLFF. Let it go! Let it go! I'll get rid of the deer. It won't be here tomorrow mornin'.

WULKOW. If somebody sees it hangin' there—that won't be settled with money.

MRS. WOLFF. We found that deer dyin' . . .

WULKOW. Sure—in a snare, I'll bet.

MRS. WOLFF. Nothin' of the kind! You'll get no place with that! Why should we give ya everything for nothin'? We work till we got no breath left. We have to sit hour after hour in the snow, not to speak of the risk we run there, in the pitch dark. That's no fun.

WULKOW. I've already got four of them, otherwise I'd say 15 marks.

MRS. WOLFF. Well, Wulkow, there's no business with us today. Ya just go nice and quiet to the next house. We worked like slaves to drag it across the lake . . . almost got stuck fast in the ice. We couldn't move backwards or forwards. We can't give something like that away for nothin'.

WULKOW. Well, am I gettin' rich from it? Shipping is hard work. And poachin'—that's bad business. If ya get caught, I'll be right in with ya. I've been workin' for forty years now. And what've I got today? Rheumatism. When I get up early in the mornin', I howl like a young dog. I've been wantin' to get me a fur coat for years. The doctors all advised me to, because I'm sufferin' so. But I haven't been able to buy one yet, Mrs. Wolff! Not up to now. And that's as true as I'm standin' here.

ADELHEID. (*To her mother.*) Did Leontine tell ya. . . .

WULKOW. Well, I'll say 16.

MRS. WOLFF. Naw! 18. (*To* ADELHEID.) Now, what did ya say?

ADELHEID. Mrs. Krueger's bought a fur coat that cost 500 marks. A beaver coat.

WULKOW. A beaver coat?

MRS. WOLFF. Who bought it?

ADELHEID. Mrs. Krueger—for Mr. Krueger for Christmas.

WULKOW. The girl works for the Kruegers?

ADELHEID. Not me, my sister. I won't go into service.

WULKOW. If I could have one like that. I've wanted to get ahold of one like that for a long time. I'd even give 60 thalers for it. I'd rather put it out for a fur coat than for doctor bills and medicine. Then I'd get some fun out of it.

MRS. WOLFF. Ya only need go over to Krueger's, Wulkow. Maybe he'll give it away.

WULKOW. No, not willingly. But like I said, I'd sure like to get my hands on a coat.

MRS. WOLFF. Oh, sure. I'd like to have one like that myself.

WULKOW. What is it now? 16?

MRS. WOLFF. Nothin' under 18. That's what Julius said. I don't dare take 16. When he gets something in his head. . . . (JULIUS *comes in.*) Well, Julius, didn't ya say 18?

JULIUS. What did I say?

MRS. WOLFF. Ya don't hear so good again, do ya? Ya said not under 18. I shouldn't take less for the stag.

JULIUS. I said that? . . . . Oh sure, the deer. Yes. Um-hm. That certainly ain't too much.

WULKOW. (*Taking out money and counting.*) Well, let's finish it. 17 marks. Is that right now?

MRS. WOLFF. You're a real swindler. I said so when ya came to the door. You only needs to put your foot in the door and somebody's cheated.

WULKOW. (*Unfolds a sack which he had hidden under his coat.*) Now help me stick it in here. (MRS. WOLFF *helps put the deer in the sack.*) And if ya ever hear anything about gettin' some—I mean, well—well, a fur like that for example. I could easily pay ya 60—70 thalers.

MRS. WOLFF. Ya really ain't quite right in your head. . . ! How'd I come by such a coat?

A MAN'S VOICE. (*Calls from outside.*) Mrs. Wolff! Mrs. Wolff! Are ya still awake?

MRS. WOLFF. (*Frightened like the others, whispers tensely.*) Quick, hide, hide. Get into that room. (*She pushes everyone into the back room and shuts the door.*)

MAN'S VOICE. Mrs. Wolff! Mrs. Wolff! Are ya asleep already?
(MRS. WOLFF *puts out the candle.*)

MAN'S VOICE. Mrs. Wolff! Mrs. Wolff, are ya awake yet?
(*The voice fades away singing:*) Mornin' glo-ow, Mornin'
glo-ow.

LEONTINE. That's only "Mornin' Glow," Mama!

MRS. WOLFF. (*Listens a while, softly opens the door and listens again. Then she shuts it quickly and lights the candle. She lets the others in again.*) It was only Mitteldorf, the deputy.

WULKOW. What the devil—you got nice acquaintances.

MRS. WOLFF. Now, see that ya get away, Wulkow.

ADELHEID. Mama, Mino's started to bark.

MRS. WOLFF. Quick, quick, Wulkow! Hurry! In back, through the vegetable garden. Julius will open the gate. Julius, go and open it.

WULKOW. And like I said, if ya should get hold of a beaver coat. . . .

MRS. WOLFF. Yes, of course, but hurry!

WULKOW. If the Spree don't close, I'll be back from Berlin in three—four days. I'll lay with the boat down below.

ADELHEID. By the big bridge?

WULKOW. Where I always lay. Well, Julius, stagger ahead.
                                                              Exit.

ADELHEID. Mama, Mino's barkin' again.

MRS. WOLFF. (*At the stove.*) Oh, let him bark.

A long drawn out cry in the distance. "Goin' over."

ADELHEID. Somebody wants to cross the Spree, Mama.

MRS. WOLFF. Well, go get Papa, he's down by the river.
("*Goin' over*" *is heard again.*) Take Papa the oars. He ought to let Wulkow get away a bit first.

Exit ADELHEID *with the oars.* MRS. WOLFF *works industriously a while, alone.* ADELHEID *returns.*

ADELHEID. Papa had oars down in the boat.

MRS. WOLFF. Who wants to cross so late at night?

ADELHEID. I think it's that stupid Motes.

MRS. WOLFF. What? Who is it, girl?

ADELHEID. It sounded like Motes' voice.

MRS. WOLFF. (*Loudly.*) Run down and tell Papa to come up. That stupid Motes can stay down there. He don't need to be snoopin' around my house.

ADELHEID *exit.* MRS. WOLFF *hides and puts away all evidence of the venison episode. She puts a cover on the stewpan.* ADELHEID *comes back.*

ADELHEID. Mama, I was too late. I hear them talkin'.

MRS. WOLFF. Who is it?

ADELHEID. I told ya—the Moteses.

MRS. *and* MR. MOTES *appear one after the other in the door. Both are average height. She is an alert young woman, perhaps thirty years old, modestly, but nicely clad. He wears a green hunting jacket, his face is healthy but has a blank expression. He wears a black patch over his left eye.*

MRS. MOTES. (*Calls in.*) My nose is frozen blue, Mother Wolff.

MRS. WOLFF. Why do ya go walkin' on such a night? Ya got enough time in the day.

MOTES. Wonderfully warm here.—Who has time during the day?

MRS. WOLFF. Well, you.

MOTES. Do you think I live on my pension?

MRS. WOLFF. I don't know what ya live on.

MRS. MOTES. Oh, don't be so cross, Mother Wolff. We wanted to ask about our bill.

MRS. WOLFF. You've asked me about that more than once.

MRS. MOTES. Well, we're asking you again. What's the harm in that? We'll have to pay sometime.

MRS. WOLFF. (*Surprised.*) Ya want to pay?

MOTES. Mother Wolff acts quite surprised. Did you think we would skip out on you?

MRS. WOLFF. Oh, I wouldn't think anything like that. If ya want to be so good, we can figure it for ya right away. It'll be eleven marks and thirty pfennigs.

MRS. MOTES. Yes, yes, Mother Wolff. We're getting money. The people around here will be surprised.

MOTES. Something here smells like roast rabbit.

MRS. WOLFF. Cat, maybe. That's more likely.

MOTES. Let's take a look at it! (*He is about to take the cover off the stewpan.*)

MRS. WOLFF. (*Stops him.*) No snoopin' in my pots.

MRS. MOTES. (*Who has been looking around suspiciously.*) Mother Wolff, we've found something, too.

MRS. WOLFF. I haven't lost nothin'.

MRS. MOTES. Then look at these. (*She produces two wire snares.*)

MRS. WOLFF. (*Without losing her composure.*) Are those snares?

MRS. MOTES. We found them quite close to here. Hardly twenty steps from your garden.

MRS. WOLFF. Oh, the poachin' that's goin' on here!

MRS. MOTES. If you keep an eye open, you could really catch the poacher.

MRS. WOLFF. Them things are none of my business!

MOTES. If I ever catch such a rascal, I'll give him something to remember—I'd show him no mercy and denounce him.

MRS. MOTES. Mrs. Wolff, have you got a few fresh eggs?

MRS. WOLFF. Now? In the middle of the winter? They're awful rare.

MOTES. (*To* JULIUS, *who now enters.*) Forester Seidel's caught another poacher. He'll be taken to the city jail in the morning. That fellow's got courage. You've got to say that. If it weren't for my accident I could be head forester today. And I'd show those bastards what's what!

MRS. WOLFF. Many a person's had to pay for that.

MOTES. Yes, if you are afraid, but I'm not. I've already denounced a few of them. (*Fixing his eyes sharply on* MRS. WOLFF *and her husband.*) And I'm just waiting for a few more. I've almost got my hands on them. The ones laying snares needn't think that I don't know who they are. I know them all right.

MRS. MOTES. Did you bake, maybe, Mrs. Wolff? We just can't stand bakers' bread.

MRS. WOLFF. Ya wanted to pay your bill, I thought.

MRS. MOTES. Saturday, for sure, Mother Wolff. My husband has been made an editor for the journals on hunting and forestry.

MRS. WOLFF. Oh, sure, I know what that means.

MRS. MOTES. Well, I'll tell you, Mrs. Wolff, we've left Krueger's.

MRS. WOLFF. Yeah, ya went because ya had to.

MRS. MOTES. We had to? Hubby, did you hear? (*She forces a laugh.*) Mrs. Wolff says we had to leave Krueger's.

MOTES. (*Red with anger.*) You'll find out why I left there —the man's a cutthroat and a profiteer.

MRS. WOLFF. That I don't know. I couldn't say about that.

MOTES. I'm just waiting until I get proof. He'd better watch out for me. He and his bosom friend, Dr. Fleischer. He in particular. If I only wanted to say the word, they'd put him under lock and key. (*He begins to withdraw at the beginning of his speech. When he finishes, he leaves.*)

MRS. WOLFF. The men have quarreled again, have they?

MRS. MOTES. (*Apparently confidential.*) There's no joking with my husband. If he gets something into his mind, there's no stopping him. He's on good terms with the Judge. What about the eggs and the bread?

MRS. WOLFF. (*Reluctantly.*) Well, five's all I've got. And a bit of bread. MRS MOTES *puts the eggs and the half loaf of bread in her handbag.*) Are ya satisfied?

MRS. MOTES. Certainly. Are the eggs fresh?

MRS. WOLFF. As fresh as my hens've laid them.

MRS. MOTES. (*Hastily, in order to catch up with her husband.*) Well, good night. Money next Saturday.

Exit.

MRS. WOLFF. Sure, sure. That's fine. (*Shuts the door. Half-aloud.*) Hurry up and get out. Them people with nothing but debts. (*At the stewpan.*) What business is it of theirs what we eat? Why don't they look into their own pots? Go to sleep, girl.

ADELHEID. Good night, Mama. (*Gives her a kiss.*)

MRS. WOLFF. Well, ain't ya goin' to give your Papa a good night kiss?

ADELHEID. Good night, Papa. (*Kisses him. He grumbles.* ADELHEID *leaves.*)

MRS. WOLFF. I always have to tell her that. (*Pause.*)

JULIUS. Why did ya have to give them people all our eggs?

MRS. WOLFF. Do ya want me to make an enemy of that fellow? Make him your enemy, Julius, and I tell ya he's a dangerous fellow. He has nothin' to do but spy on people. Come on, sit down and eat! Here's a fork. Ya don't understand such things. Ya'd better look out for your own affairs! Ya left the snares right in back of the garden! They were yours?

JULIUS. (*Angrily.*) Yah. Sure.

MRS. WOLFF. Just so that stupid Motes could find them there easy. You'll lay no more snares here close to the house, do ya understand? Maybe they'll think we laid 'em.

JULIUS. Stop your chatterin'. (*Both eat.*)

MRS. WOLFF. The wood's all gone, too, Julius.

JULIUS. I guess ya want me to go way back into the woods.

MRS. WOLFF. Well, at least we ought to get busy right away.

JULIUS. I can't even feel my bones no more. Let whoever wants to go. It's all the same to me.

MRS. WOLFF. You men always talk big, but when it comes to it, ya don't do nothin'. I work three times harder than you do, all of ya put together. If ya ain't goin' out no more tonight, Julius, there's no helpin' it, ya'll have to go tomorrow. Are the climbin' irons sharp?

JULIUS. I lent 'em to Karl Machnow.

MRS. WOLFF. (*After a pause.*) If ya only wasn't such a coward.—Then we could have a few loads of wood in a hurry.—And we wouldn't have to work so hard.—And we wouldn't have very far to go neither.

JULIUS. Let me eat a bite, will ya?

MRS. WOLFF. (*Gives him a cuff on the head.*) Don't always

be so miserable. I'll be nice to ya. (*She brings forth a bottle of whiskey and shows it to him.*) Here! See what I brought ya. Now give me a smile. (*Pours her husband a full glass.*)

JULIUS. (*Drinks.*) That sure's . . . in this cold weather, that sure's good!

MRS. WOLFF. Now see, don't I look out for ya?

JULIUS. That sure was good . . . sure was! (*He pours himself another and drinks.*)

MRS. WOLFF. (*After a pause, starts to split wood and eats a few bites in between.*) This Wulkow—he's a real scoundrel. He always acts as if he's bad off.

JULIUS. He better keep quiet—he better—about his deals.

MRS. WOLFF. Ya heard about the beaver coat, didn't ya?

JULIUS. I—I didn't hear nothin'.

MRS. WOLFF. (*With forced lightness.*) The girl told about how Mrs. Krueger gave her husband a coat for a present.

JULIUS. Them people—they have so much. . . .

MRS. WOLFF. Oh, sure. You heard what Wulkow said. If he could get a coat like that, he'd pay sixty thalers.

JULIUS. Let'm burn his fingers hisself.

MRS. WOLFF. (*After a pause, pouring her husband another drink.*) Oh, have another drink.

JULIUS. Well, go on . . . go on. What. . . .

MRS. WOLFF *takes out a notebook and leafs through it.*

JULIUS. How much have we put aside since July?

MRS. WOLFF. Thirty thalers have been paid off.

JULIUS. Then we still have about—about. . . .

MRS. WOLFF. There's still seventy. Ya don't get very far this way. Fifty, sixty thalers all at once, if ya could put that away all at once. Then the whole place would be paid for. Then ya could borrow a hundred or two and maybe add a couple of pretty rooms. We can't take in summer guests like it is, and they're the ones that bring in the money.

JULIUS. Well, go on—an'. . . .

MRS. WOLFF. (*Resolutely.*) You're a slow one, Julius. Would ya have bought the land? Huh? Well? And if we wanted to sell now, I know we'd get at least double on it. I've got a different nature. If ya only had my nature. . . .

JULIUS. I work all right. What's the use of all this?

MRS. WOLFF. Ya don't get far with that little bit of work.

JULIUS. I can't steal. I'd just get caught.

MRS. WOLFF. You're just plain dumb, and you'll have to stay that way. Nobody said nothin' about stealin'. Nothin' ventured, nothin' gained. And if you're once rich, Julius, and can sit in a carriage, then nobody asks ya where ya got your money. Sure it'd be different takin' it from poor people. But if we really—went to Krueger's and put the two loads of wood on a sleigh and put them in our shed—them people ain't goin' to be no poorer.

JULIUS. Wood? What's this again—about the wood?

MRS. WOLFF. Ya sure don't worry yourself about nothin'. Your daughter, she can work herself to death. They made her bring in the wood at ten in the evenin', and she ran away 'cause of it. An' you don't mind. Maybe ya'd just give the child a whippin' and send her back to them people.

JULIUS. Sure I'd do it! Sure . . . that's just what you think I'd do.

MRS. WOLFF. Things like that shouldn't go without bein' punished. If somebody hits me, I say, hit 'em back.—

JULIUS. Well, did they hit the girl?

MRS. WOLFF. Well, she's run away, hasn't she, Julius? No,

no, there's no use tryin' to do anything with you. Now the wood's layin' out in the street. Well, if I said, let's go—you beat my children, I'll take your wood—ya'd make a pretty face, wouldn't ya?

JULIUS. No, I wouldn't do that. What do I care? I can do more than eat bread, too. I'll see about—there won't be no more beatin'.

MRS. WOLFF. Well, don't talk so much, and get your rope. It's better to show the people that ya've got some backbone. Everything can be done in an hour. Then we can go to sleep and everything's all right. And in the mornin' ya don't need to go into the woods. Then we'll have more wood than we need.

JULIUS. If it gets out, it's all the same to me.

MRS. WOLFF. No reason why it should! Only don't wake the girl.

MITTELDORF. (*From outside.*) Mrs. Wolff, Mrs. Wolff, are ya still awake?

MRS. WOLFF. Oh, sure, Mitteldorf, come right in. (*She opens the door.*)

MITTELDORF. (*Enters. He wears a shabby uniform and overcoat. His face has something Mephistophelian about it. His nose shows signs of alcoholic reddening. He enters softly, almost timidly. His speech is low and dragging and he talks without expression.*) Good evenin', Mrs. Wolff.

MRS. WOLFF. Ya ought to say, goodnight.

MITTELDORF. I was here once before. First I thought I saw a light, then all at once everything was dark. And nobody answered me neither. Only this time I saw a light that was a light for sure, and I came back again.

167

MRS. WOLFF. What did ya want, Mitteldorf?

MITTELDORF. (*Has seated himself, thinks a while, and then says:*) That's what I come here for. The Judge's wife wants me to tell ya something.

MRS. WOLFF. I should come and wash, huh?

MITTELDORF. (*Meditates a little, then says:*) Yes, that's it.

MRS. WOLFF. When?

MITTELDORF. Tomorrow—tomorrow mornin'.

MRS. WOLFF. You're tellin' me that at twelve o'clock tonight?

MITTELDORF. Tomorrow's the Judge's wife's wash day.

MRS. WOLFF. I got to know that a couple of days ahead of time.

MITTELDORF. Oh, sure. Don't get excited. I just forgot about it again. It's just that I've got so much to think about that sometimes I forget things too easy.

MRS. WOLFF. Well, Mitteldorf, I'll try and fix it. We get on good with each other. I guess you got enough troubles with eleven children at home. What's the use of your gettin' in bad with other people?

MITTELDORF. If ya don't come tomorrow, Mother Wolff, I'll really get it in the mornin'.

MRS. WOLFF. Rest easy—I'll come. There—have a drink. Ya can use it. (*She gives him some whiskey.*) I've got a bit of hot water. We've got to take a trip tonight after some nice fat geese over in Treptow. There's no time durin' the day. That's the way it is with us. Poor folk got to slave day and night while the rich ones lie in bed.

MITTELDORF. I've been fired, did ya know? The Judge fired me. I ain't hard enough on people.

MRS. WOLFF. You're supposed to be like a watchdog, I guess.

MITTELDORF. I'd rather not go home, 'cause when I do

there'll be a fight, and I know there's no escapin' her scoldin'.

MRS. WOLFF. Put your hands over your ears.

MITTELDORF. A man goes to the tavern once in a while, so the troubles won't get him down altogether. Now she won't let me do that neither. She won't let me do nothin'! I was just settin' there today, and somebody treated to a keg—

MRS. WOLFF. Ya won't be afraid of a woman, will ya? If she scolds ya, scold her back, and if she beats ya, beat her harder. Now come here. You're taller than me. Now hand me down them things. You, Julius, get the sleigh ready. (JULIUS *leaves.*) How often do I have to tell ya. (MITTELDORF *lifts straps and pull-lines from a high shelf.*) Get the big sleigh ready. Ya can hand the straps right down.

JULIUS. (*From outside.*) I can't see.

MRS. WOLFF. What can't ya do?

JULIUS. (*Appears at the door.*) I can't get the sleigh out all by myself. Everything's upside down. An' I can't do nothin' without a light.

MRS. WOLFF. You're at your wits end again, I guess. (*She puts a shawl around her head and chest.*) Now just wait, and I'll come and help ya. Get the lantern there, Mitteldorf. (MITTELDORF *wearily takes down the lantern and gives it to* MRS. WOLFF.) Thank ya. (*She puts a candle in the lantern.*) We'll put that in here, and then we can go. Now I'll help ya pull the sleigh out. (*She goes out with the lantern.* MITTEL-DORF *follows. She turns in the door and gives* MITTELDORF *the lantern.*) You can hold the light for us a bit.

MITTELDORF. (*Holds the lantern and singing to himself, leaves.*) Mornin' glo-ow—mornin' glo-ow . . .

Curtain

ACT TWO

SCENE: *The courtroom of* JUDGE VON WEHRHAHN: *a great, white, bare room with three windows in the rear wall. On the left wall is the entrance door. At the wall to the right is a long table covered with books, legal papers, etc.; behind it is the judge's bench. Near the middle window are a table and chair for the clerk. A wooden bookcase is to the right and close enough to the judge's seat so that he can reach it if he wants a book. Shelves full of documents cover the left wall. In the foreground, there are six chairs in a row along the left wall, their backs turned toward the audience. It is a sunny winter morning. The clerk,* GLASENAPP, *sits at his desk, scribbling. He is shabbily dressed and wears glasses.* JUDGE VON WEHRHAHN, *a file of documents under his arm, enters briskly. He is about forty years old and wears a monocle. He gives the impression of being a Junker. His official garb consists of a black, buttoned cutaway and high boots pulled over his trousers. He speaks in an almost falsetto voice and has cultivated a military abruptness of expression.*

VON WEHRHAHN. (*Nonchalantly, as if too busy for even a greeting.*) Morning!

GLASENAPP. (*Stands up.*) Your obedient servant, your Honor.

VON WEHRHAHN. Anything happened, Glasenapp?

GLASENAPP. (*Standing, leafing through some papers.*) I have to report, your Honor—. Yes, first there was—Innkeeper Fiebig. He asks for permission, your Honor, to allow dance music to be played next Sunday.

VON WEHRHAHN. Isn't that . . . tell me . . . Fiebig? Didn't he recently rent his hall. . . ?

GLASENAPP. To the Freethinkers. Quite right, my Lord.

VON WEHRHAHN. The same Fiebig?

GLASENAPP. Yes, indeed, my Lord!

VON WEHRHAHN. We'll have to curb him a bit.

MITTELDORF, *the deputy, enters.*

MITTELDORF. Your obedient servant, my Lord.

VON WEHRHAHN. Look here, once and for all—officially, I am the Judge here.

MITTELDORF. Yes, of course. At your service, my lo . . . your Honor, I mean.

VON WEHRHAHN. I'm asking you to remember this: the fact that I'm a baron is quite beside the point. At least, I am not here in this capacity. (*To* GLASENAPP.) Now, go on, I would like to hear more. Hasn't the writer, Motes, been in?

GLASSENAPP. Yes, indeed, your Honor.

VON WEHRHAHN. Well, so he was here? Then I am extraordinarily curious. I trust he intends to come back?

GLASENAPP. He'll be here again around half-past eleven.

VON WEHRHAHN. Did he, by any chance, say anything to you, Glasenapp?

GLASENAPP. He came about the case of Dr. Fleischer.

VON WEHRHAHN. Now, tell me, Glasenapp, do you know this Dr. Fleischer?

GLASENAPP. I only know he lives in Krueger's house.

VON WEHRHAHN. How long has that man been here?

GLASENAPP. I came here in September.

VON WEHRHAHN. Oh, yes, you came at the same time I did. I've been here about four months.

GLASENAPP. (*With a glance at* MITTELDORF.) I think Dr. Fleischer must have been here two years.

VON WEHRHAHN. (*To* MITTELDORF.) I don't suppose you can give us any information?

MITTELDORF. At your service—a year ago last September.

VON WEHRHAHN. What? The man moved here then?

MITTELDORF. At your service—from Berlin, your . . . your Honor.

VON WEHRHAHN. Do you know the fellow well?

MITTELDORF. I only know, a brother of his is a cashier in a theater.

VON WEHRHAHN. I didn't ask about his brother. What is the man's business? What does he do? What is he?

MITTELDORF. I can't tell ya nothin' certain there, neither. Except that people say he's sick. He probably has diabetes.

VON WEHRHAHN. It makes no difference to me what the man is suffering from. He can sweat syrup, for all I care. What is he?

GLASENAPP. (*Shrugs his shoulders.*) He calls himself a privy tutor.

VON WEHRHAHN. Private, private! Not privy! Private tutor.

GLASENAPP. Hugk, the bookbinder, has books of his. He gets some bound every week.

VON WEHRHAHN. I'd like someday to see what the man reads.

GLASENAPP. The mailman says he subscribes to twenty papers. —And there are some democratic ones among them, too.

VON WEHRHAHN. Have Hugk brought here to me some time.

GLASENAPP. Right away?

VON WEHRHAHN. When it's convenient. Tomorrow. Next day. He might bring a few of those books along with him. (*To* MITTELDORF.) You seem to be asleep all day—or does the gentleman offer good cigars?

MITTELDORF. Your Honor. . . ?

VON WEHRHAHN. Well, never mind. I know what's going on. My predecessor certainly permitted things to slip by. That'll all be changed in due time. It is disgraceful for a police official to allow himself to accept favors from anyone. Of course, you wouldn't understand that. (*To* GLASENAPP.) Didn't Motes have anything definite to say?

GLASENAPP. He didn't say anything definite to me. He thought that your Honor already knew. . . .

VON WEHRHAHN. Well, I do . . . in a very general way. I've had my eye on that man for a long time. I mean Dr. Fleischer, of course. Mr. Motes has only confirmed that my judgment of the fellow was quite correct. What kind of a reputation has this Motes? (GLASENAPP *and* MITTELDORF *look at each other.* GLASENAPP *shrugs his shoulders.*) Probably borrows a great deal, huh?

GLASENAPP. He says he has a pension.

VON WEHRHAHN. Pension?

GLASENAPP. He got shot in the eye, you know.

VON WEHRHAHN. Then it would be some kind of compensation for damages.

GLASENAPP. Begging your pardon, your Honor, I believe he has mostly the damages. No one's ever seen him with any money.

VON WEHRHAHN. (*Amused.*) Is there anything else of importance?

GLASENAPP. Only minor matters, your Honor. Somebody's given notice. . . .

VON WEHRHAHN. Very well! Very well! Have you by any chance heard anything to the effect that Fleischer doesn't guard his tongue any too well?

GLASENAPP. Not that I know of, right now.

VON WEHRHAHN. Well, that's what has come back to me— makes dangerous remarks about all sorts of people in high places. Anyhow, it will all come to light in due time. Well, now we must get to work. Yes, Mitteldorf, is there anything else?

MITTELDORF. They say there was a theft committed last night.

VON WEHRHAHN. A theft? Where?

MITTELDORF. At Krueger's.

VON WEHRHAHN. What was stolen?

MITTELDORF. Firewood.

VON WEHRHAHN. When? Last night?

MITTELDORF. Last night.

VON WEHRHAHN. Who told you this?

MITTELDORF. I heard it from . . . from. . . .

VON WEHRHAHN. Well, speak up, who told you?

MITTELDORF. I heard it . . . I heard it from Mr. Fleischer.

VON WEHRHAHN. So, you're on speaking terms with that man?

MITTELDORF. Mr. Krueger hisself told me, too.

VON WEHRHAHN. The man is nothing but a chronic complainer. He writes me at least three letters a week. Either somebody has cheated him, or broken his fence, or moved the stakes on his property. It's one vexation after another.

MOTES. (*Enters. He laughs nervously, almost continually, as he talks.*) Your obedient servant, your Honor.

VON WEHRHAHN. Well, here you are. Glad you came. Perhaps you can tell me: is anything stolen from Krueger's?

MOTES. I don't live at Krueger's any more.

VON WEHRHAHN. And you haven't heard anything from anywhere else, Mr. Motes?

MOTES. Oh, I've heard about it—but nothing definite. When I passed the house just now, they were both looking for tracks in the snow.

VON WEHRHAHN. Really? Dr. Fleischer is helping him—then I suppose they are really rather good friends?

MOTES. Heart and soul, your Honor.

VON WEHRHAHN. Yes. Now as for Dr. Fleischer—that interests me above everything else. Please sit down. I tell you, I haven't slept half the night. This affair won't let me sleep. You wrote me a letter which has excited me extremely.—That is, to be sure, a matter of temperament. It wouldn't have bothered my predecessor. For my part, I'm firmly determined to see this matter through. My mission here is to make a careful examination and to clean up the sweepings that have collected under the protection of my honorable predecessor! Doubtful characters, political criminals, dangerous to King and state—I'll make all of them cringe!—Well then, Mr. Motes, you are a writer?

MOTES. That's right. On matters dealing with forestry and hunting.

VON WEHRHAHN. Then you write for such professional journals? And are you able to earn a living at it?

MOTES. When a person's established himself, my Lord, it can be done. I am grateful for a good income.

VON WEHRHAHN. You are a trained forester, are you?

MOTES. I attended the Academy, your Honor. Shortly before the examination, I met with my misfortune. . . .

VON WEHRHAHN. Oh, yes, you wear an eyepatch.

MOTES. I lost my eye on a hunt, my Lord. A buckshot hit me in the eye, and unfortunately the blame could not be placed. I had to give up my career.

VON WEHRHAHN. Then you don't get a pension?

MOTES. No, I have managed to scrape along pretty well. My name is already fairly well known.

VON WEHRHAHN. Hm.—Perhaps you know my brother-in-law.

MOTES. Oh, indeed! Headforester von Wachsman. I've corresponded with him quite a bit, and, besides, we are members of the Society for the Breeding of Pointers.

VON WEHRHAHN. (*Somewhat relieved.*) Well then! You are acquainted with him. I'm pleased to hear that. That really makes things easier and gives a basis for mutual trust. There are no more obstacles, Mr. Motes.—You wrote me in your letter that you have had the opportunity to observe Dr. Fleischer. Tell me what you know.

MOTES. (*Clears his throat.*) When I . . . when I arrived at the Kruegers about a year ago, my Lord, I had no idea of the sort of person I would encounter.

VON WEHRHAHN. You knew neither Krueger nor Dr. Fleischer?

MOTES. No. You know how it is—in one house. I couldn't completely withdraw.

VON WEHRHAHN. What sort of people came to the house?

MOTES. (*With a significant gesture.*) Oh!

VON WEHRHAHN. I understand.

MOTES. Every Tom, Dick, and Harry—Democrats.

VON WEHRHAHN. Were there regular meetings?

MOTES. Every Thursday, as far as I know.

VON WEHRHAHN. We will certainly want to keep an eye on them.—Now you no longer associate with these people?

MOTES. It was no longer possible, your Honor.

VON WEHRHAHN. It was repugnant to you?

MOTES. It had become quite odious to me.

VON WEHRHAHN. The entire illegal manner, the impertinent

mockery of people in high places.—You finally couldn't stand it any longer?

MOTES. I remained because I thought I might be able to serve some good purpose.

VON WEHRHAHN. But you finally gave notice?

MOTES. I left. Yes, indeed, my Lord.

VON WEHRHAHN. And you made up your mind to. . . .

MOTES. I thought it my duty. . . .

VON WEHRHAHN. To inform the authorities—I find that very commendable. So he used an expression—we will record all this later—relative to an individual whose reverent position stands high with all of us.

MOTES. Certainly, my Lord, he said that.

VON WEHRHAHN. You would, if necessary, take your oath on that?

MOTES. I would take my oath on it.

VON WEHRHAHN. You may have to, you know.

MOTES. Yes, indeed, my Lord.

VON WEHRHAHN. It would be best, of course, if we could get still another witness.

MOTES. I would have to look around, my Lord. Only the man throws his money around so, that it's. . . .

VON WEHRHAHN. Oh, wait a minute, here comes Krueger. I would prefer to get him out of the way first. I am, at any rate, very grateful that you have aided me so energetically. One is thoroughly dependent on such assistance if one is to accomplish anything these days.

KRUEGER. (*Enters hastily and excited.*) My goodness, my goodness! Good day, your Honor.

VON WEHRHAHN. (*To* MOTES.) Excuse me a minute! (*Haughtily inquiring of* KRUEGER.) What is it you want?

KRUEGER *is a small man, almost seventy years old, hard of hearing. He is somewhat stooped, with the left shoulder a little lower than the other. He is, however, still very robust and emphasizes his words with vigorous gestures. He wears a fur cap which he removes in the courtroom, a brown winter coat, and a woolen scarf about his neck.*

KRUEGER. (*Bursting with anger, blurts out.*) I've been robbed, your Honor.

Recovering his breath, he wipes the sweat from his forehead with his handkerchief, and in the manner of a deaf man, stares at the Judge's mouth.

VON WEHRHAHN. Robbed? Hm!

KRUEGER. (*Already provoked.*) That's right. Robbed. I've been robbed. Two loads of wood have been stolen from me.

VON WEHRHAHN. (*Half smiling, looking around at the others, makes light of the situation.*) Nothing of the sort has happened here recently.

KRUEGER. (*His hand to his ear.*) What? Nothing of the sort? Oh, dear Lord! Then perhaps I'm just here for the fun of it.

VON WEHRHAHN. There's no need to be insulting. By the way, what's your name?

KRUEGER. (*Taken aback.*) What's my name?

VON WEHRHAHN. Yes, what's your name?

KRUEGER. You don't know my name? I think we've already had the pleasure of meeting.

VON WEHRHAHN. I'm sorry. I find it hard to recall. It would make absolutely no difference here, anyhow.

KRUEGER. (*Resigned.*) My name's Krueger.

VON WEHRHAHN. A property owner, is that right?

KRUEGER. (*Firmly, ironically, violently.*) Indeed, property owner.

VON WEHRHAHN. I must ask you to identify yourself.

KRUEGER. I—identify myself? My name is Krueger. I don't think we need to be so formal. I've been living here for thirty years. Why, every child on the street knows me.

VON WEHRHAHN. It's a matter of greatest indifference to me how long you've been living here. I only want to confirm your identity. Are you acquainted with—that man, Mr. Motes?

MOTES *half rises, with an angry expression.*

VON WEHRHAHN. Ah, I understand. Please be seated. Well, then, Glasenapp?

GLASENAPP. Yes. It is Mr. Krueger, a property owner in this district.

VON WEHRHAHN. Good.—Then some wood has been stolen from you?

KRUEGER. That's right. Wood. Two loads of pine wood.

VON WEHRHAHN. Did you have the wood in your shed?

KRUEGER. (*Becoming violent again.*) That's a special matter. That's an entirely different complaint.

VON WEHRHAHN. (*Smiling ironically and casually to the others, lightly.*) Still another one?

KRUEGER. What do you mean?

VON WEHRHAHN. Nothing. Please tell us more. Then the wood wasn't in the shed?

KRUEGER. The wood was in the garden. In front of the garden, that is.

VON WEHRHAHN. In other words, it lay in the street?

KRUEGER. It lay in front of the garden on my property.

VON WEHRHAHN. So that everyone could get to it with no trouble.

KRUEGER. And that is the fault of the maid. She was supposed to bring in the wood in the evening.

VON WEHRHAHN. Then she forgot it?

KRUEGER. She refused. And when I insisted, she ran away. Now I will bring action against her parents. I demand full damages.

VON WEHRHAHN. You may do as you please, but I assure you, it won't help you much.—Now, is there anyone you suspect?

KRUEGER. No, they're all a bunch of thieves here.

VON WEHRHAHN. Please avoid being so general. You must give me something to work with.

KRUEGER. I won't accuse anyone at random.

VON WEHRHAHN. Besides yourself, who lives at your house?

KRUEGER. Dr. Fleischer.

VON WEHRHAHN. Dr. Fleischer? Dr. Fleischer. The man is a. . . . What is he?

KRUEGER. He is very learned. A very learned man, indeed.

VON WEHRHAHN. You two are very intimate friends?

KRUEGER. It's my business who I'm very intimate with. I don't think that belongs here.

VON WEHRHAHN. Then, how are we, in the end, to determine anything? You must give me some clue.

KRUEGER. I must? Oh, my goodness, yes! I must! Two loads of wood have been stolen from me. I've simply come to report the theft. . . .

VON WEHRHAHN. You must have a suspicion. Somebody must have stolen the wood.

KRUEGER. What?—Indeed, not I! Certainly, not I!

VON WEHRHAHN. But my dear man. . .

KRUEGER. What? My name's Krueger.

VON WEHRHAHN. (*Resuming, seemingly bored.*) Ah!—Well,

Glasenapp, make a record of it. Now, what is this about the girl, Mr. Krueger? The girl has run away from you?

KRUEGER. Yes. Quite right—back to her parents.

VON WEHRHAHN. Do her parents live here?

KRUEGER. What was that?

VON WEHRHAHN. I asked if the girl's parents lived here.

KRUEGER. She's the daughter of Mrs. Wolff, the washwoman.

VON WEHRHAHN. Is that Mrs. Wolff who is washing for us today, Glasenapp?

GLASENAPP. Quite right, your Honor.

VON WEHRHAHN. (*Shaking his head.*) Very strange!—This industrious, honest person.—(*To* KRUEGER.) Is that really so? The daughter of Mrs. Wolff?

KRUEGER. She's the daughter of Mrs. Wolff, the washwoman.

VON WEHRHAHN. Hasn't the girl come back?

KRUEGER. She hasn't come back yet.

VON WEHRHAHN. Then we shall call Mrs. Wolff. Oh, Mitteldorf, you're tired perhaps? Well, walk across the yard and tell Mrs. Wolff she's to come here immediately. Please sit down, Mr. Krueger.

KRUEGER. (*Sitting down, sighs.*) Oh, my goodness! Such a life!

VON WEHRHAHN. (*Half-aloud to* MOTES *and* GLASENAPP.) I'm curious about what'll come out of this. Something here's very peculiar. I think very highly of Mrs. Wolff. That woman works as hard as four men. My wife says if Mrs. Wolff doesn't come, she has to get two women to do her washing.—And the opinions the woman expresses aren't bad, either.

MOTES. She wants her daughter to go on the stage. . . .

VON WEHRHAHN. Well, yes, there might be a screw loose

there. But it's no flaw in her character. What have you hanging there, Mr. Motes?

MOTES. Wire slings. I'm taking them to Forester Seidel.

VON WEHRHAHN. Oh, let me see one of those things. (*He holds one and examines it closely.*) It would strangle a stag slowly.

MRS. WOLFF *enters, behind her* MITTELDORF. *She is drying her hands, still wet from the washing.*

MRS. WOLFF. (*Calm, cheerful, with a fleeting glance at the wire snares.*) I'm here. What's wrong now? What do ya want with me?

VON WEHRHAHN. Mrs. Wolff, are you acquainted with this gentleman?

MRS. WOLFF. Well, which gentleman? (*Pointing with her finger to* KRUEGER.) Him there? That's Mr. Krueger. I guess I know him all right. Good mornin', Mr. Krueger.

VON WEHRHAHN. Your daughter works at the Kruegers?

MRS. WOLFF. Who? My daughter? Yes, indeed! Leontine. (*To* KRUEGER.) That is, she ran away from ya.

KRUEGER. (*Raging.*) Yes, indeed!

VON WEHRHAHN. (*Interrupting.*) Wait a minute.

MRS. WOLFF. What's happened between ya?

VON WEHRHAHN. Mrs. Wolff, now listen to me. Your daughter must return immediately to her job.

MRS. WOLFF. Oh, no. We're keepin' her home now.

VON WEHRHAHN. That's not as easily done as you think. Mr. Krueger has the right, if necessary, to call for police aid. Then we would be forced to bring your daughter back.

MRS. WOLFF. My husband's taken it into his head that he won't let her go out no more. And when my husband takes something into his head. . . . You men get mad so quick, ya know.

VON WEHRHAHN. Well, let that go for the time being, Mrs. Wolff. How long has your daughter been home?

MRS. WOLFF. Since yesterday evenin'.

VON WEHRHAHN. Good. Since yesterday. She was supposed to put wood in the shed and refused.

MRS. WOLFF. She did, huh? Refused! The girl won't refuse to do the work. I wouldn't let her get by with that.

VON WEHRHAHN. You heard what Mrs. Wolff said.

MRS. WOLFF. The girl's always been willin'. If she dared just once to refuse to help me. . . .

KRUEGER. She refused to carry in the wood.

MRS. WOLFF. Sure, draggin' in wood at half-past ten at night—anybody that'd make a mere child do that. . . .

VON WEHRHAHN. The vital point, Mrs. Wolff, is that the wood remained outside, and it was stolen last night. Now will. . . .

KRUEGER. (*Can no longer contain himself.*) You will repay me for the wood, Mrs. Wolff.

VON WEHRHAHN. That will have to be decided. Please just wait.

KRUEGER. You will pay me back every last pfennig.

MRS. WOLFF. Oh, sure. That would be a new method! Maybe I stole your wood?

VON WEHRHAHN. Now let the man calm down first.

MRS. WOLFF. Well, if Mr. Krueger comes to me about payin' for wood and such things, he'll get no place. I've always been friendly with people and nobody can complain about me. But if it must be, I can talk plain, too. I do my duty, and that's all. And nobody in the town can say anything against me. But I won't let nobody trample on me.

VON WEHRHAHN. Please don't get excited, Mrs. Wolff.

There's really no cause for it. Remain calm, quite calm. You aren't unknown to us. No one will deny that you are honest and industrious. What have you to say to the accusation?

KRUEGER. She can't say anything against it.

MRS. WOLFF. Now, it's really gettin' too thick for me. Ain't the girl my daughter? I shouldn't have anything to say about that? If you're lookin' for somebody dumb, ya don't know Mother Wolff. I'm not afraid of nobody, even if it's his Honor hisself. Much less of you, ya can believe me.

VON WEHRHAHN. I understand your excitement, Mrs. Wolff, but if you want to help matters, I advise you to remain calm.

MRS. WOLFF. To think how I've worked for these people. Ten years I did their wash. And we ain't had a fallin' out the whole time. Now all of a sudden it comes to this. Believe me, I'm not comin' to do your wash no more.

KRUEGER. And you don't need to. There are other women who can wash.

MRS. WOLFF. And ya can get somebody else to sell the fruit and vegetables from your garden.

KRUEGER. I can get rid of them, don't you worry. You ought to have taken a club and sent your daughter back to me.

MRS. WOLFF. I won't allow my daughter to be abused.

KRUEGER. Who's abused your daughter, I ask you?

MRS. WOLFF. (*To* VON WEHRHAHN.) The girl's almost a skeleton.

KRUEGER. Then she shouldn't be out dancing all night long.

MRS. WOLFF. She's been sleepin' like a log all day.*

VON WEHRHAHN. (*Across to* KRUEGER.) Where did you buy the wood?

---

* This line is not clear unless one assumes that Mrs. Wolff has not been listening to Krueger's preceding remarks.

MRS. WOLFF. Will this business last much longer?

VON WEHRHAHN. Why do you ask, Mrs. Wolff?

MRS. WOLFF. Oh, on account of the wash. If I spend my time here, I can't get finished today.

VON WEHRHAHN. That doesn't matter, Mrs. Wolff.

MRS. WOLFF. And your wife? What'll she say? You can settle that with her, your Honor.

VON WEHRHAHN. It'll only last a minute longer. Now, tell us, Mrs. Wolff, you are well known around the town— whom do you suspect of the theft? Who could have stolen the wood?

MRS. WOLFF. I really couldn't say, your Honor.

VON WEHRHAHN. And you've noticed nothing suspicious at all?

MRS. WOLFF. I wasn't home all night. I had to go to Treptow to buy geese.

VON WEHRHAHN. And what time was that?

MRS. WOLFF. Right after ten. Mitteldorf was there when we left.

VON WEHRHAHN. You didn't meet a sleigh carrying wood?

MRS. WOLFF. No, not that I know of.

VON WEHRHAHN. How about it, Mitteldorf, didn't you notice anything?

MITTELDORF. (*After some reflection.*) I didn't notice nothin' suspicious.

VON WEHRHAHN. That's understandable. I knew that beforehand. (*To* KRUEGER.) Where did you buy the wood?

KRUEGER. Why do you have to know that, I'd like to know?

VON WEHRHAHN. You can leave that to me, I think.

KRUEGER. From the Department of Forestry, naturally.

VON WEHRHAHN. There's nothing natural about that. There

are stores that sell wood. For example, I buy my wood from Sandberg. Why shouldn't you buy it from a dealer? It's almost cheaper there.

KRUEGER. (*Impatiently.*) I don't have any more time, your Honor.

VON WEHRHAHN. What's that? Time? You don't have time? Did you come to me, or I to you? Am I taking your time, or are you taking mine?

KRUEGER. That's your duty, that's what you're here for.

VON WEHRHAHN. Perhaps I'm your bootblack?

KRUEGER. Maybe I've stolen something. I don't have to stand for that tone of voice.

VON WEHRHAHN. Now look here. . . . Don't shout so!

KRUEGER. You shout, sir!

VON WEHRHAHN. You're half deaf, I have to shout.

KRUEGER. You always shout. You shout at everybody who comes in here.

VON WEHRHAHN. I don't shout at anybody. Be quiet!

KRUEGER. You put on airs here like who knows what. You annoy everybody in town.

VON WEHRHAHN. Just you wait, that will change. I'll make you even more uncomfortable.

KRUEGER. That doesn't make the least impression on me. You would like to think you're important. You want to put on airs, that's all. As if you were the king himself. . . .

VON WEHRHAHN. Here, I am the king!

KRUEGER. (*Laughs loudly.*) Ha, ha, ha, ha! I assure you, in my case you're nothing at all. You're just a simple judge, and you still have to learn how to become that.

VON WEHRHAHN. Sir, if you don't shut up this very minute. . . .

KRUEGER. You'll have me arrested? I wouldn't advise you to try that. That would be dangerous.

VON WEHRHAHN. Dangerous! (*To* MOTES.) Did you hear? (*To* KRUEGER.) And even if you plot and intrigue with all of your charming followers, you won't get me away from my post.

KRUEGER. Oh, dear God! I plot against you? You are much too unimportant for that. If you don't change, believe me, you'll cause so much trouble that you'll make things quite impossible for yourself.

VON WEHRHAHN. (*To* MOTES.) Mr. Motes, one must make allowances for his age.

KRUEGER. I ask to have a report drawn up.

VON WEHRHAHN. (*Searches through his papers.*) Would you please enter a written notice. I haven't the time right now.

KRUEGER *looks at him dumbfounded, turns energetically, and leaves without saying good-bye.*

VON WEHRHAHN. (*After an embarrassing pause.*) These people come with such trifles!—(*To* MRS. WOLFF.) You can get back to your washing now.—I tell you, my dear Motes, such a position can become difficult. If one didn't know what one stood for here, sometimes one could throw in the sponge. But as things are, one must bravely endure it. What is it in the end that one fights for? The supreme welfare of the nation.

Curtain

ACT THREE

SCENE: *About eight o'clock in the morning at* MRS. WOLFF'S *house. Water for coffee is boiling on the stove.* MRS. WOLFF *is sitting on a footstool and counting out money on the seat of a chair.* JULIUS *comes in carrying a killed rabbit.*

JULIUS. You put all that money away.

MRS. WOLFF. (*Engrossed in the counting, rudely.*) Go on, mind your own business.

Silence. JULIUS *throws the rabbit on a stool; then he picks up, rather indecisively, one object after another, and finally begins to polish a boot. A hunting horn is heard in the distance.*

JULIUS. (*Listens, then anxiously.*) I told ya to put that money away!

MRS. WOLFF. Don't bother me, Julius. Let that silly Motes blow his horn. He's in the woods and don't think about nothin'.

JULIUS. You'll be sendin' us to jail yet!

MRS. WOLFF. Don't talk nonsense. The girl's comin'.

ADELHEID. (*Enters, just out of bed.*) Good mornin', Mama!

MRS. WOLFF. Did ya sleep well?

ADELHEID. I guess ya were gone last night?

MRS. WOLFF. You must a' been dreamin'.—Hurry, get a move on, get the wood in here. Hurry up!

ADELHEID *goes toward the door, playing with an orange.*

MRS. WOLFF. Where did ya get that?

ADELHEID. From Schoebel, the grocer.

Exit.

MRS. WOLFF. Ya shouldn't take no presents from that fellow!—Now come here, Julius. Listen to me! I've got fifty-nine thalers here. That's the way it always is with Wulkow. He always cheats us out of one, 'cause he said he'd give us sixty. I'm puttin' it here in this bag, understand? Now take the spade, and go and dig a hole in back of the goat shed, but under the manger where it's dry. Then put the bag in there, d'ya hear? And put a flat stone over it. Yes, and don't be long about it.

JULIUS. I thought ya was goin' to pay something to Fischer.

MRS. WOLFF. If ya'd only do what I tell ya. And don't be long, d'ya understand?

JULIUS. Don't make me mad, or I'll show ya. I don't like it that the money should be stayin' in the house.

MRS. WOLFF. What else should we do with it?

JULIUS. Take it and give it to Fischer. Ya said we'd pay him something with it.

MRS. WOLFF. You sure are dumb. If ya didn't have me, you'd be lost.

JULIUS. You stop yellin' at me.

MRS. WOLFF. A person's got to yell at ya, you're so dumb. If ya didn't talk so dumb, I wouldn't have to yell at ya. If we take that money to Fischer now, you wait and see what would happen to us.

JULIUS. I say to hell with the whole business! What good's the money, if I've got to go to jail?

MRS. WOLFF. Now it's about time for ya to shut up!

JULIUS. Can't ya yell some more?

MRS. WOLFF. I won't get me a different mouth on account of that. You make a great big fuss, I don't know why, on account of a little thing like that. Just you look after yourself and not after me. Have ya throwed the key in the river yet?

JULIUS. Well, have I gone to the river yet?

MRS. WOLFF. It's high time ya get out. Do ya want 'em to

find the key on ya? (JULIUS *wants to leave.*) No, wait a minute, Julius. Give me the key!

JULIUS. What do ya want to do with it?

MRS. WOLFF. (*Taking the key.*) That's none of your business—that's my business. (*She sticks the key in a pocket, puts coffee into the coffee mill, and begins to grind.*) Now, go into the shed, then ya can come back and drink your coffee.

JULIUS. If I'd only known that sooner.

JULIUS *exit.* ADELHEID *comes in carrying a large apronful of wood.*

MRS. WOLFF. Where did ya get the wood?

ADELHEID. From that new pile of logs, of course.

MRS. WOLFF. Ya shouldn't bring in the new wood.

ADELHEID. (*Lets it fall in front of the stove.*) It won't hurt nothin', Mama, if it gets used up.

MRS. WOLFF. What do *you* know about it? What's the idea? You who ain't even dry behind the ears yet.

ADELHEID. I know where it come from.

MRS. WOLFF. What do ya mean, girl?

ADELHEID. I mean the wood.

MRS. WOLFF. Oh, shut your mouth. It was bought at the auction.

ADELHEID. (*Plays ball with the orange.*) Uh-huh. If that was true. It was stole.

MRS. WOLFF. It was what?

ADELHEID. Stole. That's the wood from Krueger's, Mama. Leontine told me so.

MRS. WOLFF. (*Gives her a cuff on the head.*) There's your answer. We're not thieves. Now go and study your homework. And make it good, I tell ya. I'll come in later on and look at it.

ADELHEID. (*Goes into the next room.*) I guess I can go skatin'?

MRS. WOLFF. And your confirmation lesson, have ya forgot all about it?

ADELHEID. That ain't until Tuesday.

MRS. WOLFF. It's tomorrow. And you go and learn your Bible lesson. I'll come in later and listen to ya recite it.

ADELHEID. (*Can be heard in the next room yawning loudly, then saying.*) Jesus said to his disciples, whoever has no spoon shall eat with his fingers.

JULIUS *returns.*

MRS. WOLFF. Well, did ya really do it proper, Julius?

JULIUS. If ya don't like it, do it yourself.

MRS. WOLFF. God knows, it's always done best that way. (*She pours him and herself some coffee and places the cups and bread and butter on a wooden stool.*) Now here, drink your coffee.

JULIUS. (*Sitting and cutting bread.*) If only Wulkow's got away.

MRS. WOLFF. Well, with the thaw.

JULIUS. Oh, you and your thaw. . . .

MRS. WOLFF. Even if it freezes a little, he won't get stuck. He's probably a long ways up the canal by now.

JULIUS. If only he ain't still layin' at the bridge.

MRS. WOLFF. For my part, he can lay where he wants to.

JULIUS. Believe me, that Wulkow's goin' to get hisself in quite a mess one of these days.

MRS. WOLFF. That's his business, not ours!

JULIUS. We're all in it together. Just let 'em find that coat on Wulkow.

MRS. WOLFF. What coat's that?

JULIUS. Why, Krueger's coat.

MRS. WOLFF. Stop talkin' such nonsense, do ya understand? Keep out of other people's affairs.

JULIUS. That affects me, too.

MRS. WOLFF. It affects you, rubbish! It's none of your business. It's my business, not yours. You're not a man, you're an old woman.—Here's some money, now see that ya get out. Go over to Fiebig's and drink some whiskey. I don't care if ya have a holiday. (*A knock.*) Come in, come in, whoever wants to.

DR. FLEISCHER *enters with his five-year-old-son.* FLEISCHER *is twenty-seven years old, wears a hunting suit, has coal black hair, mustache and goatee. His eyes are deep-set, his voice is soft. He continually shows an almost pathetic anxiety for his child.*

MRS. WOLFF. (*Shouting joyfully.*) My! Philipp's come to visit us! That is nice. That means a lot to me. (*She takes hold of the child and pulls off his overcoat.*) Come on, now, take off your coat. It's warm in here, ya won't freeze.

FLEISCHER. (*Anxiously.*) Mrs. Wolff, there's a draft. I think there's a draft.

MRS. WOLFF. He ain't that frail. A bit of a draft won't hurt the youngster.

FLEISCHER. No, no. Be careful. What do you think? The child takes cold in a minute. Move about, Philipp. Keep moving about.

PHILIPP *refuses to move and screams.*

FLEISCHER. Yes, Philipp, be careful or you'll be ill. You just need to move about slowly.

PHILIPP. (*Disobediently.*) I won't.

MRS. WOLFF. Oh, let him be.

FLEISCHER. Good morning, Mrs. Wolff.

MRS. WOLFF. Good mornin', Dr. Fleischer. I'm glad ya're payin' us a visit.

FLEISCHER. Good morning, Mr. Wolff.

JULIUS. And a very good mornin' to you, Dr. Fleischer.

MRS. WOLFF. You're very welcome. Won't ya sit down.

FLEISCHER. We really can't stay long.

MRS. WOLFF. Well, gettin' such nice visitors so early in the mornin'. I know we'll have a lucky day. (*Kneeling before the boy.*) Ain't that so, youngster? You'll bring us luck, won't ya?

PHILIPP. (*Excited.*) I've been to the zoo, an' I saw storks, an' 'ey bit each uver wif 'eir golden bills.

MRS. WOLFF. No, not really! You're tellin' me stories. (*Hugging and kissing the boy.*) My, child, I could eat ya. I could eat ya right up. Ya know, Dr. Fleischer, I'll just keep him here. Ain't that right? Ain't ya my boy? How's your mother, huh?

PHILIPP. She's well, an' she says hello to you, an' she wants to know will you come wash tomorrow mornin'.

MRS. WOLFF. Well, look at that. Such a boy. He can already deliver a message. (*To* FLEISCHER.) Wouldn't ya like to set down a bit?

FLEISCHER. The boy's been bothering me to go boating. Is it all right?

MRS. WOLFF. Oh, sure. The Spree is open. The girl can row him around a little.

FLEISCHER. The boy won't give me any peace. He's taken it into his head.

ADELHEID. (*Becoming visible in the door of the next room, beckons to* PHILIPP.) Come on, Philipp, and I'll show ya somethin' nice.

PHILIPP *screams stubbornly.*

193

FLEISCHER. Philipp, dear, listen, don't be so naughty!

ADELHEID. Look at the pretty orange.

PHILIPP, *a broad smile on his face, takes a few steps toward it.*

FLEISCHER. Well, run along, but don't beg!

ADELHEID. Come on, come on! We'll eat it together.

She takes a few steps toward the child, takes him by the hand, holding the orange before him with her other hand, and both go amicably into the next room.

MRS. WOLFF. (*Looking after the boy.*) This youngster, I just can't help lookin' at him. I don't know, when I see such a lad. . . . (*She takes the corner of her apron and blows her nose.*) I feel like I have to bawl.

FLEISCHER. Didn't you have a boy like that?

MRS. WOLFF. Yes, I did. But what's the good of thinkin' of that. Ya can't bring the dead back to life again.—Yes, ya see— that's the way it is—with life. (*A pause.*)

FLEISCHER. A person can't be too careful with children.

MRS. WOLFF. Even if ya are so careful—what's to be will be. (*A pause. She shakes her head.*) What have ya had to do with Mr. Motes?

FLEISCHER. Me? Nothing. What would I have to do with him?

MRS. WOLFF. I just thought. . . .

FLEISCHER. How old is your daughter now?

MRS. WOLFF. She'll finish school Easter. Would ya like her to go to work for you, Mr. Fleischer? For you, I'd gladly let her go into service.

FLEISCHER. Why not? Indeed, that wouldn't be bad at all.

MRS. WOLFF. She's become a strong girl. Even if she's still young, I tell ya, she can work as hard as anybody. And ya know—she's a bit of a hussy at times, sometimes she's no good, but she ain't dumb. She's got genius.

FLEISCHER. That's quite possible.

MRS. WOLFF. Let her recite something once—a poem or something like that. And I can tell ya, Doctor, it'll give ya goose pimples. Ya can call her in sometime if ya got visitors from Berlin. All kinds of writers come to your house, don't they? She ain't bashful, she'll start right in. She recites most wonderful—(*Changing.*) Now, I'd like to give ya some good advice. Ya won't take offense. . . ?

FLEISCHER. I never take offense at good advice.

MRS. WOLFF. Well, first—don't give so much away. Nobody thanks ya for it. Ya don't get nothin' but ingratitude.

FLEISCHER. I don't give much away, Mrs. Wolff.

MRS. WOLFF. Oh, sure, I know. And don't talk so much—it just puzzles people. They'll say you're a Democrat. And always be careful about what ya say.

FLEISCHER. How am I to take that, Mrs. Wolff?

MRS. WOLFF. You can take it any way ya want to. But ya got to be careful when ya talk. For that, a person may be in jail before he knows it.

FLEISCHER. (*Turns pale.*) Now don't fool about that, Mrs. Wolff.

MRS. WOLFF. No, no. I say this in all seriousness—and beware of that man.

FLEISCHER. What man do you mean?

MRS. WOLFF. Well, the one we've been talkin' about.

FLEISCHER. Do you mean Motes, perhaps?

MRS. WOLFF. I name no names. Ya must have had something to do with the man.

FLEISCHER. I have nothing to do with him anymore.

MRS. WOLFF. Well, ya see, that's what I thought.

FLEISCHER. No one can blame me, Mrs. Wolff.

MRS. WOLFF. I sure don't blame ya.

FLEISCHER. Impossible to associate with a swindler—a notorious swindler.

MRS. WOLFF. He's a swindler. You're right there.

FLEISCHER. Now he has moved to Mrs. Dreier's. The poor woman will soon find out where she stands. She'll be rid of what little she might have. With such a fellow . . . a regular jailbird.

MRS. WOLFF. He talks so much about. . . .

FLEISCHER. Really? About me? I'm curious.

MRS. WOLFF. Ya said something bad, I guess, about some high person or other.

FLEISCHER. Hm. You don't know anything definite?

MRS. WOLFF. He's in thick with Wehrhahn. But ya know what? I'll tell ya something. Go directly to Mother Dreier. The old witch smells a rat already. First, they lick your boots, then they eat ya out of house and home.

FLEISCHER. Oh, nonsense. The whole business is foolish.

MRS. WOLFF. Oh, you go to the Dreier woman. That can't hurt nothin'. She's told me a story. . . . He wanted to get her to lie. Then ya'd have the fellow under your thumb.

FLEISCHER. I could go there, I suppose. But then, I don't really care. The devil must be in it, if such a fellow. . . . Let him come.—Philipp, Philipp! Where are you? We must go now.

ADELHEID'S VOICE. We were lookin' at such pretty pictures.

FLEISCHER. What do you think of the story?

MRS. WOLFF. Of what story?

FLEISCHER. You mean you haven't heard?

MRS. WOLFF. (*Uneasily.*) No. Like I told ya.—(*Impatiently.*) Hurry, Julius, go, so you'll be back in time for dinner. (*To* FLEISCHER.) We butchered a rabbit today. Ain't ya ready yet, Julius?

JULIUS. Let me find my cap, will ya?

MRS. WOLFF. I can't stand it when people fool around. Puttin' off till tomorrow what ya can do today. With me, everything's got to move along.

FLEISCHER. Last night at Krueger's, . . .

MRS. WOLFF. Be quiet! Don't mention that man's name to me. I'm mad at him. He hurt me bad. The way we've gotten along, and then to make me out bad in front of them people. (*To* JULIUS.) Now, are ya goin', or ain't ya?

JULIUS. I'm goin', don't get excited. I bid ya good mornin', Dr. Fleischer.

FLEISCHER. Good-bye, Mr. Wolff. (JULIUS *leaves.*)

MRS. WOLFF. Now, as I was sayin'. . . .

FLEISCHER. He quarreled with you about how the wood was stolen, didn't he? He's been sorry about that for a long time.

MRS. WOLFF. Oh, him and his bein' sorry!

FLEISCHER. Well, I'm telling you, Mrs. Wolff, and particularly after this last business. You stand high in his estimation. It would be best if you were reconciled.

MRS. WOLFF. We could've talked reasonable. But right away to come with the police.—Oh, no!

FLEISCHER. The old folks are really up against it. The wood a week ago, today the coat. . . .

MRS. WOLFF. Well, out with the news.

FLEISCHER. They've been robbed again.

MRS. WOLFF. Robbed? Don't ya make jokes.

FLEISCHER. And indeed, a brand new coat.

MRS. WOLFF. No! Ya know next thing I'll be movin' away. There must be a gang of thieves here. Even your life ain't safe. Tch! Tch! Such people. I can't believe it!

FLEISCHER. Now you can imagine the fuss about all that.

MRS. WOLFF. Ya can't blame people for that.

FLEISCHER. And really, it was a very expensive item. Mink, I think.

MRS. WOLFF. Is that anything like beaver, Mr. Fleischer?

FLEISCHER. Oh, it might even be beaver. The folks were quite proud of it.—That is, I had to laugh to myself about it. When such things are discovered it always has a comical effect.

MRS. WOLFF. You're really bein' cruel. I couldn't laugh over something like that, Mr. Fleischer.

FLEISCHER. Well, do you think I'm not sorry for the man?

MRS. WOLFF. What kind of people they must be! It's hard to believe.—To steal from other people.—No, it's better to work till ya drop.

FLEISCHER. Couldn't you listen around a bit? I believe the coat's still in this area.

MRS. WOLFF. Well, ain't ya got nobody under suspicion?

FLEISCHER. There was a woman who washed at Krueger's. . . .

MRS. WOLFF. Mrs. Miller?

FLEISCHER. She has such a big family. . . .

MRS. WOLFF. The woman has a big family, all right, but stealin' . . . no. Pilfer a little, yes.

FLEISCHER. Naturally, Krueger fired her.

MRS. WOLFF. That's got to be cleared up, or the devil has a hand in it. Now, if only I was the Judge. The man is really dumb . . . so dumb. Believe me, I can see more with one eye shut than he can through his monocle.

FLEISCHER. I almost believe you.

MRS. WOLFF. I can tell ya something. If I had to, I could steal the chair out from under him.

FLEISCHER. (*Has risen. Calls laughingly into the next room.*) Come, Philipp. Come, we have to go now. Good-bye, Mother Wolff.

MRS. WOLFF. Get dressed, Adelheid. Row Dr. Fleischer around a bit.

ADELHEID. (*Enters, fastening the last buttons at her neck. She leads Philipp by the hand.*) I'm ready. (*To* PHILIPP.) Come here, I'll carry ya in my arms.

FLEISCHER. (*Anxiously helps dress him.*) Now bundle up well. He is too delicate. And it'll be windy on the water.

ADELHEID. I'll go ahead and get the boat ready.

MRS. WOLFF. How's your health now?

FLEISCHER. Much better since I've been living out here.

ADELHEID. (*In the doorway, calls back.*) Mama, Mr. Krueger.

MRS. WOLFF. Who?

ADELHEID. Mr. Krueger.

MRS. WOLFF. It ain't possible!

FLEISCHER. He wanted to come to see you this morning.

Exit.

MRS. WOLFF. (*Throws a glance at the pile of wood and begins swiftly to put it away.*) Come on girl, help me put the wood away.

ADELHEID. Why, Mama? Oh, on account of Mr. Krueger.

MRS. WOLFF. Why else, ya silly goose? The way it looks around here. Is that fittin' on a Sunday mornin'? What would

Mr. Krueger think of us. (KRUEGER *appears, excited.* MRS. WOLFF *calls to him.*) Mr. Krueger, don't look around. Everything looks so terrible here.

KRUEGER. (*Hastily.*) Good morning! Good morning! Never mind! You work all week, you can't have everything cleaned up on Sunday. You're an orderly woman. You're an honest woman, Mrs. Wolff. And let's all forget about what's happened between us.

MRS. WOLFF. (*Touched, drying her eyes with the corner of her apron.*) I never had nothin' against ya. I always liked to work for ya. But when ya was so violent—a person couldn't help gettin' mad.—I'm sorry about it.

KRUEGER. You come back and wash for us. Where is your daughter, Leontine?

MRS. WOLFF. She went to take some cabbage to the postmaster.

KRUEGER. Send the girl back to us. Instead of twenty, she'll get thirty thalers. We were always satisfied with her. Let's forgive and forget everything. (*He extends his hand.* MRS. WOLFF *shakes it.*)

MRS. WOLFF. All this wouldn't have been necessary. The girl's really a dumb one. Us old ones always got along all right.

KRUEGER. Then this affair is settled. (*Catching his breath.*) Now, at least my mind's at rest. Now, tell me—about what's happened to me—what do you say to that?

MRS. WOLFF. Well, you know . . . no, I can't really say.

KRUEGER. Now we have this von Wehrhahn—annoying honest citizens, inventing vexations and tricks. If that man doesn't stick his nose into everything!

MRS. WOLFF. Everywhere but where it should be.

KRUEGER. I'm going there now and file a complaint. I won't give up. This thing's got to be cleared up.

MRS. WOLFF. Don't give up, Mr. Krueger.

KRUEGER. And if I have to turn everything upside down, I'll get my coat back, Mrs. Wolff.

MRS. WOLFF. Things have got to be cleaned up here, so there'll be peace in this place. They'd steal the roof over your head.

KRUEGER. Well, think, for heaven's sake! Two such thefts in two weeks. Two loads of wood like you've got there. (*He picks up a piece.*) Such good, expensive wood, Mrs. Wolff.

MRS. WOLFF. Oh, I get so mad I could scream. What a pack of thieves here. . . . What the hell! Oh, well. Leave me in peace!

KRUEGER. (*Angrily waving the piece of wood in the air.*) And if it costs me hundreds of thalers, I'll get on the trail of those thieves. They won't escape going to jail.

MRS. WOLFF. That would be a blessin'. Honest to God!

Curtain

ACT FOUR

SCENE: *In the courtroom.* GLASENAPP *sits at his place.* MRS. WOLFF *and* ADELHEID *are waiting for the Judge.* ADELHEID *holds a package on her lap wrapped in linen.*

MRS. WOLFF. He's late again today.

GLASENAPP. (*Writing.*) Patience! Patience!

MRS. WOLFF. Well, if he comes so late again, he won't have time for us today, neither.

GLASENAPP. My God! With your trifles there! We have other important things to do.

MRS WOLFF. I've got lots of important things to do, too.

GLASENAPP. That's no way to talk. That won't work here.

MRS. WOLFF. Oh, just put on a few more airs. The girl was sent here by Krueger.

GLASENAPP. That business about the coat again, I suppose?

MRS. WOLFF. That's right!

GLASENAPP. The old fellow's got something for once. Now he can really go to it, the bow-legged old grumbler.

MRS. WOLFF. All *you* do is grumble; better see if ya can find out something.

MITTELDORF. (*Appears in the door.*) You're supposed to come over, Glasenapp. The Judge wants to ask ya something.

GLASENAPP. Must I be interrupted again? (*Throws down his pen and goes out.*)

MRS. WOLFF. Good mornin', Mitteldorf.

MITTELDORF. Good mornin'.

MRS. WOLFF. What keeps the Judge so long?

MITTELDORF. He's writin' a whole book full, Mother Wolff. And it's important stuff—I tell ya. (*Confidentially.*) And ya know something's in the air. What, I don't know. But there's something.—That I know for sure.—If ya only pay attention, ya'll find out. It strikes, and when it strikes, Mrs. Wolff, then —it has struck. No, like I said, I don't understand nothin' about it. That's all new stuff. Everything's new. And I don't understand the new stuff. Something's got to happen. It can't go on like that. The whole place'll have to be cleaned out. I don't understand things no more. The judge that's dead was a loafer compared to this one. I could tell ya plenty, but I ain't got no time. He'll miss me. (*Goes to the door, turns once more, and says:*) It strikes, Mother Wolff, ya can believe me.

Exit.

MRS. WOLFF. Well, if he ain't gone nuts. (*A pause.*)

ADELHEID. What am I supposed to say? I forgot.

MRS. WOLFF. What did ya say to Mr. Krueger?

ADELHEID. Well, that I'd found this package here.

MRS. WOLFF. Then ya don't need to say nothin' different here. Just be bold and firm. Ya ain't shy other times.

WULKOW (*Comes in.*) I wish ya good mornin'.

MRS. WOLFF. (*Stares speechless at* WULKOW, *then:*) No, Wulkow, you must be crazy! What are ya doin' here?

WULKOW. Well, my wife's had a little one. . . .

MRS. WOLFF. She had what?

WULKOW. A little girl. I had to come here to register it.

MRS. WOLFF. I thought ya'd be way up the canal by now.

WULKOW. And I wouldn't mind that myself, Mrs. Wolff. If I had my way, I'd be there, too. I cast off right away. And when I come to the locks, I could go no farther. I've been waitin' for the Spree to open up. Two days and nights I laid there, until this with my wife came along. Then there was nothin' to do but come back.

MRS. WOLFF. Is your boat down at the bridge again?

WULKOW. Like always. Where else would it be?

MRS. WOLFF. Leave me out of it.

WULKOW. Oh, if only they ain't suspectin' nothin'.

MRS. WOLFF. (*To* ADELHEID.) Go get me 10 pfennigs' worth of thread from the store.

ADELHEID. I'll get it when I go home.

MRS. WOLFF. You'll go now and don't ya talk back.

203

ADELHEID. I ain't a little girl no more.

Leaves.

MRS. WOLFF. (*Hurriedly.*) Then ya laid up at the locks?

WULKOW. Two whole days—like I told ya.

MRS. WOLFF. You're plumb crazy . . . wearin' that coat in bright daylight.

WULKOW. Me? Wearin' the coat?

MRS. WOLFF. Yeah, wearin' the coat in broad daylight. For the whole place to know what a nice fur coat ya got.

WULKOW. That was way out in the country.

MRS. WOLFF. A quarter of an hour from our house. My daughter saw ya settin' there. She had to take Dr. Fleischer out rowin' and he got suspicious at once.

WULKOW. I don't know about that. That's none of my business. (*Some one is heard coming.*)

MRS. WOLFF. Shh, be on your guard now, Wulkow.

GLASENAPP. (*Comes in hastily, somewhat like the Judge. Asks* WULKOW.) What is your business?

VON WEHRHAHN. (*Still outside.*) What is it you want, little girl? Did you come to see me? Then go in. (VON WEHRHAHN *allows* ADELHEID *to enter before him, and follows.*) I don't have much time today. Ah, yes, you are the young Wolff girl. Well, sit down. What is your business?

ADELHEID. I've got this package. . . .

VON WEHRHAHN. Well, wait a minute. . . . (*To* WULKOW.) What is your business?

WULKOW. I'd like to announce a birth.

VON WEHRHAHN. A registration. The books, Glasenapp. No, I think I'll settle this other affair first. (*To* MRS. WOLFF.) What is this with your daughter? Has Krueger boxed her ears again?

MRS. WOLFF. No, he ain't gone that far.

VON WEHRHAHN. What is wrong then?

MRS. WOLFF. It's about the package. . . .

VON WEHRHAHN. (*To* GLASENAPP.) Hasn't Motes been here yet?

GLASENAPP. Not up to now.

VON WEHRHAHN. I can't understand! Well, girl, what is it?

GLASENAPP. It concerns the stolen coat, your Honor.

VON WEHRHAHN. Oh, yes. That's impossible today. Who can do everything at once? (*To* MRS. WOLFF.) She can tell me about it tomorrow.

MRS. WOLFF. She's already tried twice to talk to ya.

VON WEHRHAHN. Then in the morning she can try for the third time.

MRS. WOLFF. Mr. Krueger won't let her alone no more.

VON WEHRHAHN. What has Mr. Krueger to do with it?

MRS. WOLFF. The girl went to him with the package.

VON WEHRHAHN. What sort of rag is this? Show me.

MRS. WOLFF. It has to do with the coat. I mean, that's Mr. Krueger's idea.

VON WEHRHAHN. Well, what's in it?

MRS. WOLFF. A green vest of Mr. Krueger's.

VON WEHRHAHN. You found it?

ADELHEID. I found it, your Honor!

VON WEHRHAHN. Where did you find it?

ADELHEID. It was when I was goin' with Mama to the train station. I was goin' along, and there. . . .

VON WEHRHAHN. That will do. (*To* MRS. WOLFF.) You leave it here. We will come back to it tomorrow.

MRS. WOLFF. It'd be all right with me. . . .

VON WEHRHAHN. And not with. . . ?

MRS. WOLFF. Mr. Krueger is just too anxious about it.

VON WEHRHAHN. Mr. Krueger, Mr. Krueger.—I don't care about him. The man actually bothers me. One can't hurry such things. He's put up a reward. It's been officially entered in the records.

GLASENAPP. The man isn't satisfied with anything.

VON WEHRHAHN. What does that mean: Not satisfied with anything? We have taken down the facts of the case. He suspected his washwoman. We searched her house. What does he want? The man should be quiet. Now, as I said, tomorrow I shall be at your service.

MRS. WOLFF. It's all the same to us. We'll come again.

VON WEHRHAHN. All right, tomorrow morning.

MRS. WOLFF. Good mornin'.

ADELHEID. (*Curtsies.*) Good mornin'.

MRS. WOLFF *and* ADELHEID *leave.*

VON WEHRHAHN. (*Burrowing into some documents, to* GLASE-NAPP.) I'm curious to see what will come of this. Mr. Motes now wants to supply witnesses. He says that Mrs. Dreier, the old witch, was once present when Fleischer made irreverent remarks. How old would you say this Dreier woman is?

GLASENAPP. About seventy years old, your Honor.

VON WEHRHAHN. A bit touched, do you think?

GLASENAPP. Well, that depends. She still seems to have her wits about her.

VON WEHRHAHN. I tell you, Glasenapp, it would be a great pleasure to me to clean up properly, so these people will take note whom they are dealing with. Who was not present at the Emperor's birthday? Fleischer, of course. The man, I am sure, is capable of the worst things, even if he gives such an innocent appearance. One knows them, of course, these wolves in sheep's clothing. They wouldn't harm a fly, but when it counts, these bastards blow up entire cities. We'll make it hot for them here, though.

MOTES. (*Enters.*) Your obedient servant.

VON WEHRHAHN. Well then, how do things stand?

MOTES. Mrs. Dreier will be here around eleven o'clock.

VON WEHRHAHN. This matter will create quite a stir. They'll say, Wehrhahn has his hand in everything. Well, thank heaven I am prepared for that. I am not in this position for my pleasure. I wasn't put here for the fun of it. The people think that a judge is nothing more than a glorified jailer. Then they may put some one else here. Of course, the gentlemen who appointed me know well enough with whom they are dealing. They know the complete seriousness of my conception of the office. I consider my office a holy calling. I have drawn up a report for the prosecuting attorney. If I send it off this noon, an arrest warrant will be here the day after tomorrow.

MOTES. Now everybody will be down on me.

VON WEHRHAHN. You know, my uncle is a senator. I will speak to him about you. Confound it! Here comes Fleischer! What does the man want now? Do you suppose he smells a rat? (*A knock.* VON WEHRHAHN *shouts.*) Come in!

FLEISCHER. (*Enters pale and excited.*) Good morning! (*There is no answer.*) I would like to make a report in connection with the most recent theft.

VON WEHRHAHN. (*With the penetrating stare of a police official.*) You are Dr. Fleischer?

FLEISCHER. Quite right. My name is Joseph Fleischer.

VON WEHRHAHN. You want to make a report to me?

FLEISCHER. If you will allow me, I would like to do that. I have, in fact, observed something which might possibly lead to the trail of the fur coat thief.

VON WEHRHAHN. (*Drums his fingers on the table and looks at the others with an expression of mock astonishment, provoking them to smile. Indifferently.*) Now then, what have you observed that is so important?

FLEISCHER. Well, if you have decided beforehand to put no value on my information, I would prefer to. . . .

VON WEHRHAHN. (*Rapidly, haughtily.*) What would you prefer to do?

FLEISCHER. I would prefer not to speak.

VON WEHRHAHN. (*Turns silently and as if not understanding to* MOTES. *Then changing, in an off-hand manner.*) My time is somewhat in demand. I'll have to ask you to be brief.

FLEISCHER. My time is taken up, too. Nevertheless, I felt it my duty. . . .

VON WEHRHAHN. (*Interrupting.*) You felt it your duty. Good. Now tell us what you know.

FLEISCHER. (*Mastering himself.*) Yesterday I went out in a boat I got from Mrs. Wolff. Her daughter sat in front.

VON WEHRHAHN. Does that have any bearing on the case?

FLEISCHER. Yes, indeed . . . in my opinion.

VON WEHRHAHN. (*Impatiently drumming his fingers.*) All right, all right. Let's get on with it.

FLEISCHER. We rowed close to the locks. A boat was lying there. The ice, we saw, was blocked up at the locks. It seems the boat was fast there.

VON WEHRHAHN. Well, that is of little interest to us. What is the point of the whole thing?

FLEISCHER. (*Containing himself with great effort.*) I must confess that this manner. . . . I am here entirely voluntarily to offer my service to the authorities, to give. . . .

GLASENAPP. (*Impertinently.*) His Honor hasn't the time. You should use fewer words. You should make it short and sweet.

VON WEHRHAHN. (*Violently.*) Come to the point. What do you want?

FLEISCHER. (*Mastering himself.*) I am eager to have this business cleared up. And in the interest of old Mr. Krueger, I will. . . .

VON WEHRHAHN. (*Yawning, disinterested.*) The light blinds me. Pull down the shades.

FLEISCHER. On the boat was an old man—probably the owner of it.

VON WEHRHAHN. (*As before, yawning.*) Yes, most probably.

FLEISCHER. This man sat on deck in a fur coat that I took from the distance to be beaver.

VON WEHRHAHN. (*As before.*) I might have taken it to be marten.

FLEISCHER. I rowed as far as possible and could then see it rather well. The boatman was a shabby, dirty fellow, and the coat didn't seem at all made for him. It was a brand new one. . . .

VON WEHRHAHN. (*Apparently just waking up.*) I'm listening, I'm listening.—Well. . . ? And what then?

FLEISCHER. What then? Nothing!

VON WEHRHAHN. (*Apparently coming to life again.*) You wanted to make a report to me. You spoke of something important.

FLEISCHER. I told you what I wanted to say.

VON WEHRHAHN. You told us a story here about a boatman who wears a fur coat. Well, boatmen occasionally wear fur coats. That's not news.

FLEISCHER. You can think what you like. Under these circumstances, I am finished. (*He leaves.*)

VON WEHRHAHN. Have you ever seen anything like it? The man is extremely stupid. A boatman wears a fur coat. Has the man really gone suddenly insane? I own a beaver coat myself. I'm certainly not a thief on account of that. Confound it! What is that again? There isn't to be any peace today. (*To* MITTELDORF, *who stands at the door.*) From now on, you will let no one in. Mr. Motes, do me the favor, please, of going over to my apartment. We can confer there without being disturbed.—This Krueger—for the hundredth time. He acts as if he's been bitten by a tarantula. If the old ass is coming to plague me, I'll throw him out the door.

KRUEGER, *accompanied by* FLEISCHER *and* MRS. WOLFF, *is visible in the open door.*

MITTELDORF. (*To* KRUEGER.) His Honor can't be seen, Mr. Krueger.

KRUEGER. Nonsense. Can't be seen! Who cares? (*To the others.*) Go on, go on. I'll see about this. (*All enter;* KRUEGER *comes in first.*)

VON WEHRHAHN. I would like to ask for a little more quiet. As you see, I still have business to transact here.

KRUEGER. Go ahead and transact it. We can wait. Then, perhaps, you will transact business with us, too.

VON WEHRHAHN. (*To* MOTES.) Please then, in my apartment. —And if you should see Mrs. Dreier, I would rather hear her there, too. You can see yourself that it's impossible here.

KRUEGER. (*Pointing to* FLEISCHER.) This gentleman knows something about Mrs. Dreier, too. He can even give you a written statement.

MOTES. Your obedient servant, sir. I had best take my leave.

Exit.

KRUEGER. This man needs to take his leave.

210

VON WEHRHAHN. You will kindly keep your remarks to yourself.

KRUEGER. I'll say it again: the man is a swindler!

VON WEHRHAHN. (*As if he did not hear, to* WULKOW.) Now then, what is it? First I will take care of you. The books, Glasenapp! Wait a minute! I will get rid of this first. (*To* KRUEGER.) I will dispose of your case first.

KRUEGER. Yes, I will most urgently ask you to do that.

VON WEHRHAHN. We will entirely disregard the "most urgently." And what is your complaint?

KRUEGER. No complaint. I have no complaint at all. I come to lay claim to my proper rights.

VON WEHRHAHN. What would your proper rights be?

KRUEGER. My proper rights, your Honor. The rights that I have as the victim of a theft, that the authorities give me aid in restoring my stolen property.

VON WEHRHAHN. Has aid been refused you?

KRUEGER. No, indeed not. That can't be done, of course. But, nevertheless, I see that nothing has happened! There has been no progress in the case.

VON WEHRHAHN. Do you believe that it can be done in a minute?

KRUEGER. I believe nothing of the sort, your Honor. If that were true, I wouldn't come here. Rather, I have definite evidence. You don't take an interest in my case.

VON WEHRHAHN. I could interrupt you now. To listen to any more of this kind of thing lies outside my duties as an official. For the time being, however, go on.

KRUEGER. You couldn't interrupt me at all. As a Prussian citizen, I have rights, and if you interrupt me here, there are other places to talk. You don't take an interest in my case.

VON WEHRHAHN. (*Apparently calm.*) Would you please prove that?

KRUEGER. (*Pointing to* MRS. WOLFF *and her daughter.*) Here, this woman came to you. Her daughter found something. She didn't shy away, your Honor, although she is a poor woman. You sent her away once, and today she is back again. . . .

MRS. WOLFF. He said he had no time, the Judge did.

VON WEHRHAHN. Oh, please. Go on. . . !

KRUEGER. I'm far from being finished. What did you tell the woman? You quite simply told her that you had no time for her now. You didn't listen to her daughter. You don't even know the least of the circumstances. You know nothing at all about the entire incident.

VON WEHRHAHN. Now, I must ask you to moderate yourself somewhat.

KRUEGER. I am moderate. I am very moderate. I am much too moderate, your Honor. I am really much too moderate a man. What else should I say to such a thing? What kind of an investigation is this? This gentleman here, Dr. Fleischer, has come to you with an observation he made. A boatman wearing a beaver coat. . . .

VON WEHRHAHN. (*Raising his hand.*) Wait a minute. (*To* WULKOW.) Aren't you a boatman?

WULKOW. I've been a boatman for thirty years.

VON WEHRHAHN. Are you frightened? You're so jumpy.

WULKOW. I've had a bit of a scare.

VON WEHRHAHN. Do the boatmen on the River Spree often wear fur coats?

WULKOW. A lot of 'em has fur coats. Sure.

VON WEHRHAHN. The gentleman there has seen a boatman who stood on deck in a fur coat.

WULKOW. There's nothin' suspicious about that, your Honor. There's a lot of 'em has pretty fur coats. I've even got one myself.

VON WEHRHAHN. Well, you see, the man has a fur coat himself.

FLEISCHER. But certainly not a beaver coat.

VON WEHRHAHN. You didn't see enough for that.

KRUEGER. What? Has this man got a beaver coat?

WULKOW. There's plenty, I can tell ya, that's got the finest beaver coats. And why not? We all make enough money.

VON WEHRHAHN. (*Full of triumph, with unaffected indifference.*) Well. (*Lightly.*) Please continue, Mr. Krueger. That was only a small digression. I only wanted to show you the importance of such an "observation."—You see, the man has a fur coat himself. (*Violently again.*) It doesn't, therefore, even in our wildest dreams, occur to us to say that he has stolen the coat. That would be an absurdity.

KRUEGER. What? I don't understand a word of it.

VON WEHRHAHN. Then I'll have to talk somewhat louder. And since I am talking, I would like, at the same time, to say something to you—in my capacity, not as an official, but simply as a man like you, Mr. Krueger. An honorable citizen should husband his trust more—should not call on the testimony of people. . . .

KRUEGER. Are you talking about my associates. . . ?

VON WEHRHAHN. Yes, indeed. Your associates.

KRUEGER. Then look to yourself. You associate with such people as Motes, whom I've thrown out of my house.

FLEISCHER. The man who waits in your apartment—him I've shown the door of my house.

KRUEGER. He cheated me out of my rent.

MRS. WOLFF. There ain't many around here he ain't cheated blue, out of pfennigs and marks and thalers.

KRUEGER. The man has a regular system of revenue collection.

FLEISCHER. (*Pulls a paper from his pocket.*) The man's ripe for the district attorney, too. (*He lays the paper on the table.*) I beg you to read through that.

KRUEGER. Mrs. Dreier herself has signed that paper. He wanted her to give false testimony.

FLEISCHER. She was to have testified against me.

KRUEGER. (*Taking hold of* FLEISCHER.) He is a blameless man and this scoundrel wants to ruin him. And you extend your hand to the man.

All talk at once.

VON WEHRHAHN. Now I'm at the end of my patience. What business you have with the man is no concern of mine. (*To* FLEISCHER.) Please remove that piece of paper there.

KRUEGER. (*Alternately to* MRS. WOLFF *and* GLASENAPP.) That's the friend of his Honor, the Judge. That is his informant. A fine informant. A gangster, we should say.

FLEISCHER. (*To* MITTELDORF.) I'm accountable to no man. What I do and don't do is my business. With whom I associate is my business. What I think and write is my business.

GLASENAPP. It's impossible to understand a single word. Your Honor, perhaps I should get the sheriff? I'll run over at once. Mitteldorf!

VON WEHRHAHN. Quiet, please. (*They become quiet. To* FLEISCHER.) Will you please remove that piece of paper?

FLEISCHER. (*Does it.*) The paper there goes to the district attorney.

VON WEHRHAHN. You may do with it what you wish. (*He*

214

stands up and takes MRS. WOLFF'S *package from the case.*)
Now, let's get this affair out of the way. (*To* MRS. WOLFF.)
Where did you say you found this thing?

MRS. WOLFF. Oh, I didn't find it, your Honor.

VON WEHRHAHN. Who did then?

MRS. WOLFF. My youngest daughter.

VON WEHRHAHN. Why didn't you bring her along?

MRS. WOLFF. She was here before, your Honor. I can bring
her over in a hurry.

VON WEHRHAHN. That would only delay the business considerably. Hasn't the girl told you anything?

KRUEGER. You said she found it on the way to the station.

VON WEHRHAHN. Then the thief has probably gone to Berlin.
We would have a difficult time finding him there.

KRUEGER. I don't believe that at all, your Honor. Fleischer
here has the right opinion. The whole business with the package is meant to throw us off.

MRS. WOLFF. Oh, yes! That's quite possible.

VON WEHRHAHN. Now, Mrs. Wolff, you aren't so stupid
about other things. Stolen goods go straight to Berlin. The
coat was sold in Berlin even long before we knew here that
it was stolen.

MRS. WOLFF. No, your Honor, I can't help it. There I ain't
quite of your opinion. If the thief is in Berlin, then I'd like
to know what was the use of losing a package like this?

VON WEHRHAHN. One doesn't always lose things intention-
ally.

MRS. WOLFF. Oh, just look at this package once. Everything's
packed together so nice, the vest, the key, the piece of
paper. . . .

KRUEGER. I believe the thief is here in this town.

MRS. WOLFF. (*Backing up* KRUEGER.) That's right, Mr. Krueger.

KRUEGER. (*Now strengthened.*) I certainly believe that.

VON WEHRHAHN. It's a pity. I am not inclined to your view. I have had far too much experience. . . .

KRUEGER. What? Much experience? Ha!

VON WEHRHAHN. Certainly. On the basis of this long experience, I know that this possibility is hardly to be considered.

MRS. WOLFF. Well, well. A person shouldn't be sure about a thing like that, your Honor.

KRUEGER. (*With reference to* FLEISCHER.) He has seen a boatman, however. . . .

VON WEHRHAHN. Oh, don't bring up that story. That would mean for twenty policemen to do nothing but search houses day after day. I would have to search every single house.

MRS. WOLFF. Then start right in with mine, your Honor.

VON WEHRHAHN. Well, isn't it ridiculous, then? No, no, gentlemen, that won't do. We would never get anywhere that way. You must give me an entirely free hand. I already have my suspicions, and, in the meantime, I will just sit back and watch. There are a few shady characters here I have had my eye on for a long time. They travel in the early morning to Berlin with heavy packs on their backs and return in the evening with them empty.

KRUEGER. Those are vegetable women that carry their packs on their backs.

VON WEHRHAHN. Not only the vegetable women, Mr. Krueger. Your fur coat probably went the same way.

MRS. WOLFF. That's quite possible. Nothin' in the world's impossible.

VON WEHRHAHN. Well, then. Well? You wanted to register.

WULKOW. A little girl, your Honor.

VON WEHRHAHN. I will do my utmost.

KRUEGER. I'll give you no peace, your Honor, until I recover my coat.

VON WEHRHAHN. Well, what can be done will be done. Mrs. Wolff can listen around a bit.

MRS. WOLFF. I don't understand much about such things. But if things like that don't come out—no, no, there ain't no security at all.

KRUEGER. You're quite right, Mrs. Wolff, quite right. (*To* WEHRHAHN.) I beg you to inspect the package well. There is some handwriting on the slip which might lead to a discovery. And the day after tomorrow, early in the morning, I'll be back to ask about it. Good-bye!

Exit.

FLEISCHER. Good-bye!

Exit.

VON WEHRHAHN. (*To* WULKOW.) How old are you? Good-bye, good-bye!—Those two fellows are crazy. (*To* WULKOW.) What is your name?

WULKOW. August Philipp Wulkow.

VON WEHRHAHN. (*To* MITTELDORF.) Go over to my apartment. The writer Motes is sitting there waiting. Tell him I'm sorry, but I have other things to do this morning.

MITTELDORF. Then he shouldn't wait?

VON WEHRHAHN. (*Roughly.*) He's not to wait! No!

Exit MITTELDORF.

VON WEHRHAHN. (*To* MRS. WOLFF.) Do you know the writer Motes?

MRS. WOLFF. So much that I'd rather keep quiet. I don't know much good to tell ya.

VON WEHRHAHN. (*Ironically.*) But much more about Fleischer?

MRS. WOLFF. He really ain't a bad man.

VON WEHRHAHN. You should be a bit cautious.

MRS. WOLFF. Now, you know I ain't good at that. I'm always direct, your Honor. If I wasn't always comin' right out with what I've got to say, I could be a lot farther along now.

VON WEHRHAHN. It hasn't done you any harm with me.

MRS. WOLFF. With you, I suppose not, your Honor. You can stand an honest word. There's no use tryin' to hide anything from you.

VON WEHRHAHN. In short, Fleischer is an honorable man.

MRS. WOLFF. That's a fact. Yes, that's a fact.

VON WEHRHAHN. Well, you think about what you have said today.

MRS. WOLFF. And you think about it, too.

VON WEHRHAHN. Good. We shall see. (*He stands up and stretches his legs. To* WULKOW.) This is our industrious washwoman here. She thinks all men are like her. (*To* MRS. WOLFF.) But, unfortunately, that isn't the way of the world. You look at all men from the outside. People like myself look somewhat deeper. (*He takes a few steps, then stops before her and puts his hands on her shoulders.*) And it's as true when I say here, Mrs. Wolff is an honest soul, as it is when I tell you with the same certainty, your Dr. Fleischer is an extremely dangerous fellow.

MRS. WOLFF. (*Resigned, shakes her head.*) Well, I don't know. . . .

Curtain

Rinehart Editions

Addison and Steele, SEL. FROM THE TATLER & THE SPECTATOR 87

AMERICAN THOUGHT: CIVIL WAR TO WORLD WAR I 70

ANTHOLOGY OF ENGLISH DRAMA BEFORE SHAKESPEARE 45

ANTHOLOGY OF GREEK DRAMA: FIRST SERIES 29

ANTHOLOGY OF GREEK DRAMA: SECOND SERIES 68

ANTHOLOGY OF ROMAN DRAMA 101

Arnold, SELECTED POETRY AND PROSE 62

Austen, PRIDE AND PREJUDICE 22

Balzac, PÈRE GORIOT 18

Benét, S. V., SELECTED POETRY & PROSE 100

THE BIBLE: SEL. FROM OLD & NEW TESTAMENTS 56

Brontë, Charlotte, JANE EYRE 24

Brontë, Emily, WUTHERING HEIGHTS 23

Brown, C. B., ARTHUR MERVYN 112

Browning, Robert, SELECTED POETRY 71

Bunyan, THE PILGRIM'S PROGRESS 27

Burke, REFLECTIONS ON THE REVOLUTION IN FRANCE 84

Butler, THE WAY OF ALL FLESH 7

Byron, SELECTED POETRY AND LETTERS 54

Chaucer, THE CANTERBURY TALES 65

Coleridge, SELECTED POETRY AND PROSE 55

COLONIAL AMERICAN WRITING 43

Conrad, LORD JIM 85

Conrad, NOSTROMO 111

Cooper, THE PIONEERS 99

Cooper, THE PRAIRIE 26

Crane, RED BADGE OF COURAGE, SEL'D PROSE & POETRY 47

Dante, THE DIVINE COMEDY 72

Defoe, MOLL FLANDERS 25

De Forest, MISS RAVENEL'S CONVERSION 74

Dickens, GREAT EXPECTATIONS 20

Dickens, HARD TIMES 95

Dickens, OLIVER TWIST 115

Dreiser, SISTER CARRIE 86

Dryden, SELECTED WORKS 60

Eliot, ADAM BEDE 32

Eliot, SILAS MARNER 114

ELIZABETHAN FICTION 64

Emerson, SELECTED PROSE AND POETRY 30

ENGLISH PROSE AND POETRY 1660–1800: A SELECTION 110

Fielding, JOSEPH ANDREWS 15

FIFTEEN MODERN AMERICAN POETS 79

Flaubert, MADAM BOVARY 2

FOUR MODERN PLAYS: FIRST SERIES, Ibsen, Shaw, O'Neill, Miller 90

FOUR MODERN PLAYS: SECOND SERIES, Ibsen, Wilde, Rostand, Gorky 109

Franklin, AUTOBIOGRAPHY AND SELECTED WRITINGS 12

Frederic, THE DAMNATION OF THERON WARE 108

Garland, MAIN-TRAVELLED ROADS 66

Godwin, CALEB WILLIAMS 103

Goethe, FAUST: PART I 75

Goethe, SORROWS OF YOUNG WERTHER, NEW MELUSINA, NOVELLE 13

Gogol, DEAD SOULS 5

GREAT ENGLISH AND AMERICAN ESSAYS 34

Hardy, FAR FROM THE MADDING CROWD 98

Hardy, THE MAYOR OF CASTERBRIDGE 9

Hardy, THE RETURN OF THE NATIVE 39

Hauptmann, THREE PLAYS: The Weavers, Hannele, The Beaver Coat 52

Hawthorne, THE HOUSE OF THE SEVEN GABLES 89

Hawthorne, THE SCARLET LETTER 1

Hawthorne, SELECTED TALES AND SKETCHES 33

Howells, THE RISE OF SILAS LAPHAM 19

Ibsen, THREE PLAYS: Ghosts, Enemy of the People, Wild Duck 4

Irving, SELECTED PROSE 41

James, Henry, THE AMBASSADORS 104

James, Henry, THE AMERICAN 16

James, Henry, SELECTED SHORT STORIES 31

Johnson, RASSELAS, POEMS, & SELECTED PROSE 57

Keats, SELECTED POETRY AND LETTERS 50

Lincoln, SELECTED SPEECHES, MESSAGES, AND LETTERS 82

LITERATURE OF THE EARLY REPUBLIC 44

London, MARTIN EDEN 80

MASTERPIECES OF THE SPANISH GOLDEN AGE 93

Melville, MOBY DICK 6

Melville, SEL'D TALES AND POEMS 36

Milton, PARADISE LOST AND SELECTED POETRY AND PROSE 35

MODERN AMERICAN LITERATURE 53

Newman, THE IDEA OF A UNIVERSITY 102

Norris, Frank, MC TEAGUE 40

Parkman, THE DISCOVERY OF THE GREAT WEST: LA SALLE 77

PLUTARCH—EIGHT GREAT LIVES 105

Poe, SELECTED PROSE AND POETRY, REV. 42

POETRY OF THE NEW ENGLAND RENAISSANCE, 1790–1890 38

Pope, SELECTED POETRY AND PROSE 46

RINEHART BOOK OF SHORT STORIES 59

RINEHART BOOK OF VERSE 58

Robinson, E. A., SEL. EARLY POEMS AND LETTERS 107

Roosevelt, F. D., SPEECHES, MESSAGES, PRESS CONFERENCES, & LETTERS 83

Scott, THE HEART OF MIDLOTHIAN 14

SELECTED AMERICAN PROSE, 1841–1900 94

SELECTIONS FROM GREEK AND ROMAN HISTORIANS 88

Shakespeare, FIVE PLAYS: Hamlet; King Lear; Henry IV, Part I; Much Ado about Nothing; The Tempest 51

Shakespeare, AS YOU LIKE IT, JULIUS CAESAR, MACBETH 91

Shakespeare, TWELFTH NIGHT, OTHELLO 92

Shaw, SELECTED PLAYS AND OTHER WRITINGS 81

Shelley, SELECTED POETRY AND PROSE 49

SIR GAWAIN AND THE GREEN KNIGHT 97

Smollett, HUMPHRY CLINKER 48

SOUTHERN STORIES 106

Spenser, SELECTED POETRY 73

Sterne, TRISTRAM SHANDY 37

Stevenson, MASTER OF BALLANTRAE 67

Swift, GULLIVER'S TRAVELS 10

Swift, SELECTED PROSE AND POETRY 78

Tennyson, SELECTED POETRY 69

Thackeray, HENRY ESMOND 116

Thackeray, VANITY FAIR 76

Thoreau, WALDEN, ON THE DUTY OF CIVIL DISOBEDIENCE 8

Trollope, BARCHESTER TOWERS 21

Turgenev, FATHERS AND CHILDREN 17

Twain, THE ADVENTURES OF HUCKLEBERRY FINN 11

Twain, ROUGHING IT 61

Vergil, THE AENEID 63

VICTORIAN POETRY: Clough to Kipling 96

Wharton, HOUSE OF MIRTH 113

Whitman, LEAVES OF GRASS AND SELECTED PROSE 28

Wordsworth, THE PRELUDE, SEL'D SONNETS & MINOR POEMS, Rev. & Enl. 3